GREAT EXCAVATIONS
JOHN ROMER'S HISTORY OF ARCHAEOLOGY

This book is affectionately dedicated to Norah Romer
and Alan and Rita Aylwin, and to the fond memory
of Eileen Aylwin and Louis Romer.

First published in the United Kingdom in 2000 by Cassell & Co,
Wellington House, 125 Strand, London, WC2R 0BB

A CIP catalogue record for this book is available from the British Library.
ISBN 0 304 35563 1

Art Editor: Austin Taylor
Designer: Nigel Soper

Printed and bound in Great Britain

Jacket photographs: Images supplied by Elizabeth Romer,
the Royal Geographical Society and Images Color Library

GREAT EXCAVATIONS

JOHN ROMER'S HISTORY OF ARCHAEOLOGY

CASSELL&CO

Contents

Introduction

Stand on the cliffs of western Thebes upon the upper Nile and in a single glance, you can see a landscape of two million years spread out before you. On the east bank of the river, the hotels' neon signs flash international welcomes. On the west bank, just a half mile into the desert beyond, the shadows of a few thin trenches mark where French archaeologists have excavated flint hand axes as old as any on the planet. Between the hotels and the trenches stands the vast sun-bleached temple of King Ramesses III. High up on its walls is a scene of harvest home, still bright with ancient paint: great Ramesses standing in a field cutting graceful sheaves of wheat with a little copper sickle chased with gold. Like most of the ancient Egyptians' ritual implements, the design of this sickle is from an age much older than the pharaohs. The earliest-known examples, from around 11,000 BC, being made of wood or bone all set with rows of tiny cutting flints. Microscopic examination shows that these flints, that archaeologists call microliths, have so-called 'sickle polish' on them – a burnish made by the constant brushing of the stems of wild wheats, harvested in the long millennia before the age of farming.

Neither Ramesses III nor any of his court knew anything of these archaeological continuities, just as they knew nothing of the two million year-old axes that the French archaeologists would find in the thin trenches in the desert behind their temple. What they did know, however, was that there had been a time before their state had existed, a time when tools were not made of bronze, but flint and wood and bone; and their elaborate rituals held within them a deep sense of continuity with these distant ages, a part of the cosmic past and present.

The fixing of human creation in a specific time and place, the coming of Judaism, Christianity and Islam shattered such immediate and uncomplicated links with our primaeval forebears. Until the rise of archaeology, the span of Western history hardly extended beyond the stories of the Bible and the ancient Greeks. Most Westerners of course, believed the history held in the Book of Genesis; that the human race was directly descended from the sons of Noah, who, like Eve and Adam before them, had come perfect into a world designed for their exploitation and delight.

Neither were these the unthinking tenets of a rigid faith. It was also a matter of intellectual convenience. From St Augustine to Madame de Staël, Beethoven and George Washington, most people saw little point in extending human history into unknown millennia for which there seemed to be no evidence at all. Before the age of archaeology, intelligent Westerners believed that the human race was five thousand years old, and quite separate from other life on the planet. Human history was conveniently contained in a few thousand printed pages, a time-frame of some 250 generations in which all of human history had taken place. And that perhaps, is part of the reason why the Europeans of the eighteenth century were more self-assured, less anguished about their place in the order of creation, than we are today.

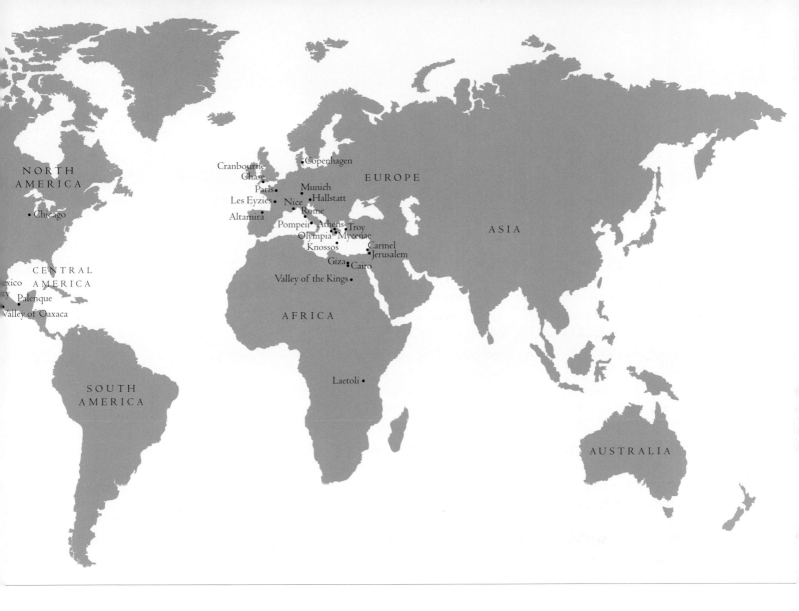

ABOVE: *The map above shows some of the archaelogical sites discussed in this book.*

PAGE FOUR: *Excavating the archaeologists. Egyptian workmen excavating the ruins of a photographic laboratory used during the excavation of the Valley of the Kings in the first decade of the last century. Along with fragments of contemporary newspapers and many personal effects, they found hundreds of fragments of broken glass negatives, a unique record of the archaeological history of the Valley of the Kings.*

Archaeology has changed all that. It has shown us all our most ancient ancestors. It has provided every nation on the planet with thousands of years of previously unknown history; with scientific and entirely novel narratives, with continuities of time and evolution wider and deeper than any pharaoh ever dreamt of. And we have all been changed. At first glance then, though archaeologists might seem to be harmless romantics dabbling in the relics of the past, in reality, they practice one of those rare disciplines that has the power and the authority to change the way that people feel about themselves, their country and their race. For archaeologists sift through the ancient dust of our identity. And that perhaps is the reason why so many governments invested such large sums to transform the pursuit of eighteenth- century gentlemen into a complex modern science; archaeology acts directly on the popular imagination.

This book aims to provide a history for archaeology itself: to describe the central attitudes of some of its founders, scientists and visionaries; to describe some of the myths and histories that they have made for us and tell also, why they made them the way they did. This then, is not a collection of tales of archaeological discovery but the history of archaeology itself – a science born in a Jane Austen world and set between Europe and the Middle East, whose passionate practitioners, a mix of soldiers and scholars, country squires and hard colonials, vicars, architects and statesman, transformed an innocent pastime into a worldwide science.

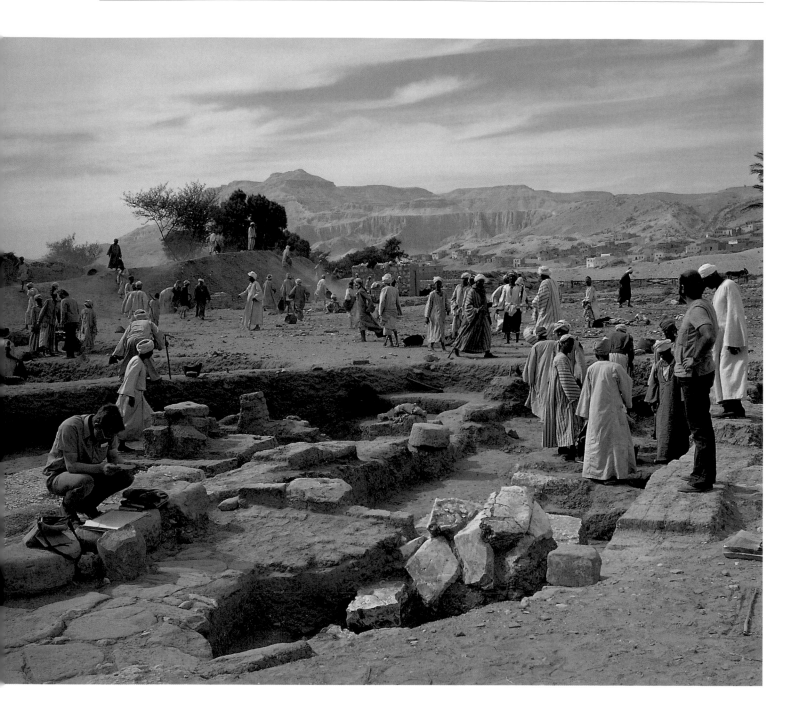

It is a tale that is hardly ever told. For the history of archaeology cannot be held in a single simple story line of a scientific development in the manner of a history of nuclear physics, the motor car or the kings and queens of England. For archaeology is not and never has been, a single subject but a complex gathering of skill and science, held together with the dubious glue of historical interpretation. Glyn Daniel, archaeology's most eminent historian, once described his subject as an 'art-cum-craft-cum-science'. It is not surprising, therefore, that the various residues of archaeology, the treasures and relics of the past are held in such a wide variety of institutions, from private galleries of art and public libraries, from museums of natural history to churches, temples, national treasures and the greatest museums of the world.

LEFT: *Staff of the German Archaeological Institute in Egypt excavating the mortuary Temple of the Pharaoh Seti I at Thebes in Upper Egypt in the 1970s. The archaeologists and their foreman scrutinise the progress as local villagers clear away the loose dirt in the traditional manner, using their agricultural tools. The surviving architecture and objects are recorded and measured as they are uncovered, and lines of labourers carry off the dirt in traditional Egyptian baskets.*

Neither can the history of archaeology be conveniently divided into the separate stories of the rediscovery of the past of individual countries or cultures. That would bypass those magical events, those quantum jumps through space and time, when knowledge gained in the excavation of one culture is cross-related to another, sometimes with astonishing results. Just as each and every country has its own ancient history, so it also has its own history of archaeology, and all these together spin and turn like a maze in and around upon itself.

Like all good mazes though, there are direct routes to the centre. Born of the nineteenth-century West, archaeology has always had a handful of constant themes within it, themes as insistent as a steady drumbeat that have haunted and inspired archaeology since its beginnings, and still remain.

For the most part, the universal themes of archaeology have had very little to do with the popular myths that presently surround the profession, myths that archaeologists such as Heinrich Schliemann and Howard Carter themselves perpetuated, and Indiana Jones' scriptwriters have subsequently embroidered. Yet these underlying themes are the real roots of the passions that drove men and women into the jungles of America, had them faking ancient skulls in Dorset, and travelling steerage from Europe to the Middle East equipped with a trowel, a camera and a compass.

Each of this book's five sections describes the history of one of these basic themes in archaeology: the search for treasure trove; the search for the origins of humankind and civilisation; the search for 'scientific' proof of the truth of ancient writings and of holy scripture; and the constant continuing search for ancient pedigree for every modern nation, every modern culture. And always, universally, above all others, the single re-occurring question: 'What were our ancestors really like?'.

My own career in archaeology began in the 1960s, in that same vast temple of King Ramesses III at western Thebes, drawing scenes from the life in the royal harem, scenes cut in the most exquisite relief high up on the temple's gateway. One cold spring morning, as I was gratefully lolling into tea-break drowsiness serenaded by clouds of chirping sparrows, my boss and co-worker suddenly leapt to his feet and with a growled 'goshdernit,' walked over to a broken wall which we had both been rather dolefully regarding over the rims of our Egyptian tea cups. Dropping to his knees and all the while repeating his archaic oath in intonations rising from incredulity to exultation, the archaeologist regarded a fragmentary relief upon the stones through the bottom half of his bifocals.

There were just two of us working at the temple that morning, so Dr Charles Francis Nims of the University of Chicago was forced to deliver his impromptu lecture on his discovery to an entirely ignorant audience of one. As far as I can remember, he had noticed a detail in a scene that showed a pharaoh of the Late Period performing a mysterious archaic ritual that many scholars assumed had died out in much earlier ages. Nims' impromptu observation had changed his ideas on the purposes and meaning of that ritual forever.

This was my first real lesson in archaeology: that there can be no fixed truths in history, or in its explanation. That the most ancient past and our understanding of it is always in a constant state of change. Archaeology is the process of that unending investigation.

JOHN ROMER
Aiola, Tuscany, 2000

PART I

Into the Past

Herculaneum Docks: 1980

I N 1980, ITALIAN ARCHAEOLOGISTS EXCAVATING ancient Herculaneum found fresh evidence of the catastrophe that, nineteen hundred years before, had obliterated half the cities on the Bay of Naples in showers of lethal ash and flowing lava. The end had come at night, and so fast that many citizens had died unknowing in their beds. Hundreds though, woken perhaps by explosions in the volcano of Vesuvius high above the bay, had fled to the city's dockside where they were killed by hurricane-force winds of superheated poison gas.

On the ancient beach nearby, under seventy feet of hard volcanic pumice and half a mile from the modern seaside, the archaeologists found the remnants of an upturned boat completely filled with corpses. Beside the stern lay the skeleton of a man whose bones showed distortions, probably resulting from a life spent manning a heavy steering oar. This then, had been a living Charon, taking his last boat-load of passengers from the dying city.

LEFT: *The skeletons of heaped bodies lying as they fell on Tuesday, 24 August AD 79, excavated by Italian archaeologists in the early 1980s inside a dockside cellar of the city of Herculaneum.*

RIGHT: *Long buried in volcanic ash and lava, then cut from the plastered walls of an ancient house at Herculaneum, this group portrait shows a Roman matron and two young girls, perhaps her daughters, and a maid, presumably a family slave. Such paintings gave eighteenth-century Europe vivid glimpses of the living world of the little town whose physical remains were being slowly excavated from Vesuvius' rock-hard lava.*

PREVIOUS PAGE: *This nineteenth-century photograph shows the streets of Pompeii standing once again in the Neapolitan sunlight, in the omnipresent shadow of Vesuvius.*

A middle-aged woman lay upon the dockside. She had fallen from a great height, a victim apparently, of the earthquakes that accompanied Vesuvius' eruption. Although she crouched as she had fallen through the air to minimise the impact, her legs still hit the ground with such force that the upward thrust of her knees had broken both her shoulder bones. Two splendid belts, a military sword and a little hoard of coins identified a nearby corpse as that of a Roman solider, a rare survival from a society where cremation was the rule. He had been a well-fed cavalry man, with a wound in his thigh and a jaw bone damaged when three of his front teeth had been knocked out.

Huddled together in a dockside storeroom, holding hands, were what appeared to be the

LEFT: *A sea-gull's view of the ancient seaside villa of the city of Herculaneum. Due to later volcanic activity, the water is now half a mile away. In a direct link with its most ancient past, the ruins of the ancient city trapped in some seventy feet of rock-hard pumice, now run directly beneath the town of Resina, renamed now, as Ercolano, in honour of its archaeological predecessor.*

bodies of a single household: three men, four women and some children, one of them a three-year-old with gold and pearl earrings; another, a five-year-old in urgent need of a visit to a dentist. Beside them, still cradling a tiny bejewelled baby, lay the body of an older girl. Grooves in her teeth showed that when she had been very young, she had almost died of illness or malnutrition; scars on her long bones also showed that she had suffered long, hard labour; she was probably a family slave, still protecting the youngest member of her household after two millennia.

Silent images of ancient life, the drama of real history, of life, not death, lying deep within the earth.

The Theatre of Herculaneum: 1736. Into the Past

Modern archaeology began at 123 Corso Resina, Ercolano, just a few hundred yards from the ancient dockside of Herculaneum. Built for the nineteenth-century tourist trade, a grandiose nineteenth-century façade still covers the mouths of some huge shafts excavated in the 1740s in a search for ancient marbles, which as local people knew, lay buried in the ground, deep in an ancient flow of grey volcanic pumice.

Long before that time, of course, Europeans of a dozen different countries had studied and collected ancient relics, and dug into the earth in hope of finding more. Others too, had studied ruins and inscriptions. Right around the world indeed, there have always been historians and antiquarians — the earliest known museum catalogues were made in eleventh-century China, where there was a venerable tradition of connoisseurship, of collecting old and ancient things. No one though, had ever drawn these things together; no one had ever abandoned treasure-hunting to tease the stories, styles and people of the past from beneath the silent earth.

Excavations of a sort, more accurately described as an entrepreneurial treasure hunt, had started at a well on the eventual site of the Corso Resina as early as 1705, when the then owner of the land, an Austrian cavalry officer, ordered his workmen to excavate a series of desultory shafts into the pumice, to search for ancient statues. In 1736, however, a new king, Charles, a Bourbon prince of Spain had come to Naples with his German Queen, Maria Amalia, to rule the ancient kingdom of the 'Two Sicilies'. And he bought the Austrian officer's land to form part of a royal hunting park.

Charles' court already knew of the Austrian officer's secret statue mine; the Queen indeed, had already seen three marvellous Roman statues that had been taken from it at the court of Dresden. So the royal antiquary, Count Marcello Venuti of Cortona, was sent down a rope into the dark well of the Austrian's statue mine to examine what was locally known as a buried 'Temple of Hercules'. Down there in the dark, however, deep in the lava of Vesuvius, Venuti found the living past, and archaeology was born.

On that very trip, when this first literate visitor to that ancient place in some seventeen centuries read the inscriptions that earlier fortune hunters had believed, had named a temple dedicated to the god Hercules – M. NONIO M. F. BALBO PR. PROCOS. HERCVLANENSES – he saw that these were not temple texts at all, but dedications in a public theatre, a theatre presented to the city of Hercules – Herculaneum – by one Mammianus Rufus – A...MAMM...RVFVS.II. VIR.QUIN THEATRE. ORCH. DE SVO....Here then, it was clear, was not an isolated temple, but part of a city that had been completely buried by Vesuvius' eruptions. At Venuti's suggestion, officers in the army of the new king took over the Austrian excavations. Under the careful eye of military sappers, armed with picks, chisels, iron bars and the occasional charge of gunpowder,

BELOW: *A Mexican tourist of the 1860s, one of tens of thousands of visitors of the day, standing on the dark stage of the buried amphitheatre of Herculaneum where, a century earlier, Count Marcello Venuti had read the name of the buried city on a statue base.*

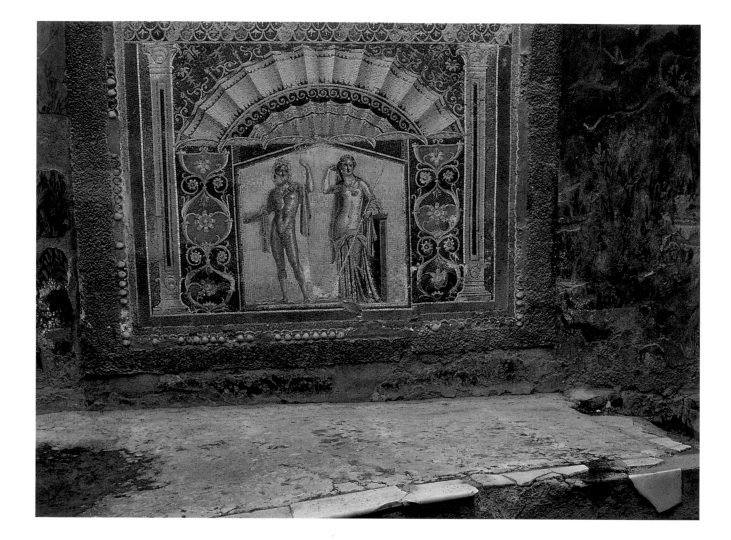

criminals, gangs of Turkish slaves and other prisoners of state were set to mine the rock-hard lava, still filled with pockets of deadly, ancient gas. The work was hard and dangerous.

From the beginning though, their haul was tremendous; their mine shafts cut through ancient buildings made of rare marbles from Europe, Africa and Asia, all of them perfect elements of classical architecture, and as fresh as the ancient day they were made. More statues came to light as well; women, athletes and portraits of individual Greeks and Romans, many of them still standing on their original bases. There were huge fragments of bronze equestrian statues too, some of them judged to be finer than the famous monuments of Rome. Slowly, very slowly, the miners cut tunnels down into the very streets and houses of the ancient town of Herculaneum. Now the chain gangs walked through villas of an ancient middle class, through libraries and shops, through public baths and market places, stripping paintings and mosaics from the ancient walls as they went. Fascinated with the products of their sculpture mine, the king and queen spent hour after hour with their ever-growing collections of antiquities, which they had housed in the private apartments of a newly built palace nearby.

Count Marcello Venuti published a report on the unveiling of the embalmed city in Naples in 1748: *A description of the first excavations at the antique City of Herculaneum rediscovered in*

ABOVE: *A sumptuous courtyard mosaic in a townhouse of Herculaneum showing the gods Neptune and Amphitrite, one of several similar mosaics made by travelling Greek craftsmen for a prosperous middle class, in this instance a wine and cereal merchant. This splendid scene would have been the backdrop to the evening meal of the shopkeeper's family, taken in the open air, in the small courtyard behind his shop and living quarters.*

the vicinity of the Royal Villa at Portici. Offering a brief history of the excavations, then identifying the city from the inscription in the theatre, Venuti's text then moves to more traditional concerns, tracing the mythic history of ancient Herculaneum in the texts of ancient classical authors and concluding with erudite expositions on the subject matter of some of the paintings they had excavated. It is the world's first archaeological report.

By this time, scholars all over Europe were complaining that the unique discoveries on the Bay of Naples were being kept a secret, and that the royal excavators appeared to be both damaging and stealing the priceless relics of antiquity. Charles and his ministers, however, were unmoved, regarding the statue mine as a natural asset, more valuable than any other of the kingdom, and at their complete disposal. Clearly such a treasure mine needed to be guarded and discreetly screened from public view. So the French and German scholars who travelled to Naples to see the excavations and its treasures usually published literary laments about the secrecy and mendacity surrounding the royal excavations. Generations of English antiquarians too, who went to live at Naples, wrote accounts on what they were allowed to see, and purchased splendid objects stolen from the mines.

King Charles, who even had Venuti's modest effort banned from the book shops of his kingdom, saw little need to please anyone on earth except his queen and his confessor. Leaving the care of the excavated treasures to the Neapolitan civil service, Venuti meanwhile had retreated back to Tuscany. A few years later, however, realising that such publications brought nothing but lustre to the throne, and fame to his collections, the king engaged another antiquary, *Professore* Ottavio Baiardi, to write official notices of the ongoing excavations. In what has become a standard archaeological practice, Baiardi began by attempting to ban all unauthorised volumes on Herculaneum on the grounds that the information they contained was the exclusive property of the king. The problem was though, that the great grand publications of the excavations that Baiardi issued contained little archaeological information and large amounts of dubious scholarship. One critic complained that Baiardi had covered Herculaneum in 'a much denser shroud than that of the lava'.

With mounting impatience, the king then formed the Accademia Ercolonese to study and publish the treasures of ancient city. Over forty years, this little group of scholars, produced eight huge volumes – *Le Antichitá di Ercolano Esposte* – that successfully separated wordy old-fashioned academic scholarship from lively accounts of the excavations, accompanied by maps and illustrations of the finds. It was the first time that the results of archaeological excavations had been recorded in a careful and consistent manner, a yardstick for those early archaeologists who first found inspiration at this buried city.

The influence of these large impressive books can hardly be over-estimated. For centuries, the artists and architects of popes and kings had employed the grandiose forms of Roman antiquity; forms known only from great Roman ruins and ancient texts. Although neither Baiardi nor Venuti had realised it, the royal excavations gave form and substance to more private ghosts. For both the excavations and the splendid volumes of the Accademia Ercolonese revealed the most intimate daily truths of a past only previously glimpsed in the writings of the ancient Romans – that same lost literary Elysium indeed, that had educated and amused all Europe for so many centuries! Here then, for the first time, were the very chairs and braziers, the beds and plates and money boxes, the thimbles, the jars and shops of real ancient Romans. The truth perhaps, behind the legend; the other half of the past.

Archaeology's vast potential and something of its power and fascination too, was slowly sliding into view.

Naples: 1763
Europe Intrigued

A FEW YEARS AFTER VENUTI DESCENDED INTO THE DARKNESS of the theatre at Herculaneum, engineers digging a canal some miles to the south in the plain along the bay, uncovered an ancient street lined with ruined houses. The discovery was shown to the officers mining Herculaneum, and over the next few years the archaeological attentions of the court of Naples were switched to 'la Civitá', as the new excavation site was called. Here, in the green fields of Vesuvius' lower plain, the soil was soft and easy, the ruins buried in just twenty feet or so of loose and fertile dust. Here the past could be brought to light with far less effort. Although the work gangs were small and erratically employed, the excavations at 'la Civitá' proceeded month by month, street by street. Soon it was clear that an entire city lay under this sunny plain – a city whose ancient name, Pompeii, was rediscovered on an inscription in 1763, and immediately celebrated by the great engraver Giambattista Piranesi in a famous print.

Despite the efforts of the king, Naples' long-lost cities were becoming famous all over Europe and attracting many visitors. Scholars especially, were thrilled that this lightly buried city in the plain was that same city of Pompeii whose fiery ending had been so vividly

RIGHT: *Preserved by the eruption of Vesuvius, this first-century Roman painting from an ancient villa on the Bay of Naples shows the area before the catastrophe of AD 79; an ancient landscape similar to the Bay of Naples today, a riotous mix of harbours and civic and private architecture running from the seaside up into the surrounding hills. The artist shows us that ancient boat crews sometimes lowered their sails while in dock to serve as umbrellas in the summer sun. The arches in the sea probably represent the quays of the Imperial port of Puteoli, Rome's chief port for many centuries and its gateway to the ancient East. And on the docksides all around, are rows of villas, public promenades and a great high lighthouse, the remains of which are all still buried beneath the modern port of Pozzuoli, a little to the north of Naples, along the bay.*

LEFT: *Sir William Hamilton's fine contemporary plate of the excavation of the Temple of Isis at Pompeii in 1765. The remains of the little building, the corpse of its priest and all the paraphernalia of the ancient Egyptian religion, fired the imaginations of novelists and philosophers from Bulwer Lytton and Sigmund Freud, to Madame Blavatsky and Cecil B. De Mille.*

described by several ancient Roman writers. All at once the eighteenth century was faced with the reality of a well-known literary event that had taken place, the ancient authors wrote, on 24 August, AD 79, when the volcano of Vesuvius had blown itself to pieces, killing the famous author Pliny, and clothing the entire city in an ash-grey shroud.

Unlike the deep dark mines of Herculaneum, at Pompeii excavators entered the ancient houses through the front door and in daylight. Inside they found an astonishingly fragile past, a past of surprising detail and unexpected beauty. Standing to their full height, the houses of the city were still furnished. Withered plants still filled their gardens and their trellises. Dishes of uneaten food lay on the ancient dining tables, coins too, on wine shop benches, boiled eggs in the provision shops, bread in the bakers' ovens, thimbles at the tailors. Here too, were the remains of many of the ancient Pompeians and their slaves, still lying where they had fallen, choked by volcanic fumes and buried in a rain of pumice.

ABOVE: *Excavations at Pompeii in May 1961 revealed further evidence of the ancient tragedy; men, women and children lying hunched together in death.*

Pompeii became the first and by far the greatest archaeological sensation the world has ever known, and its effect on European taste was deep and long lasting. For over a century, artists, architects, potters and furniture-makers all over Europe drew immediate inspiration from the ancient buried cities around the Bay of Naples. Adams' designs for English stately homes, Marie Antoinette's apartments, Wedgewood's pottery, the paintings of Ingres and David, the furniture of Chippendale and Versailles were all influenced by the styles of these buried cities. An influence that continues to this day, its colours, forms and patterns have entered the European bloodstream and are now part of our daily life.

Unlike Herculaneum, Pompeii also became one of the most celebrated sights of Europe, the real ancestor of the modern tourist trade, and still incidentally, the most visited ruin in

LEFT: *The open courtyard of an anonymous Pompeiian house, the so-called 'House of the Little Fountain'. Such excavated glimpses of the living ancient Roman past have influenced architectural design throughout the Western world ever since the first excavations at Pompeii in the eighteenth century.*

BELOW: *The stairway of the Temple of Jupiter of Rome, on the main square of Pompeii. Worn down during the 160 years of their active existence, buried for some sixteen centuries and dug out by Bourbon galley slaves, the steps now stand again in the Neapolitan sunlight.*

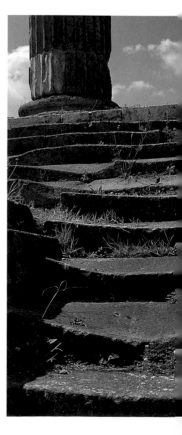

the world. What most amazed the early visitors both to Pompeii and the palatial museum that King Charles later built at Naples to exhibit his collections, were the traces of the ancient Pompeians themselves. About one tenth of the city's ancient population, some 2000 souls, had been trapped inside the dying city. Quite often their vanished bodies, voids now in the crisp volcanic ash, were recast in plaster to bring their death to life again.

Here then, laid out for public delectation, were a thousand cinematic tableaux. Nor was this merely the exhibition of the contents of the brothels and other scandalous erotica so common in the ancient city. Trapped in the temple of the Vestal Virgins, you could view a cast of a woman's body that had been gnawed by her pet dog, when the animal had survived its mistress. Across the road, at the temple of Egyptian Isis, whose excavation had been the sensation of the 1760s, you could view an ancient priest, axe in hand, still trapped inside a room beside the temple. Inside the pretty Isis Temple, still gaudy with its original decorations, all the ritual paraphernalia of the Egyptian cult lay where it had been buried on 24 August, AD 79: the burnt offerings on the altar and the lotuses in their pond; the garlands of flowers, the sacred ibises, musical instruments and esoteric imports from Egypt.

From Madame de Staël to Mark Twain, most nineteenth-century novelists, at some time in their lives were fascinated by Naples' buried cities. For visitors, their ancient streets were filled with nineteenth-century romances like Bulwer Lytton's phenomenal success of 1834, *The Last Days of Pompeii*, which drew together many of the dead cities' most famous tableaux and attractions. Years later, Lytton returned to the romantic, yet at the same time profoundly archaeological notion, of life lying deep in the earth; *The Coming Race*, tells of a mysterious underground people called the Vril, who had powers of telepathy and telekinesis.

LEFT: *The gardens of the so-called 'House of the Scholars' at Pompeii. The remarkable state of conservation of remnants of ancient garden plants in Pompeiian houses is now enabling archaeologists to replant many of the original species.*

BELOW: *A miller's workshop at Pompeii, with his storage jars for grain, and the heavy millstones cut from local volcanic tufa. Excavators have found the remains of the paired donkeys used to turn these millstones, still tethered, having fallen where they were working when Vesuvius exploded in AD 79.*

Just as the city of Pompeii inspired Nietzsche to recommend his readers to 'build your house on the slopes of Vesuvius', and tempted Freud to turn his analytic power on the best-selling novel *Gradiva, a Pompeiian Fantasy*, a century on, Bulwer Lytton's Pompeiian books influenced Madame Blavatsky, earth mother to the theorists of the Nazi party and later, to many New Age faiths as well.

The romance, the drama that the excavation of Pompeii brought to light provided archaeology with its fundamental inspiration; that living history and forgotten wisdom – not mere graves and death – lay buried in the silent earth. A revelation beautifully celebrated, along with Mediterranean light and fruitfulness, by Percy Bysshe Shelley in his 1816 'Ode to Naples', archaeology's first and probably its greatest poem:

> *I stood within the City disinterred;*
> *And heard the autumnal leaves like light footfalls*
> *Of spirits passing through the streets; and heard*
> *The mountain's slumberous voice at intervals*
> *Thrill through those roofless halls;*
> *The oracular thunder penetrating shook*
> *The listening soul in my suspended blood;*
> *I felt that Earth out of her deep heart spoke-*
> *I felt, but heard not: through white columns glowed*
> *The isle-sustaining ocean-flood,*
> *A plane of light between two heavens of azure!*

Copenhagen: 1816
Ordering the Ageless Past

IN EUROPE'S NORTHLANDS, BEYOND THE LIMITS of the Roman Empire, excavation was a very different thing. Although there were many misty and mysterious ancient monuments, and rich and curious treasures to be found in them, the northern European past was dumb, and therefore ageless. No ancient chronicles described its peoples or its kings; there were few written texts at all in fact, before Christianity arrived in Scandinavia a thousand years ago. Nothing then, to identify the buried citadels and towns that lay below the gently swelling fields. And no identity outside of legend, for the ancient dead that lay buried in numberless grassy graves.

'Our antiquity is wrapped in a thick fog, and belongs to a space and time we cannot measure,' wrote Rasmus Nyerup, the librarian of the University of Copenhagen and an assiduous collector of Danish antiquities. 'We know it is older than Christianity, but by a couple of years? a couple of centuries? or even by more than a millennium? we can do no more than guess'.

The urge to reach, to know this silent past inspired the birth of scientific archaeology. In 1807, within a year of his despairing remarks, Nyerup was given charge of an embryonic national collection of antiquities, sent for the most part, from the private collections of dilettante excavators who, for generations, had been digging randomly in the ancient mounds that stood in their thousands in the Danish fields and along the fjords. Nyerup stored the new collection in the university library, which was housed in the loft of the cavernous brick church, the Trinitatis, in central Copenhagen. He could find no order in it, and did little more than catalogue the antiquities as they arrived. Ten years later, the new curator, Christian Thomsen described the national collections on his arrival as lying 'in parcels, wrapped in scarves, lying on unpainted shelves, in cupboards, on window shelves, without the least plan or order. Neither was there money, nor anyone who had ever made plans of similar collections'.

A bluff man with a twinkle in his eye who dressed, like Beethoven, in the careless manner of the day, Christian Jürgensen Thomsen, the son of a wealthy merchant and banker, had from his youth, a deep passion for collecting and antiquarianism. Although lacking a university education, Thomsen was possessed of the tenacity, the energy and good sense of a successful entrepreneur of his time, and had a firm command of many languages and all the confident integrity of his class. He was moreover, of completely independent means. A lifelong bachelor, a coin collector from childhood with a mass of contacts right through Europe and Russia, Thomsen was also possessed of an especial genius for system analysis. In fact, this apparently unlikely figure was the perfect person to organise the tangled mass

RIGHT: *One of the most celebrated images of archaeological history. Drawn by Magnus Petersen in 1846, Christian Jürgensen Thomsen is seen standing in the museum galleries of the Christiansborg Palace, the first in the world to display the objects of an archaeological collection according to their place in Thomsen's system of the Stone, Bronze and Iron Ages. Affable and friendly, 'old Thomsen', as he was affectionately called, is seen showing the collections to a group of visitors. He advised museum curators to educate and enthuse the public, especially country people who often found buried relics in their fields. 'Archaeology,' said Thomsen, 'depends upon reliable information about the associations in which the artefacts were found'.*

of antiquity that he had inherited from Nyerup; and this he quickly did by dividing it into three basic groups, which he called 'ages'; the Stone, Bronze and Iron Ages were born.

At a single stroke, in the library of the University of Copenhagen, the ageless north was given an order, a history, something that successive generations working with additional material could change and modify, accept or reject, by reasoned argument. In short, Thomsen's simple system of classification was the first step in the creation of the modern science of archaeology.

The framework of the Three Age System was based initially, as are many good ideas, on intuition and experience. Thomsen's three 'ages' were not arbitrary divisions of the collections into three heaps of objects made of stone, bronze and iron, not simply the naming of arbitrary epochs – why then, were there no ages of pottery, or glass or bone, some early critics asked. Thomsen had simply identified those three materials that related, in a most basic way, to the northland's tangible progress, and named his ages after the three materials used by the ancients for the cutting edges of tools and weapons. In naming his three ages as he did, he realised that he might appear to be simply harking back to the ancient Greek and Roman writers who had written that before their own times, there had been an age of bronze, before that, an age of stone. Thomsen, however, used these classical labels much as Freud would later do in psychoanalysis, that is, as an embellishment and explication of a genuinely novel theory.

Magnus. P.
1846.

Thomsen's second breakthrough, one yet more important for the development of archaeology, was a process that he describes as arranging 'what was found together, and what was not'. In other words, he did not treat the objects in the collection in isolation, but as part of a group of objects that had been buried together at a single moment in time, usually in a single grave. This was the real key to building his Three Ages into a complete system that encompassed objects of other materials and types. Fortunately Nyerup's antiquarians had usually numbered and listed the contents of individual graves that they sent to Copenhagen, as Thomsen described, 'in parcels, wrapped in scarves, without the least plan or order'.

Thomsen quickly found pattern and order in these burial groups. His 'Stone Age', for example, was not only composed of the objects from those burials in which tools and weapons were made of stone and nothing else, but also included all the other objects from these graves as well, of amber, wood and gold, and copious pottery too — and all of them were labelled 'Stone Age'. From the fragmentary descriptions of the antiquarians who had collected them, Thomsen was even able to make the basic archaeological observation that many of these Stone Age burials had been placed in stone-lined underground chambers. Slowly, a picture of three distinctive ancient cultures was coming into view. 'That the Stone Age,' Thomsen later wrote, 'was the earliest in which we find our regions to have been inhabited by human beings seems established beyond all doubt, as is also the fact that the people must have borne a relationship to savages.'

A few of Thomsen's 'Iron Age' objects, on the other hand, bore Latin inscriptions that showed that some of the burials of that age were of approximately the same era as the Roman Empire. In the Iron Age too, Thomsen noted, the dead had sometimes been placed in wooden chambers accompanied by horses and even on occasion, by boats. Many of the Danish Iron Agers, he also noted, were cremated.

The beautiful burials of Thomsen's 'Bronze Age', his intermediate age between stone and iron, he noted, contained no iron at all and no silver either, and only simple beads of glass, rather than the complex glass vessels that were sometimes found in many of the Iron Age burials. The first cremations too, seemed to have taken place in the Bronze Age; this perhaps, Thomsen suggested, reflecting the arrival of another race in Denmark with different attitudes to death.

In the years after 1816, when Thomsen became curator, the national collections swelled to some 1500 pieces, flooding out of the little rooms beside the library. Accordingly, Thomsen's system slowly grew in sophistication, always surviving the acid test of absorbing novel objects and new-found grave groups without contradicting the established pattern. Like, it seemed, always did appear with like; and this from tombs all over Denmark. The ability of the Three Age System to enlarge and subdivide, to encompass fresh discoveries and new cultures, was the single overwhelming reason for its astonishing influence and longevity in Old World archaeology.

After some twenty years of collecting and arranging the national collections, Thomsen wrote a brief account of his system in a museum guide — known nowadays simply as the *Ledetraad* — prepared when the national collection was moved from its overcrowded quarters in the university library to a royal palace. By that time though, the outlines of Thomsen's scheme were known throughout northern Europe, having spread by word of mouth, in Thomsen's own letters and in friendly conversations with other curators from Germany and Scandinavia. Although it bore little relationship to any other history ever written, the Three Age System provided a brand new sort of history, one independent of written texts, yet a unique narrative of ancient ages that had been lost, as Nyerup had observed, in the silent northern mists. But was it really true? Was Thomsen's Three Age System just the abstract divisions of a museum display, or had it, in some pale way, reflected ancient realities?

Denmark: 1836–1886
Worsaae's Misty Mounds

THE PRACTICALITY, THE REAL IMPORTANCE of Thomsen's Three Age System was quickly proven in the excavations deep in the misty mounds of Denmark, of Jens Jacob Worsaae, one of Thomsen's museum assistants and a precocious genius in his own right. At fifteen Worsaae was excavating and publishing reports of his discoveries. At twenty-two, in 1843, he published an influential history of Danish prehistory based entirely on the underlying narrative implied by Thomsen's Three Age System, which was admired and imitated by archaeologists all over Europe. Time and time again, working in stone chambers deep in Danish mounds, excavating in fields and bogs and by the seaside, Worsaae's results were the same. Stratum upon stratum, lying one upon the other in the earth, burials that Thomsen's Three Age System identified as Bronze Age were found above those of his Stone Age and underneath those of his Iron Age. So an idea born in a museum, a simple system of classification had been proved by excavation in the field. Reality had corresponded with theory, and the modern science of archaeology had begun.

Along with proving the worth of Thomsen's Three Age System, Worsaae had also demonstrated the fundamental value of the principle of stratigraphy to archaeology. The notion that the layers, or strata in the earth, provided a relative time chart, a history of the site that could also be tied to grander schemes like the Three Age System. The technique of excavating and recording by stratigraphic layers is now a universal archaeological method employed in ice and desert, north and south, Old World and New from Jericho to Mexico. Stratigraphy and the relative chronologies it generates works everywhere.

Why though, was modern archaeology born in Denmark? Above all perhaps, because in this small continuously embattled country studded with ancient mounds and local myth, ancient history and modern national identity were uniquely intertwined long before the age of Thomsen and Worsaae. After northern Europe's counts and princes had visited the Bay of Naples and seen the rich dramas of the buried cities, the history in the earth, it was hardly surprising that similar archaeological sentiments were inspired at home, with several Danish kings and princes showing growing interest in the ancient monuments of their predecessors, however silent and mysterious their histories.

In 1776, the woods surrounding the royal hunting lodge of Jaegerspris close by Copenhagen were transformed into a memorial to national genius. From Tycho Brahe to Dr Bartholin, the names of a hundred eminent Danes were memorialised in sylvan neoclassical memorials thrown like enormous chess pieces into the glades of one of northern Europe's

OPPOSITE PAGE: *One of the hundreds of ancient mounds to be seen on the road from Copenhagen to Jaegerspris. Just as they had all over Europe, local antiquarians have dug about in such intriguing earthworks for centuries.*

oldest forests. Nor were the legendary Danish kings forgotten. At the forest's edge, a splendid Bronze Age barrow with a stone-lined burial chamber was transformed into a circular eighteenth-century formal French garden, hedged with dainty fences and topiary, and studded with marble memorials inscribed with royal names – Skiold, Harald Hildetand, Gorm, Wittekind and the like. It was traditionally believed that these ancient mounds, the mounds from which most of the objects of national collections would later came, covered the temples and the burial places of ancient Danish heroes.

Locked in desperate wars with first England then Prussia, which threatened to absorb the land of Denmark, the Danish kings and ministers employed the relics of local ancient history to help forge an individual national identity, a process that began with the adoption of Danish as the exclusive language of the court. In 1805, ministerial decrees ordered that a list of all ancient mounds of Denmark, the haunt and wonderment of generations of local antiquarians, be carefully catalogued and surveyed. In 1807, the same year that Rasmus Nyerup was appointed as the first curator of the National Danish Collection, most of Copenhagen was destroyed by a bombardment of the British Navy, part of Nelson's war against Napoleon, whom the Danish supported.

At his appointment, Thomsen was not merely faced with a simple problem of the classification of antiquity, but with giving shape and history to the silent Danish past. The government picked the right man for such an awesome undertaking; by the time of his death in 1865, Thomsen had established and organised all the major national museums to house the relics of Danish history. Not surprisingly, in his own country he is celebrated for more than the invention of the Three Age System, for which he is internationally renowned.

That these early archaeologists understood their role and the role of archaeology in this growing sense of nineteenth-century nationalism shows clearly in their writings. Worsaae, for example, wrote that a nation could only respect itself and its independence when it understood its ancient history; only then would the national character be truly revealed, only then would people be inspired to live and work in harmony and prosperity for the honour and well-being of their country and, above all, fight for its independence.

Not surprisingly perhaps, in 1847 Worsaae became the world's first professional archaeologist, the Archaeologist Royal, appointed by his friend, Frederik VII, King of Denmark. It is hardly surprising too, that the world's first professional archaeologist was not only supplied with a salary, but a military-style uniform. Only in 1854, when a university appointment was arranged for him, did the archaeological bandwagon hit the academic road; its roots, however, were in national history, and to some extent, remain so to this day.

Worsaae's diaries proudly describe a long series of grandiose excavations undertaken with the king, excavations accompanied by soldiers and brass bands, with armchairs set beside deep trenches dug under Worsaae's supervision by estate workers and military sappers. Excavations often undertaken alongside the king's relentless military manoeuvres, sometimes on the great Bronze Age fortification of the *Dannevirke* itself, which at that time, still separated Denmark from the state of Prussia.

'When I heard that the King was out on manoeuvres but would be back for lunch I took a carriage in order to report at Falkenberg Castle. Halfway there I met a large force of soldiers and His Majesty, who bade me welcome and ordered me to proceed to the camp

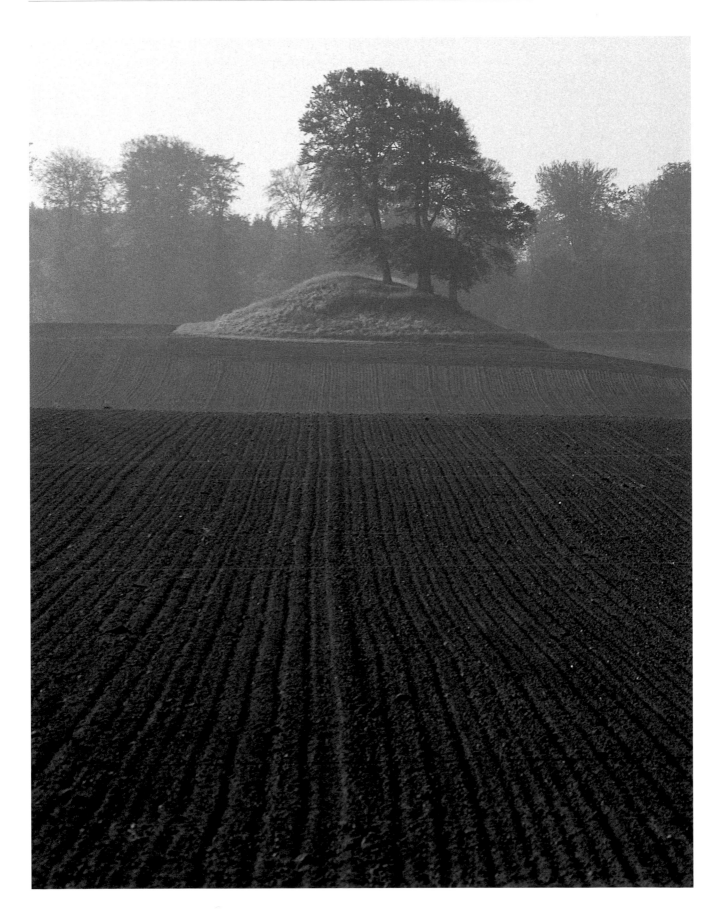

and report myself as a member of the Court. Tomorrow morning the King will inspect my drawings and discoveries with respect to the *Dannevirke*. It amuses me mightily that the foreign officers cannot believe that I am an antiquary. With my uniform and decorations I am normally taken for a diplomat. They little know how right they are. . .It was heartening for a good Dane to see our army once more gathered under the *Dannevirke*, prepared to defend the ancient frontier. . .Later we took a brisk walk to Isted Wood, where we visited a passage-grave of unusual dimensions. . .'

Sometimes, Worsaae tells us, the king would tip-toe away to salt the excavations with objects of the wrong age and thus puzzle his learned friend. Not for a moment though, would this jolly monarch have fooled the learned Dr Worsaae; by that time northern antiquity was most carefully organised.

Old Thomsen, as he had been affectionately known, was of another age with neither the ambitions nor the in-built limitations of the academics. He, of course, was very wealthy; in his fifty years directing, organising and conserving Denmark's various national collections, he was never paid a penny for his labours. Neither was he interested in fame or professional advancement. He simply did not care to write, frequently offering the opinion that there were too many books in the world. When he was young, the beginnings of Danish history had been explained in terms of a biblical emigration of bricklayers fleeing from God's destruction of the Tower of Babel, a cleric's bookish calculations dating their arrival in Copenhagen in 2266 BC precisely. All this, of course, had been quietly swept away by Thomsen's little *Ledetraad*.

Unlike Thomsen, Dr Worsaae was relatively poor and in a hurry. Not surprisingly, he was greatly annoyed when Thomsen, who had admiringly dubbed him his 'heaven-stormer', refused him a salary for his work at the museum. After the two men had parted, Worsaae obtained the paid position of Archaeologist Royal in an audience with the Danish king. Before that, however, he had acted as a roving ambassador for the new Danish scholarship, using Thomsen's Three Age System as the basis of a new science, a profession for scholars all over Europe. By the 1860s Worsaae's numerous publications had been joined by a flood of other books, journals and the papers of international archaeological congresses at which, until his death in 1886, Worsaae was an honoured guest.

This then, was the birth of a new kind of history-making. Pragmatic, nationalistic and above all, materialistic, the new science of archaeology was designed to trace humankind's material progress in a scientific way and that, decades before Darwin's evolutionary writings! As the archaeologist Sir Mortimer Wheeler observed with perhaps only half his tongue in his cheek, Darwin's evolutionary theories were the result of the application of archaeological concepts to the natural world.

Yet for all of that, this revolutionary northern history still had no fixed dates. As far as fixed chronology was concerned, the situation was exactly as Rasmus Nyerup had written before Thomsen had begun his work: was this new prehistory older than Christianity, by a couple of years, a couple of centuries or by more than a millennium?

BELOW: *Juliane-Hoj, a Bronze Age barrow on the royal estate of Jaegerspris that Danish princes have converted into a shrine to honour legendary national heroes, the old mound being cut with three steps, and encircled with memorial stones and trees. The notion of creating such an extraordinary archaeological curiosity may well have occurred to its architect, Johannes Wiedewelt in 1776 after a visit to Rome where he saw a similarly circular mausoleum, the mock tomb of a Roman emperor, in the gardens of the Villa Medici.*

Hallstatt: 1846. White Gold and the History of the Fibula

THE LAKE OF HALLSTATT LIES DEEP IN THE AUSTRIAN ALPS, just south of Salzburg. Until 1875, when a road was blasted out of the mountains, the only way in to the town of Hallstatt was by boat across the lake. In spite of its remoteness, two and a half thousand years ago this little town was a centre of European trade, a bridge, a link, between the classical cultures of the Mediterranean with their carefully compiled chronologies, and the undated cultures of ancient northern Europe. The mountains that stand high over Hallstatt are filled with salt. For millennia, the people of the town climbed up to them from their lakeside to mine the 'white gold', to clean it in mountain waterfalls and sell the refined results to the kitchens of all Europe. This salt, however, was not just used for savour; in ages before canning and refrigeration, salting was a fundamental method of preserving fish, pork, bacon and ham. That French ham was popular in ancient Rome and Sicily was due to Alpine salt mines such as Hallstatt; the town's very name indeed, it has been suggested, is derived from an archaic Mediterranean term for salt.

Nineteenth-century Hallstatt miners often found relics of their prehistoric forebears as they tunnelled their mountain; set fast in the salt that, in the damp darkness of the mine shafts, soon filled every void. Stubs of ancient torches burnt down to their handles, piles of wood shavings used for kindling, tools and baskets, even bowls of ancient food with the remains of dishes in them that are still prepared in Hallstatt to this day. Occasionally, they found the preserved bodies of ancient miners killed in long-forgotten accidents, and reburied them in Hallstatt's cemeteries down by the lake.

In November 1846, a young engineer employed by the state mining company, one Johann Ramsauer, was supervising a group of labourers digging road gravel from a meadow in the high green valley of the salt mines. Unexpectedly, a few feet beneath the surface, his workmen uncovered a skull and a bizarre bronze earring; soon after they had laid bare two large shallow graves; two circular basins with smooth mud floors, each one with skeletons laid lengthways on their backs, accompanied by jewellery, pots and daggers, and heavy ancient swords. The nearby cottagers told Ramsauer that they often found such things when they dug in their vegetable gardens; it seemed that this archaic cemetery was very large. A careful man, Ramsauer made measured drawings of the graves and sent them, along with their contents, to his immediate superiors in Vienna. In the way of civil servants, the collection was passed on to the relevant government department; in this instance the Offices of the Imperial Cabinet of Coins and Antiquities whose custodian, Baron von Sacken, was most intrigued.

What von Sacken saw was that Ramsauer's graves were pre-Roman in date and probably related to the northland's Bronze and Iron Ages. Unlike the northern collections, the

Austrian state museums held very few archaic antiquities in them, so von Sacken quickly arranged state funding for Ramsauer and a small team of workmen and artists to continue the excavations by the salt mines. At times, it must have seemed as if the work would never end. For twenty-five years, in the most careful and sustained archaeology of the time, Ramsauer supervised the excavation and recording of almost a thousand of these curious graves set in the high mountain valley. Many of the graves proved to be elaborate affairs, multiple burials beneath stone structures that resembled houses. Some graves contained interments, others cremations; some contained bronze weapons, others iron. All in all, they yielded more than six thousand objects — jewellery, pins, weapons, ceramics and cauldrons — all taken from the burials which, to the amazement of visiting archaeologists, Ramsauer and his artists meticulously recorded in beautiful watercolours.

So bizarre, were these strange graves in their cloud-filled cemetery that the Austrian Emperor Franz Joseph came to Hallstatt to view the excavations. Engineer Ramsauer, by temperament a natural-born field archaeologist, received a medal from him. Over the years von Sacken and other antiquarians issued learned tomes describing the discoveries.

There were two main theories as to who these ancient people in the grave field were; were they the 'Warrior Lords of the Salt' or simply the families of Hallstatt miners whom the salt mines had enriched? Recent excavations proved the latter to be true. Enormous heaps of animal bones found beside the ancient mine entrances show that the ingenious ancient Halstatters had not merely exported their salt, rowing it across their lake and carting it both north and south, but had organised extensive summer pasturing on the mountainsides, driving great herds of animals on to the fields beside the mines, which were butchered each autumn before the snows, salted, then sent for export. In recent excavations inside the mines, archaeologists working with jack hammers have reopened the salted-up ancient workings, and have recovered tiny fragments of rich cloth that give a picture of these early capitalists wearing imported robes embellished, like the burials in the grave field, with elaborate imported goods.

ABOVE: *The mountain slopes above the little Austrian town of Hallstatt, where a Bronze Age cemetery was skilfully excavated in the 1840s by a local mining engineer, providing Scandinavian archaeologists with a vital link between the historically well-known cultures of the ancient Mediterranean and the anonymous cultures of northern Europe. The platforms are the remains of the nineteenth-century salt works. Modern methods remove the salt by dissolving and pumping: the only miners presently working in these mountains are archaeologists re-excavating the ancient mineshafts.*

LEFT: *The lake of Hallstatt traversed by a traditional salt boat, Until the coming of the railways, such transport was the only way of travelling to the miners' houses on the lakeshore.*

In Ramsauer's day, however, Hallstatt's greatest gift was not the recovery of a slice of ancient life, but the fact that the ancient burials promised to provide fixed dates for part of Thomsen's Three Age System.

That both bronze and iron weapons were buried in the grave field showed that its inhabitants had spanned the cusp of those two ages – or, as the northern antiquarians would say, that it had been in use from the late Bronze to the early Iron Age. That most of the objects from the graves, which were assumed to be of local manufacture, were clearly related in both their materials and designs to the antiquities of Denmark, of Germany and of Sweden provided an immediate connection to the northern antiquities and the Three Age System. A few objects, on the other hand, connected these same tombs with ancient cultures to the south, and some of these could be given fixed dates – rare imports from ancient

Greece, modest bronzes of the fourth century BC. From Italy too, there were some Etruscan bronzes of similar date. That there were no ancient Roman objects at all in any of the graves simply served to confirm this early date; Ramsauer's gravefield had fallen out of use, probably in the fourth century BC, long before the Romans came.

Even as Ramsauer continued his work at Hallstatt, other similar sites were being discovered in the Alps. Linked to the contents of the Hallstatt graves by their material and design, the heaps of majestic weapons dredged from Lake Neuchâtel close by the village of La Tène, extended this same Bronze Age craft tradition further back in time, whilst finds of older imports from the south provided earlier fixed dates of the seventh to eighth centuries BC.

Some of Worsaae's northern colleagues had recognised Hallstatt's importance from the first years of the excavations. They eagerly visited the grave field where they marvelled at Ramsauer's delicate and tireless field work; then they travelled to the Imperial collections in Vienna to draw and measure, comparing his finds with others from the north. By the 1860s, Swedish archaeologists had christened the indigenous objects from Ramsauer's grave field as the 'Hallstatt Culture' and had given it an approximate lifespan between 800–400 BC.

To make such simple histories, a small group of northern archaeologists passed their lives studying the vast harvests of such archaic cemeteries, forging analytic keys to unlock the past. These pioneers invented the word 'typology', that now-common term used to describe a method of arranging groups of similar objects by their changes in design, such as you may order, say, motor cars, in sequences from old to recent. They compared thousands of ancient graves, analysing the materials, patterns and techniques of their contents, correlating their relative stratigraphies, and attempting always, to place the dates obtained from rare sites such as Hallstatt into their general schemes of European history. Such work is slow and often library-bound; here then, something of the image of the dusty scholar was born. Yet these same cataloguers were building grand histories from odd fragments of ancient daily life

Slowly then, in the 1860s and 1870s, the later history of the Three Age System was fixed in real-time. What though, of earlier ages? Half of Thomsen's Three Age System, the Stone Age and the early Bronze Age, still lacked any dates at all. In all the world, the unlettered past extended back no further than the eighth century BC. In 1881, however, an Englishman on a Cook's Tour in Egypt gave the northern past another thousand years of history.

Thebes: 1881
Pitt Rivers' *terminus ante quem*

E ARLY IN MARCH *1881*, a certain Augustus Henry Lane Fox Pitt Rivers took a tour down the Egyptian Nile to Thebes. The General, as he was known, for he had been an army man and fought in the Crimea, had come into an enormous fortune. In consequence, he had just moved house from Earl's Court to Kensington and taken possession of the largest and most ancient of estates in all of southern England. Now he was taking a holiday.

Pitt Rivers was an archetypal Victorian. Ruthless, eccentric, intelligent and naive; a quick, cold sceptic who reserved his passion for his lifelong devotion to archaeology, especially in the silky hills of northern Dorset. Never a man to waste an opportunity – the General once stopped a shoot on his estate and had his startled guests down on their knees searching for flints – on that day at Thebes, on his way to the Valley of the Kings, he spotted the key to a basic archaeological problem. By the roadside he noticed some flints of types that were common in European excavations where they were generally labelled as being from Thomsen's dateless Stone Age. At Thebes, however, they were firmly embedded in the architecture of ancient Egyptian tomb chapels that were cut from a bed of compacted sand and rubble brought down by ancient floods. This, he realised, was incontrovertible evidence that the European Stone Age was at least as old as ancient Egypt, for the beds of gravel that held the ancient flints were far older than the ancient chapels.

For many centuries, most antiquarians and geologists had simply assumed that the worked flints they found had been made in very distant times. The General though, was interested in hard evidence; evidence he said, capable of standing up in a court of law. What he had seen that day at Thebes was that the date of the ancient tomb chapels provided the latest possible date – a *terminus ante quem* in archaeological jargon – for the dates of the flints' own manufacture. Now in 1881, these tombs had already been given dates by egyptologists; they had been described in an ancient Egyptian papyrus written by a team of tomb inspectors around 1000 BC when these tombs were already some five centuries old. All Pitt Rivers had to do was to demonstrate that the position of the flints embedded in the walls of these tombs was genuinely ancient.

Enlisting a fellow traveller, the geologist J. F. Campbell, to serve as a witness, on 4 March, 1881, Pitt Rivers set off on a little excavation. Almost immediately, he found what he was looking for; man-made flints embedded so firmly and deeply in the walls of the ancient tombs that they could not possibly have been set into them at a later date. While the geologist and his man-servant set about extracting some of them for measuring

ABOVE: *This typical Theban flint, labelled in the typography Pitt Rivers employed for his archaeological work, stands as solid proof of his Theban researches in 1881, when archaeology was finally able to prove that the European Stone Age was at least as old as pharaoh's Egypt.*

RIGHT: *General Augustus Henry Lane Fox Pitt Rivers DCL, FRS, FSA, stares confidently at a world of which he was a leading member; a photograph taken about 1890, when the General's epoch-making excavations and publications were well under way.*

and drawing, Pitt Rivers and his artist surveyed and drew the architecture of the tombs, and the topography and geology of the gentle valley, which they mapped for half a mile. The extracted flints, the General's hard evidence, were each numbered and boxed for storage in the South Kensington Museum at London. Within the year, a brief scientific report, with fine drawings of the flints and the relevant parts of the plain of Thebes together with some sample tomb plans, were published in the *Journal of the Anthropological Institute* in London: Thomsen's northern Stone Age was at least as old as 1500 BC.

This Medalet was designed for me by Dr. John Evans, Treasurer of the Royal Society, and President of the Society of Antiquaries, to whom I am also indebted for valuable assistance and advice on many occasions. It has been placed near the bottom of the greater number of excavations made by me since 1880, together with a few coppers and other objects, and the date has usually been stamped on it with a punch.

Today perhaps, the General's Cook's Tour excavation may seem pedantic. In 1881, after all, the year in which Bartók and Picasso were born and the motor car was being developed, all sensible people, from Charles Darwin to Thomas Edison agreed that such man-made flints as those that the General had found were very ancient. What the General had done, however, was to *prove* that assumption.

And that, ultimately, is what the *science* of archaeology is all about. That is why it is different from religion, New Age theorising and those who put their faith in visions and opinions. As the General well knew, at its very root archaeology is the slow process of gathering proof about the past from the silent earth. In Egypt, at a single stroke, he had doubled the real time span of European prehistory. After Egypt, on his recently inherited estates in Dorset, Pitt Rivers transformed the rough and tumble of contemporary excavation into a precise science.

Cranbourne Chase: 1880–1900. Stalking Darwin

Rushmore House, Pitt Rivers' country seat at the centre of his vast north Dorset estate, was a modest enough dwelling for what in the 1870s, was one of the richest families in England. It was an unhappy household: the General's wife counted every penny, complained about the cost of archaeology and fought continuously with her children and her husband. Apart from occasional wild forays into family life – whipping a daughter, disinheriting an errant son but always honouring their debts – the General devoted himself to the past.

Cranbourne Chase was an ancient hunting park, nearly thirty thousand acres of beautiful rolling countryside, a grazing ground for royal deer, untouched by farmers since early medieval times. In consequence, its hills and woods were covered with a wondrous variety of archaeological remains. When the General's men dug pits for trees designed to tame the windy Chase, ancient skulls appeared, glistening white in the black earth. Ancient pottery too, littered the chalk downs; the General once found some fragments of imported Roman tableware, shining in the fresh dirt of a mole hill, evidence of a buried Roman farmstead.

In his former career as a professional soldier, Pitt Rivers oversaw the British army's change of weaponry from the Brown Bess of the Waterloo troopers to the first Enfield rifle used later during the First World War. In those days

ABOVE: *Sown by Pitt Rivers throughout the trenches of his excavations on Cranbourne Chase, these little disks may be called the seeds of modern archaeology.*

BELOW: *The excavating team at Pitt Rivers' last dig in December 1897 at Iwerne, close by the boundaries of Cranbourne Chase, where a small Roman villa was unearthed. The team consists of a supervisor and surveyor, G. Waldo Johnson, who stands at the left of the pick and shovel men. 'As a rule,' the General commented on his supervisors, 'I have been well served by my clerks'. The three small boys used their buckets to wash pottery fragments and any other finds.*

CRANBOURNE CHASE: 1880–1900

he had become a passionate collector of 'savage and primitive' objects, founding two enormous collections of ancient and tribal objects, that were amongst the first in Europe. Donated to Oxford University, his first astonishing assemblage – everything from baby Buddhas to shrunken heads, from Greek statues to Polynesian shields – remains the finest Victorian museum in the world. Like the Scandinavian archaeologists before him, Pitt Rivers saw processes of evolution, something similar to those that his contemporary Charles Darwin was describing in the natural world, working in these 'primitive' objects, just as he observed the same principles at work in the weaponry of war and later, in the evolution of the motor car.

To Pitt Rivers indeed, the evolution of guns and flints, of skeletons and human institutions, of phrenology and feudalism were all as one, and he wrote learnedly and trenchantly on all of them whilst serving on committees of various national societies of anthropology and organising archaeological congresses. His great ambition was to communicate his evolutionary principles, which he believed, had climaxed in the social order of contemporary European culture. It was to this end that his two museums were established. In the second of them, built on Cranbourne Chase and set around with entertainments, tea rooms, hotels, peacocks and brass bands, the General set up this characteristic notice:

> *Professors, Peddlers, Politicians and Poultry-keepers*
> *Why have you come here and what do you expect to see?*
> *Please ask yourselves these questions*
> *What are you (by race, by descent, by nationality) ?*
> *Are you civilised?*
> *Are you educated?*
> *What do you mean by civilisation?*
> *What do you mean by education?*
> *Please think*
> *We ask you to read the labels and form your*
> *opinion on the order that you see*
> *You are invited to write your remarks in the Visitors Book when you leave*

It is hardly surprising then, that archaeology, the young science that provided an entirely materialistic vision of the past, became Pitt River's final and greatest passion. In the remains of the past he could find the earliest evidence, the history of those evolutionary patterns he had already seen in armaments and anthropology. At fifty, he tells us, 'having retired from active service on account of ill health. . .I determined to devote the remaining portion of my life chiefly to an examination of the antiquities on my own property'.

The main problem in archaeology, as he saw it, was the one he had faced at Thebes; how to document precisely such vitally important buried truths as the early development of modern society. He started modestly enough, by excavating a series of small Bronze Age barrows, small funerary earth works that lay clustered throughout Cranbourne Chase. In later years, his excavations grew to include Roman farms and Iron Age earthworks, Saxon graves and medieval houses. Whatever the site, however, he always recorded every excavation with the same care and intelligence, meticulously recording evidence which, as he said, would be capable of standing up in a court of law.

The General trained a small team of excavators for this work – England's first professional

SECTION I. ACROSS BOKERLY DYKE, ON LINE A-B. OF PLAN. PLATE CLXII.
NOTE. ALL THE RELICS FOUND IN THE CUTTING AND IN THE RAMPART EXTENSION CUTTING, ARE PROJECTED INTO THIS SECTION.

SECTION 3, ACROSS ROMAN ROAD ON LINE G-H OF PLAN, PLATE CLXII.

SECTION 4, ACROSS ROMAN ROAD, 440 YARDS NORTH-EAST OF SECTION 3.

SCALE OF FEET FOR ALL SECTIONS.

archaeologists. These supervisors were paid a pittance and lived with the family at Rushmore House, albeit in the servants' quarters. Usually, there was four of them: one draftsman, sent at the General's request from the Royal College of Art; and three others, young men recruited locally, trained by the General to sketch and survey and control the diggings. Each morning, this little band set out across the Chase, led by the General, sitting bolt upright in his carriage, attended by two liveried coachmen. Following on behind, sporting Pitt Rivers' colours of blue and gold in the rims of their boaters, and sometimes, it was later recalled, riding penny-farthing bicycles, came the four young supervisors.

At the site of the excavations, this procession would meet the ten or so labourers especially drawn from the estate gangs to serve as archaeological workmen. Both men and boys were paid 12 pence a day and worked a six-day week. Sometimes they enjoyed the work. Pitt Rivers often praised their skills; years later some of them remembered him too with affection, if with a slight shiver of apprehension, for the General was a hard military master. Rain and shine, they dug on open sites on the high chalk downs and in the dark coppices of the valleys. Throughout the winter months, they cut deep trenches and cleared ancient earthworks to depths of thirty feet or so, usually excavating right down to the undisturbed natural chalk beneath. Most of the time, the General watched their progress himself. Under his direction, every object, every piece of pottery, each change of strata, however small, however insignificant, everything the General saw, was drawn and measured, placed and planned in the position in which it was found within the earth. Everything.

ABOVE: *An example of the hundreds of maps, plans and sections that the General published of his excavations. Writing from Egypt in 1892 in criticism of a colleague's work, the young Flinders Petrie advised his correspondent to 'look at Pitt Rivers' Excavations at Bokerley Dyke, [and] you will see what I mean'. The General's standard of excavation and the presentation of his findings — their very look and feel — have influenced archaeology around the world.*

In all his twenty years of excavation, Pitt Rivers found very little gold or art or ancient history. But then he was not much interested in treasure nor in ancient politics, just the processes of ancient life.

Pitt Rivers placed a special medallion in the trenches, graves and pits he excavated, before he filled them up again. Designed by his friend, the chairman of the Royal Numismatic Society, Sir John Evans, the father of the excavator of Knossos in ancient Crete, these 'medalets', as the General called them, were decorated with images from his excavations: a labourer's pickaxe, ancient pottery, a bronze axe and sword, an excavated skull and a surveyor's level. Pottery, he prophetically observed, would come to provide dates for excavations as firm as those provided by buried ancient coins: skulls, he believed, revealed detailed information about the ancient races of the Chase. Hundreds of these 'medalets' still lie buried beneath the green Dorset landscape. They are the seeds of modern archaeology; the General's complete absorption with record-making, with his ultimately unattainable goal of reproducing all traces of past activity as it existed in the earth before his excavation, entirely overwhelmed his desire to teach us about the history of social evolution.

Nothing expresses the General's absorption with the reproduction of the three-dimensional reality of his excavations than the exquisite models he ordered of his work, fastidiously accurate scale surveys sculpted in mahogany and paint, prepared by Mr Martin, the estate carpenter under the General's careful eye. At the excavation sites themselves, he often erected little stone monuments with inscriptions recording his discoveries. The same sanserif typeface used for those inscriptions also appears on his models; they are two aspects of the same reality. The same distinctive typeface is employed again in the illustrations of the four volumes, *Excavations in Cranbourne Chase*, weighty buckram tomes decorated in the Pitt Rivers livery colours, the third aspect of this extraordinary labour. To this day, the

BELOW: *With his carriage awaiting his return, in military style and great good order, General Pitt Rivers and his men excavate the ditch at Wor Barrow on the edge of Cranbourne Chase in the autumn of 1893. Some sixty years later, Sir Mortimer Wheeler described this excavation as 'the first long barrow scientifically excavated — and still one of the few'. No mean praise from a man who described another archaeologist's work as similar to 'digging for potatoes'.*

General's books stand as a benchmark of archaeological excellence.

Although others may think it all a waste of time, the General prophesied that there was no knowing the needs of future archaeologists, and in the 1950s armchair archaeologists revisited the General's plans and models to reconstruct some of the ancient realities which he had excavated and recorded, but never really understood. All the information that they needed was at hand.

The four volumes of *Excavations at Cranbourne Chase* also show an extraordinary prescience; his text shows a wide range of practical interests in ancient life that archaeology has only taken up again within the last few decades. In one line he notes that we have no idea when inventions as basic as the iron nail were introduced to England; in another he observes that some rough stones from his excavations served the same purposes anciently as ones used in contemporary Dorset, supporting sheds and wooden barns high above the ground. There are numerous graphs as well – how the General would have loved computers! – analysing pottery and coins; anything indeed, that could be counted and quantified. Elaborate charts and diagrams compare the excavated bones of ancient horses, oxen, pigs, sheep, dogs and deer with their modern equivalents, with bred horses and cart horses, with New Forest and Exmoor ponies, with Alderney and black Kerry cows, with wild boar, black crossbred pigs and twelve kinds of sheep and deer. Such preoccupations with the interaction of people with their environment and following changes in both through long ages is uncannily modern (*see pages 204–11*). In a series of moving paragraphs, Pitt Rivers even shows us that he instinctively saw himself as part of these same social processes, abruptly breaking off in the middle of a brilliant description of the excavation of a medieval hunting lodge to expiate, in typical eccentric prose, upon some contemporary changes in the hunting laws. Then it is that you see the roots of this strange Victorian, which so nourished his archaeology.

Like Thomsen before him, Pitt Rivers was, as contemporary academics would have said, 'self-taught'. Like many of his intellectual peers, the General stood outside academia and

BELOW: *Sir Mortimer Wheeler's now-classic diagram, first published in 1954 in his influential* Archaeology from the Earth, *showing how careful excavation and recording of an archaeological section can provide a time-chart, a history of the site, even if the ground has been extensively disturbed, as it had been in Wheeler's celebrated Indian excavations of the late 1940s. The division of objects by type and by their location in related strata is the mainstay of archaeological excavation to this day. Similarly, linking a series of different stratigraphic sections into a single continuous 'sequence' provides archaeologists with the potential to link different digs together in a single relative history.*

showed no desire to enter or affect it. His immediate impact therefore, on mainstream archaeology, was negligible. Although several of his assistants continued working as archaeologists after his death, serving as curators of local museums and archaeological societies, they hardly affected the growing academic mainstream whose standards of excavation for thirty years and more were well below those of the General.

And yet his overall effect has been profound, not the least upon Middle Eastern archaeology, a discipline he personally deplored as taking funding away from the 'primary study of the British race'. Chance meetings with the young Flinders Petrie, who later become the doyen of Egyptian archaeologists — they first met on the General's Cook's tour of Egypt, when Petrie was surveying the Pyramids — slowly turned into a fruitful relationship, with Petrie taking his new young wife down to Rushmore to meet the old man in 1899, the year before his death.

The effect of the General's books on Petrie and hence on Middle Eastern archaeology, had been deep and lasting. In a letter describing the low quality of British excavation in Egypt, young Petrie had observed in a postscript that 'If you look at Pitt-Rivers' *Excavations at Bokerley Dyke* [part of a *Cranbourne Chase* volume], you will see what I mean'. The content, the order, the very look and feel of most of Petrie's archaeological publications reflect the General's deep influence upon him. Although the General's lavish excavations were impossible goals for Petrie to attain in the hard and lonely conditions of nineteenth-century Egypt, they provided Petrie with a yardstick, an epitome of good archaeology.

The General even influenced Petrie's greatest single contribution to archaeological method, a system of relative dating, of 'Sequence Dating', as Petrie called it (*see further, page 152*). Petrie's identification of design changes on early Egyptian pottery bears close resemblance to some of Pitt Rivers' observations concerning the decoration on a Roman-British pot from Cranbourne Chase. Such 'evolutionary' changes of design, the General had commented, 'afford an example of one of those transformations of ornament of which such numerous examples occur in savage and early art, and of which many specimens are shown in my museum at Oxford'.

Pitt Rivers' work was rediscovered by a new generation of archaeologists in the late 1940s who, in the volumes of Cranbourne Chase, found to their great surprise that the General had established methods of excavation and recording that had hardly been bettered. Shortly after this discovery, Mortimer, later Sir Mortimer Wheeler, began to organise his excavations and publications along lines pioneered on Cranbourne Chase, although Wheeler later extended them to dizzy new heights in England and in India. In 1954, Wheeler placed Pitt Rivers securely in the mainstream of archaeological development in his slim volume that became a standard textbook on archaeological technique — an evolutionary process that the 'maestro,' as Wheeler dubbed the General, would have undoubtedly approved.

Piltdown: 1912. The Missing Link and Dawson's Dawn Man

I N THOSE LAST COMFORTABLE YEARS before the beginning of the First World War, it must have seemed that archaeology had come of age and was engaged in the making of a brand new history for the West; a dispassionate history, as the General would have said, built firmly upon expert science and archaeological evidence capable of standing up in a court of law. By that time of course, Darwin's theories had largely swept away traditional Western visions of human origin. The Bible's gentle universe, Adam and Eve, theology and scripture, had been replaced by the developing jargons of a young academic establishment that had taken control of archaeology, anthropology and anatomy. Modern people who wished to know about the past read the works of scientists, not priests; they wanted facts not myths or theories.

In the London offices of the Royal Geographical Society there is a portrait of a group of Edwardian gentleman of just this same time. They are observing a seated man in a laboratory coat who is showing them a human skull. Gesturing with one hand, his index finger making a scientific point, in the other, he holds a pair of anatomical dividers. His audience is fascinated. On the wall behind them all is a small portrait of Charles Darwin, deep-browed father of popular evolutionism and saintly patron of this eminent group of scientists. However, although most of them do not know it, the skull they stare at is a forgery, and one of their company is, perhaps, the greatest archaeological forger of all time, he who made the Piltdown Man.

In 1912, in a triumphant press conference, complete with a reconstructed 'meet your ancestor' portrait, some of these same men, Britain's finest anatomists, gathered around this skull and pronounced it the 'missing link' of Darwin's evolutionary chain; the ugly half-way house between our man-monkey ancestors and *Homo sapiens*. Darwin's scientific prophecy had been fulfilled and at a single stroke, the archaeology of the human race was given new dimension. All the brutish bones previously found in France and Germany had come from later geological strata. The Piltdown skull, however, 'excavated' in Sussex and dated by the gravels in which it was 'found', was believed to be at least 100,000 years older than all of those, and more than that, he had been English! Although he would surely have been critical of the poor quality of the excavation that purported to have brought Mr Piltdown back into the light, Pitt Rivers, who had died a decade earlier, would have been delighted with this discovery that corroborated so many of his deepest beliefs about science and the human race.

And that perhaps, is why such a clumsily forged mock Stone Age skull, with 'a substance resembling chewing gum' stuck in its teeth, with file marks on its jaw and false tinting which,

RIGHT: *Whodunnit? In all likelihood the Piltdown Skull was forged by one or more of the eminent Edwardians shown in this painting by John Cooke. The white-coated Sir Arthur Keith perhaps, intently measuring the fake? Or Sir Grafton Elliot Smith, standing at Keith's right shoulder, who performed the celebrated autopsies on Egypt's royal mummies? Or the amateur prehistorian Charles Dawson, standing at Keith's other shoulder, on whose estate the famous fake was excavated? It may, however, have been made by someone not present in this painting. Dawson's novelist neighbour, Sir Arthur Conan Doyle, a keen practical joker; or the Jesuit philosopher and archaeologist, Teilhard de Chardin, who found one of Piltdown's teeth himself, and later excavated another now-mysteriously vanished skull of 'early man'. Piltdown might have appealed to Teilhard's religiosity as well as his sense of humour. Without fresh evidence, however, it is likely that the forger's identity will never be known.*

the National Gallery later declared to be similar to Vandyke Brown, fooled the archaeological establishment for more than forty years. It served so many different purposes. Made to fill a gap in scientific theory, Piltdown Man flattered contemporary English visions of the ancient past, made celebrities of the archaeologists who found and studied it and advertised the power of the developing science of archaeology. It even served to shift the centre of the science of prehistory away from the Continent to England. Billed as 'the first Englishman', the 'discoveries' at Piltdown effectively made Britain the world centre of evolutionary archaeology for decades. No longer were international congresses on human prehistory conducted in French and held in France. After Piltdown, those foreign scholars who came to England to attend academic gatherings were taken down to the Sussex gravel pits at Piltdown and encouraged to sieve out more evidence of the world's prehistory for themselves.

At Piltdown's ill-tempered exposé in the 1950s, a sadly pugilistic affair awash with accusations and recriminations, a vast battery of scientific establishments joined together to prove the wicked forgery: the British Museum's Department of Geology and Minerals; Oxford University's Department of Human Anatomy; the Atomic Energy Department, the Geological Survey and the Physics Department of King's College, London; the Government Chemist's Department; Oxford University's Microchemical Department; not to mention the National Gallery and the Soil Survey. Quite coolly and with the most admirable detachment, science saved its reputation!

Yet the fraud of the Piltdown skull was detected and revealed only when evolutionary archaeology had no further use for it, when it had become something of an anachronism. Although there had been many doubts and disagreements as to Piltdown's importance in the evolutionary scheme, up until that time no one had imagined that they were the bones of a very false prophet. Although Pitt Rivers' science could indeed stand up in a court of law, the language and assumptions that grew up around it could be filled with myth and fantasy. Even the General himself had dug to scientifically prove beyond all doubt that the order of the Victorian state of which he was a leading member was a 'natural' order, sanctioned by millennia of social evolution. 'The law that Nature makes no jumps,' the General once observed in his transparent, if elliptic prose, 'can be taught by the history [gained by archaeology!] of mechanical contrivances, in such a way as at least to make men cautious how they listen to scatter-brained revolutionary suggestions.' Was archaeology then, really as abstract a science as Pitt Rivers claimed, or was it simply a humanistic discipline? Could archaeology indeed, take place at all without a programme to 'interpret' its discoveries?

The Vézère Valley: 1863. Lartet and Christy Arrange the Ancestors

ALTHOUGH PILTDOWN TEMPORARILY ECLIPSED the Continent's role in the recovery of early human history, it could never have replaced it. Half a century before the Piltdown forgery, French archaeologists were already developing the language and classifications that their archaeological successors still use to describe parts of the Stone Age; eras of the human past are still stamped with French provincial names. Compared with Pitt Rivers, French archaeology was poor; these excavators though, were not interested in recording all surviving traces of human activity existing in the soil of France. They were looking specifically for relics of human prehistory, in recovering what they considered to have been the dawning of the human race.

Édouard Lartet, the greatest of these archaeologists and now called the father of prehistory, was a French lawyer-turned-archaeologist born in south-western France in 1801, and of the same generation as Thomsen. He was the man who more than any other, uncovered the astonishing cultures of European prehistory from some thirty thousand years ago. Lartet's most important work was undertaken in the Dordogne in the few years before he died in 1871. He was well prepared. For more than twenty years, ever since retiring from the law at the age of 33, he had excavated in his home region of the Pyrenees. A quarter-century before Darwin published his theories of human evolution, Lartet had already proposed that the bones of ape-like creatures he had found just ten miles from his house, were ancestors of the human race. Excavating sites of a much later period, he had earlier suggested that some small engravings he had found, a bone engraved with the figure of a deer, had been drawn by people of the Stone Age, the first time such a suggestion had ever been put forward. By 1850, Lartet's discoveries and speculations had made him a scientific celebrity and he was elected to the *Académie*. Then in short order he had suffered a series of attacks by its most eminent members, some of whom were still Creationists, and many of whom mistrusted the growing science of archaeology, which seemed to be taking history away from traditional historians.

Such bitter debates, Lartet realised, could only be resolved by placing the ever-growing number of prehistoric archaeological discoveries into a single chronology, 'after the names' as he put it 'recently adopted by

RIGHT: *Édouard Lartet was the first prehistorian to realise that prehistoric people had drawn images of the animals that they hunted. This plate from* Reliquiae Aquitanicae *shows some of the animal bones excavated by Lartet and Christy, engraved with vivid images of horses and reindeer.*

LEFT: *This lovely lithograph, an illustration from Lartet and Christy's sumptuous* Reliquiae Aquitanicae *was published in 1875, the year that Christy died. It shows the centre of the riverside village of Les Eyzies, nestling beneath the rock shelters that still hold innumerable relics of early man. The ruined chateau above the village has now been rebuilt as the National French Museum of Prehistory; its celebrated sculpture of a noble savage looks out from beneath the shelter of the swinging cliff.*

archaeologists in their divisions of Stone, Bronze and Iron Age'. It was also clear to him that the Age of Stone needed a detailed relative time chart of its own, so that the various discoveries, the different ancient cultures already excavated in Europe could be placed in broad chronological order, much as Thomsen had done for Danish prehistory. Lartet's long years of excavation led him to realise that stratigraphy alone, layer on layer through time, could place the relics of these various diverse cultures into a pattern of prehistory.

After receiving a box filled with an exceptionally rich collection of ancient flints and bones gathered by a friendly fossil hunter from the natural rock shelters of the beautiful valley of the River Vézère, Lartet travelled to the sleepy village of Les Eyzies at the heart of that region to take a look for himself. There was, of course, no shortage of Stone Age sites in Europe at that time; Lartet's previous work in the Pyrenees had been exceptionally rewarding. The wonder of the calm Vézère Valley at the heart of the Dordogne region lay in the sheer spans of time over which the ancient sites had been used, the sheer depth and consistency of their undisturbed strata. In the immediate area of a grand cave known locally as La Madeleine, was a riverside rock shelter whose strata were studded with anciently made flint tools. Such extraordinary caves – and there were many more – were chock-full of remains that, we now know, span the last half million years. For Lartet the archaeologist, they promised to provide a single guidebook to the entire late Stone Age, layer upon layer, epoch after epoch. This then, was a place to excavate.

At Les Eyzies, Lartet joined an English friend, Henry Christy, who would finance the excavation. A retired banker some ten years younger than Lartet, Christy had been travelling the world for many years, often in the company of scholars who were in the process of founding the modern science of anthropology (*see page 149*). A devout Quaker, Christy's previous ambition had been to tease out something of the origins of modern religion, of social and ethical development, by studying the so-called 'primitive' races of mankind. Like Pitt Rivers, however, whom he knew and liked, Christy had been entirely fascinated by Darwin's theory of evolution. All at once, he had realised that the origins of humankind's moral development were best studied archaeologically, and that Édouard Lartet, whom he had also known for years, was the best-placed scholar in Europe to aid this investigation.

Before their meeting at Les Eyzies, they had organised their archaeological expedition around a precise agenda; an English ethnographer teamed with the French archaeologist to order and perhaps even to part explain the rise of humankind. Though, just two years later Christy was dead and Lartet too died shortly after, in the brief time they worked together in the pretty valley of the Vézère, they revolutionised prehistoric archaeology.

Such work traditionally began by making a sounding, *sondage*, that classic French approach to excavation, where a number of small pits are dug throughout a site to locate the most fruitful places to excavate. They used local farmers for their labourers, quiet ingenious people who were fascinated by the ancient relics that the archaeologists dug out of their sheep pens, and in the caves in which they kept their hay, their onions and potatoes. Some of these same caves and sheep pens have since lent their names to variants of similar ancient cultures and vast epochs of prehistory found right around the world.

Lartet and Christy excavated two small rock shelters in their first season, two gentle hollowings in the cliffs beside the slow-flowing river where Stone Age people had sat and slept, made fires, flaked their flints and eaten their food. In the first trench that they made, they found flints of a type previously only known from excavations made thirty years earlier in Cornwall; this then, was the first evidence of the real possibility of linking all such sites into a single history. In the rear of the other rock shelter called Laugerie-Haute, part of which had been anciently blocked and sealed by a rockfall from the cliff above, they found a little dirt-filled cave, which they discovered as they dug into its many strata, held some fourteen feet of human history beneath its floor – charcoal and wood ash, bone, flint and white sea shells set in dark organic stains in the earth, the tell-tale shadows of ancient human life. At the top of the trench, they excavated flints of a type they had found earlier in the first rock shelter. Beneath, they found types of flints that Lartet had already excavated in the Pyrenees and dubbed as aurignacian, after the Cave of Aurignac where he had first found them. Beneath these yet again, right on the bedrock, they found types of flint that no one had ever seen before. In a single season then, they had joined their work with that of two other excavations and set them all in a single sequence; the first relative time chart of the Stone Age. When they relayed their discoveries in both French and English scientific journals, the news was greeted with amazement.

The following season at La Madeleine, on the low lush banks of the Vézère, Lartet and Christy excavated some more of the same distinctive flint tools that they had found the previous season. Beneath these they found flints and artefacts of another unknown culture, and this they named the Magdelanian, after the great rock shelter above. Here too, Lartet found more evidence of Stone Age art – an engraving of a mammoth cut on a piece of mammoth tusk.

At another rock shelter called Le Moustier high above the valley floor, looking down upon the red roofs of a medieval hamlet, they found flints of the same type that they had found at the bottom of their cut in Laugerie-Haute during the previous season. Here, however, the flints lay in strata just under the top soil. Beneath them then, lay the remains of yet earlier, completely unknown epochs of human history. Even as they started into these lower levels, they found new types of flint tool, of the variety now called mousterian. Since Lartet and Christy's day, relics of the Mousterian culture have been found on every continent on earth and have been associated with an extinct species known as Neanderthals who emerged around 150,000 years ago and were therefore close contemporaries of early *Homo sapiens*. Beneath the mousterian strata, Christy and Lartet found other, yet simpler and larger

ABOVE: *Lartet and Christy's drawings of some of the flints that they excavated in the little rock shelter of Le Moustier, the archaeological site outside Les Eyzies that has since lent its name to a culture called the Mousterian, that has now been found across Europe, Asia and North Africa. These flints are associated with Neanderthal populations and are dated, approximately, to around 40,000 years ago.*

tools, these of a type they realised excitedly, that had long been famous in the circles of prehistoric archaeology, having been excavated many decades earlier from gravel beds beside the River Somme.

As the rest of the archaeological establishment watched in fascination, Lartet and Christy joined all known archaeological prehistory in a single sequence, a relative time chart for the cultures of the European Stone Age. Though they had no dates for their tables, Lartet and Christy had placed the remains of 'primitive man' into an ordered succession based upon the stratigraphic sequences in which they were found. Lartet named a number of 'periods' after the animal bones that they found beside the various flint tools; the Bear, Bison, Mammoth and Reindeer ages; Christy, however, preferring more anthropological classifications based upon human habitat, divided them into a Drift Period, a Cave Period and so on. Both of them though, realised that these various divisions actually reflected widely varying physical environments, when humans and their ancestors alternatively shivered through Ice Ages and luxuriated in sunny times of plenty. They also understood that as the ancient animals, as the excavated flora and fauna of the strata had changed with the climate, so the flint tools had been adapted age by age, to suit these changing circumstances.

Les Eyzies is still a fundamental location for prehistorians. Nowadays, the lazy Vézère is called the 'River of Man'; the little town beside it, the 'Centre of World Prehistory,' housing the French National Museum of Prehistory whose relics span the last hundred thousand years of human history. Set beneath a line of natural rock shelters, the museum and the tourist shops in the high street sit side-by-side with shelters covering other more recent excavations. To the surprise of visiting archaeologists, many of the descendants of Lartet and Christy's workmen still own their now-famous excavation sites and care for them assiduously. Some indeed, have been transformed into museums, and the farmers into their curators.

Years before he had gone to work in the Dordogne, Christy and his anthropological friends had invented the notion that contemporary primitive societies, the cultures of modern savages, were simply less evolved manifestations of more developed peoples, such as modern Europeans. After Lartet and Christy's excavations began to give the Stone Age internal shape and narrative, it seemed to many people that prehistoric history might simply be the beginnings of this same process – the very beginning of humanity's 'evolutionary' journey from prehistoric savagery, or 'idiocy' as one eminent professor of anatomy described it, to modern-day intelligence.

From Marx to Freud and down on to today, this simple notion that confuses modern tribal peoples with ancient humans has had tremendous influence, usually to the detriment of all concerned. When an anatomist observed that Piltdown's strange-shaped jaw would have rendered him incapable of speech, an archaeologist responded that this would have no bearing on his tool-making abilities; such archaic 'primitives' after all, would have no use for speech! Small wonder that earlier, when Lartet found drawings on fossil bones and suggested that they had been made by ancient human beings, no one took him seriously. These Stone Age people, after all, were at a 'lower' stage of evolution and quite incapable of making such fine things. Years later too, when another archaeologist discovered extraordinary paintings on the walls of caves, no one seriously believed that such things were made by ancient savages. As archaeologists uncovered scientific evidence of the past, their 'scientific' theories conspired to make it dumb again and the Bible's stories were replaced by another simpler and un-Christian set of legends.

Altamira: 1879
An Unimagined Past

FROM CONAN DOYLE TO INDIANA JONES, a handful of plots occur repeatedly in archaeological fiction, plots that have gained such power that the modern media often cast their accounts of real-life archaeological expeditions into the same moulds: young man with a dream finds a tomb in the desert; children chasing a little dog discover secret caves; a peasant's plough turns up ancient treasure trove; theories that attracted ridicule are proved true after their inventor dies. And once in a while, some of these tales come true.

The story of the Cave of Altamira is just one such story. It begins on the coast of northern Spain in the 1860s on the estate of a Spanish noblemen, Señor Don Marcelino Santiago Tomás Sanz de Sautuola, with the sudden disappearance of a dog following a wounded fox to ground on the limestone downs above the town of Santillana del Mar. From the faint barking that followed the animal's brusque exit from the world, the poacher realised that his dog had crawled into a hidden hole, which are common enough in that area. Amongst low scrub beside a small rock fall, the hunter found the gap, squeezed himself through its small opening and found the Cave of Altamira.

Though very large and dry and dark, there seemed to be little in the cave but the hunter's dog. A few years later, with the poacher's identity forgotten, one of Don Marcelino's estate labourers told his *padrone* about the cave upon the hill of Altamira. Like many other Europeans of his day, Don Marcelino was interested in archaeology, and in geology and ancient history. Taking two men to clear the entrance for him, he visited the hidden cave and when the doorway was enlarged to let in the light, he saw the thick deposits on the floor; evidence, it seemed to him, of previous habitation. Don Marcelino took some bone fragments from the floor of the cave which he later showed to his friend Vilanova y Piera, Professor of Geology at the University of Madrid, who confirmed his suppositions. They were bones of long-extinct animals – bison, wild horse and reindeer, – hunted in the European Stone Age, and had been split lengthways to extract their marrow. Like Pitt Rivers, his exact contemporary, Don Marcelino was the proud possessor of an untouched archaeological site!

In 1878, visiting the Universal Exhibition of Paris, one of a long series of gigantic international fairs, Don Marcelino had been especially intrigued by a large display of prehistoric objects from the Dordogne, assembled by one of Edouard Lartet's protégés. Realising that he too possessed this same material in the Cave of Altamira, in the following spring he reexamined the cave floor and was immediately rewarded. Along with bones and teeth and shells lying on the surface, there were flints of what he now recognised as belonging to Lartet's Magdelanian Culture. Further back, in the darkness of the cave he found the bones of a gigantic bear, some black marks on the walls, and what appeared to be the pigment that had made them, held on the curve of a shell. Side chambers off the main cave, whose plan somewhat resembled a lumpy intestine, held further evidence of ancient habitation: ashes, the marks of fire, more bones. Don Marcelino decided to excavate.

Some days later, so Don Marcelino has fondly recorded, his daughter Maria came with him to the cave with Robot, her little dog. Bored by her father's digging and scraping, she wandered off into the darkness behind the excavations. Suddenly she reappeared uttering, so legend says, archaeology's most magic words: '*Papá, Papá, mira toros pintados!*' and her father went to see what had made her so excited. Shining his lamp up into the high darkness of the natural vault he saw the *toros* for himself; a great herd of bison, grand, gorgeous and entirely lively, painted on the ceiling of the cave, as fresh as new.

Don Marcelino first doubted they were ancient. Then he realised that the bison and some of the other animals portrayed were all extinct in Europe but had been a staple of the diet of the ancient people whose remains he was presently engaged in excavating. He was reminded too, of the French discoveries of Lartet and others, engraved animal bones whose tiny images bore faint resemblance to these extraordinary paintings. Don Marcelino quickly revisited Vilanova in Madrid, who came to Altamira and confirmed his friend's enthusiastic description of the paintings.

Next, Don Marcelino employed a visiting artist to make copies of the paintings and in 1880 published a scientific monograph on his cave, *An account of certain prehistoric discoveries in the Province of Santander*, with detailed descriptions of the flints, the animal remains and finally, copies of the paintings. First his essay met with silence, then with derision. Don Marcelino de Sautuola did not seem to understand; 'Primitive man', one contemporary academic stated 'was little more than a gorilla, incapable of conceiving arts and sciences'. Half idiot, entirely unintelligent, 'primitive' man may possibly have scratched small drawings on the bones of

RIGHT: *One of the great palaeolithic bulls painted on the ceiling of the cave of Altamira. No photograph can adequately express the sensation of entering this cave, whose bright colours and marvellous draughtsmanship have earned it the somewhat dubious title of the 'Sistine Chapel of prehistory'.*

animals he ate. That, as someone said, would be 'the dawn of art'; but never these hugely splendid paintings in Don Marcelino's cave. On discovering that a painter had been hired to help prepare the publication, the great Émile Cartailhac, the leading French prehistorian of the day and professor of prehistory at Toulouse University, suggested that Don Marcelino had commissioned the paintings to concoct a hoax; alternatively, it was suggested, they were the work of some off-duty Roman legionaries. Yet something must have pricked the French successors of Lartet, the learned professors of prehistory of Bordeaux and Toulouse who were united against the Spanish publications, for scientific cartwheels were turned to explain away the disturbing pictures

Don Marcelino quickly retired from this unseemly fray and never again participated in academic discussion. However, his professor friend, Vilanova y Piera, could hardly afford such sanguine behaviour and mounted a virtually unassailable defence of the Altamira paintings that was greeted at best with shrugs, at worst with sheer abuse. When Don Marcelino died in 1888 and Vilanova y Piera a few years later, the paintings in the Cave of Altamira were still completely unaccepted by the archaeological establishment.

Then in 1895 the French prehistorian Émile Rivière visited Altamira and was amazed at what he saw. Further investigations in the Dordogne rock shelters produced evidence of pigment marks and scratching on the walls and ceilings which fortified Rivière's conviction that Altamira's paintings were completely genuine. That same year, Rivière published an account of paintings and rock engravings discovered in a Dordogne cave called La Mouthe, a cave that previous to its excavation, had been completely sealed, then opened by two archaeologists to reveal a deep dark wonderland of silent prehistory, dancing with engraved animals, horses and horned cattle, scenes painted, so the flints and artefacts from the cave suggested, in the later Stone Age. Just as Don Marcelino had excavated shells employed to hold the pigment used to paint Altamira's bison, so now Rivière reported, the archaeologists of Le Mouthe had also excavated a small lamp engraved with an ibex, apparently used by the ancient artists to light their work.

Rivière's report started an avalanche of similar discoveries, gaggles of French prehistorians now found any number of caves with similar images in them, although none of these were anything like as grand as Altamira. (Only in 1940 would some boys follow their dog into the French caves at Lascaux, whose paintings rival Altamira.) Only then were Don Marcelino's discoveries finally embraced by the prestigious *Association Française pour l'Avancement des Science*, which had sprung Jesse-like from the work of Lartet and served to authenticate all new discoveries. In 1902 Don Marcelino himself was vindicated. Led by a contrite Professor Cartailhac, a small procession of French academics wound their way to Don Marcelino's country house close by to Altamira Hill and there they met Maria, by then a married woman, and made apology to her. Cartailhac's celebrated paper '*Les Cavernes ornées de dessins: La grotte d'Altamira. Mea culpa d'un sceptique*' appeared in the scientific journal *L'Anthropologie*. As with the Piltdown exposure half a century later, academia somehow managed to emerge with all its feathers shining.

As far as the Stone Age is concerned, Rivière's discoveries helped to liberate archaeologists from older notions of the stupidity of 'lower' stages of 'evolution'. Far from being 'the dawn of art', however, as some suggested, Altamira and its contemporary monuments show sophistication of eye and hand, of technique and genuine experience that, happily, has so far resisted all explanation. Like the animals they portray, these vast images just *are*; that is, they are a vivid part of ancient experience, animals seen by people who knew them intimately.

Carmel: 1929
Neolithic Revolutions

IN 1927 OFFICIALS OF THE BRITISH ADMINISTRATION IN PALESTINE chose to use the great grey cliffs, the ancient coral reefs of biblical Carmel as a quarry for the new stone quays of Haifa Harbour. Soon after blasting had begun, Charles Lambert, assistant director of the Mandatory Department of Antiquities in Palestine, came to see if anything ancient and of value was being destroyed. Trenching some of the caves at that time still used by Palestinian shepherds, he found the first Stone Age art outside Europe: 'A sickle blade handle carved,' as Lambert reported, 'with a young animal...which faintly reminds one of the painted bison in the cave of Altamira'. Lambert had also seen that the sickle implied reaping, not an occupation of the Altamira painters: here then, was evidence of very early agriculture. Lambert's astute comments led a succession of scholars to confirm Carmel's importance to archaeology: 'It must not only be reserved for investigation by those most competent in such matters', decreed the British Administration, 'but must, after investigation, be preserved as a permanent monument'.

BELOW: *The cliffs of Mount Carmel in northern Israel. The shelter covers the present archaeological excavations of the University of Haifa. The tip of earth beyond marks the excavations of earlier archaeologists.*

A year later, funds had been procured from an enthusiastic industrialist and the great prehistory archaeologist, Dorothy Garrod had set up camp beneath the Carmel cliffs and begun six seasons of excavation in and around the caves. She found that engineers had already started blasting part of the cave the shepherds called *Mugharet el Skhul* – the Cave of the Kid – where they had kept their herds of sheep and goats. Trial trenches showed flints of the type called mousterian. Shortly afterwards the first skeleton was found and identified as a three-year-old male Cro-Magnon, a skeletal type found earlier in the Dordogne and very close to modern *Homo sapiens*. In all, some fourteen skeletons were taken from the cave. Over the millennia, however, they had become cemented into a rock-hard limestone breccia. Using drills and chisels Garrod's team had to cut them in great blocks from the rock which were sent to the Royal College of Surgeons, where a team of anatomists led by Professor Arthur (later Sir Arthur) Keith, spent years of careful work cutting them from their stony shrouds.

The results were revolutionary. These were the first complete near-modern human skeletons to be found, the first look then, at our immediate ancestors, men, women and

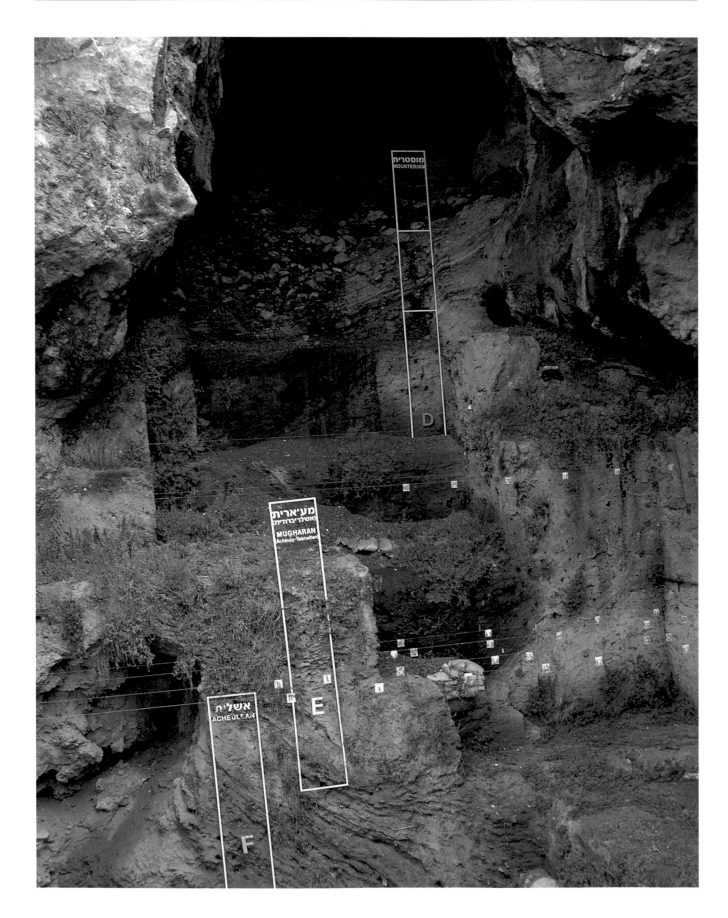

children. And, as Keith and others noticed, they were closer yet to modern humankind than the Cro-Magnon skeletons from the Dordogne.

In a nearby cave, called el Tabun, 'the oven', because of its circular bellying shape, Garrod excavated an astonishing seventy feet of fill, representing untold ages of habitation – a standing section that is one of the most moving sights of prehistoric archaeology in the world. (Today we know that all of human civilisation, the last ten thousand years, is represented by the last few inches of this cut.)

By the 1930s, archaeology had become extremely sophisticated with an academic jargon all of its own. Listen to Garrod describing a single substratum, labelled Eb, in this cave: 'A very interesting feature of Tabun Eb is the presence of a group of implements of Upper Palaeolithic type. These include Chatelperron points, end scrapers and gravers...I consider them to be due to contact with a very early Aurignacian rather than a development *in situ* of the Acheulo-Mousterian industry.' Underneath the obfuscation though, complex excavations like that of Garrod's at Carmel, were beginning to pinpoint passages and events in early human history previously unrecorded, yet fundamental to an understanding of the development of the human race.

In the Carmel caves for example, high above the most ancient levels of habitation, Garrod excavated a settlement and graves of a culture, a society she called Natufian; people of the era when, as Lévi-Strauss has said 'the discovery of those civilised skills which form the basis of our daily lives was made'. Today, the bulk of the food that humans eat, the animals we farm and domesticate are largely those farmed by Garrod's Natufians. All at once then, the archaeological establishment was faced with clear evidence of what had been the single most important event of human history, an event that Gordon Childe, the greatest archaeological theorist of Garrod's time, dubbed the 'Neolithic Revolution'. Now, just as no one knew precisely, the dates of Thomsen's Stone, Bronze and Iron ages, so no one at the time of the Carmel excavations had any way of knowing when this Neolithic Revolution had occurred.

There were other surprises too, and other questions buried in the Carmel caves. Deep down in el Tabun, Garrod had found the single grave of a Neanderthal woman. As with many such burials, the care of the interment seems to provide the first evidence of concern for the dead; the first evidence perhaps, of human faith. Flints found in association with this grave showed Garrod that it was approximately contemporary with the burials in the nearby cave of el Skhul, whose skeletons however, were anatomically much closer to modern *Homo sapiens*. Had these two communities of cave dwellers, Neanderthals and early humans, been contemporaries or even neighbours? Had they fought? Had they interbred? Why had the stronger, larger-brained Neanderthals died out?

By the early 1940s, all sorts of racial and cultural theories were fighting for space around the world. Even the archaeological 'savage' was on the march again: Garrod herself noting that during a lecture when she had speculated upon the beginnings of farming in the Levant, Nazi archaeologists had left the room *en masse*. True or not, for those young Germans, the notion was entirely unacceptable. In the earlier days, the answers to such archaeological questions would have been resolved around arguments involving the interrelationship of archaeological strata. By Garrod's time though, archaeology was so precise, that these well-worn tools were no longer sufficient; the new archaeology badly needed real, finite dates.

ABOVE: *Modern archaeologists from Haifa digging beneath the spoil heaps of the excavations of the 1920s, excavating part of a cemetery of some of the first-known farmers in world history.*

OPPOSITE PAGE: *The archaeological section in the Cave of el Tabun in the cliffs of Carmel in northern Israel, first excavated by Dorothy Garrod in the 1920s. The extraordinary depth of the archaeological stratum, which is nearly fifty feet deep, is partly the result of sand and water washing down through the cave from its roof for the last 300,000 years. The last ten thousand years of human history, from the invention of farming and cities, down to the deposits left by Palestinian shepherds in the 1920s, is held in a foot of earth just below the original floor of the cave, beneath the natural arch of the cliffs.*

Los Alamos and Chicago: 1947
Hard Time

THE FIRST ATOMIC BOMB EXPLODED AT 5:30 in the morning of 16 July, 1945, some 120 miles south of Albuquerque in New Mexico; a flash of light, a wave of heat, a tremendous roar and a ball of fire, followed by a mushroom cloud rising 40,000 feet above a desert whose surface was turned to glass. Along with so many miseries, the Bomb produced, as is usual with military research, several unexpected spin-offs. For the history of archaeology, that mushroom cloud signified a coming earthquake: for Willard F. Libby, one of the Los Alamos scientists later used an essential step in the creation of the atomic bomb to make a ruler to measure out the distant past in years.

In 1947, working at the University of Chicago's Institute for Nuclear Studies, Libby was the first to measure the rate at which the radioactive isotope Carbon 14, present in all living plants and animals, decayed from the moment of death; a constant radioactive stopwatch capable of running for fifty thousand years and more. Awarded a Nobel prize for the development of what is now called Carbon 14 dating, Libby had provided prehistory with a tool that few of its earlier practitioners could have dreamed of. At last, the archaeology of Denmark and the Dordogne, of Carmel and Altamira could be placed in real-time, on a single time line.

It is difficult today, to imagine the initial effect of Libby's extraordinary gift to archaeology, just as, at first it was profoundly difficult for archaeology to accept it, so established, so entrenched were the opinions of many of its scholars. Within fifteen years of Libby's announcement of his discovery, however, the archaeological prehistory of Europe and the New World had been rewritten. Though the grave field at Hallstatt, which provided firm fourth-century BC connections between Scandinavia and the Mediterranean still stood, the dates of earlier periods were completely revised. Some of the previously accepted dates for the Bronze Age had to be raised by a thousand years and more whilst Rasmus Nyerup's rhetorical rumination, that the North was older than Christianity 'but by a couple of years? a couple of centuries? or even by more than a millennium?' was seen to have been bound by an imagination grounded in biblical histories. After Carbon 14 dating, it was no longer possible, for example, to suggest that Stonehenge had been constructed under the guidance of Bronze Age princes from the Mediterranean; its antecedents were older than the pyramids of Egypt. In short, Carbon 14 dating caused a revolution. In the process, many old histories and prejudices were blown away and a brave new past, sharp as the shining desert, was born.

A measurement of minute amounts of residual radioactivity, the accuracy of Carbon 14 dating is dependent upon the quality of the measuring equipment and the purity of the sample. In the beginning, Libby's team checked their results against two long-established

BELOW: *Dr Willard Libby, the atom bomb scientist from Berkeley, California who developed techniques that, by measuring the amounts of residual radioactivity in organic material, provided the first dates for the distant past and the beginnings of human history and evolution. In 1960 Libby was awarded a Noble prize for chemistry for his great gift to the science of archaeology.*

chronologies; ancient Egyptian written histories and an ingenious nineteenth-century Swedish system of counting the small deposits of clay known as varves – the residue of yearly melts and freezes of northern glaciers. Varve counts had long provided precise local dates for the northern Ice Ages and established prehistory's first-known absolute date of 6839 BC, reaching back further, with slightly less accuracy, some 18,000 years BP – prehistoric dates being expressed in years Before the Present. Such preliminary cross-checking showed that most dates obtained with Carbon 14 were accurate to within two hundred years.

Another cross check involved a different system of absolute dating, known as dendrochronolgy, which Arizona archaeologists had been developing from the late 1920s. Instead of counting melts and freezes, dendrochronolgy counts annual variations of growth in trees by examining and comparing the rings in a cross-section of a bough or trunk. By cross-referencing from tree to tree within a single species, rather like stratigraphy, several accurate spans of localised year-dates had been built up, an absolute chronology stretching back some several thousand years. Comparison with Carbon 14 showed that the rates of natural radioactive decay were not as constant as Libby had first imagined. As a result, a complex system of date correction was introduced.

Since the 1960s a variety of other time-measurement systems have been developed and used in archaeology. Libby's elegant and simple idea appears to have taken on a life of its own. Some systems, like Libby's, are dependent upon the rates of decay of radioactive particles, others upon the measurement of changes in the earth's magnetic field, or upon spectrum analysis. Though far less accurate than Carbon 14, Potassium-Argon dating, based again on that most convenient habit of regular radioactive decay, measures out far longer spans of time and has extended the archaeological clock some five million years.

Apart from providing a brand-new time span for prehistory, the new discipline of archaeometry, the scientific measurement of time, has efficiently disposed of many fakes and forgeries, and it has also given us new eyes. Discrepancies in the amounts of fluorine in the Piltdown gravels and the famous skull, for example, were the first evidence that they were not true contemporaries; old Piltdown himself being finally shown the door after Carbon 14 testing. Similarly, large numbers of fake ceramics and sculptures have been removed from exhibition in many of the best museums. Carbon 14 dates for the Turin Shroud have demonstrated that the great cloth is not nearly old enough to have wrapped the body of Jesus. Objects from old excavations such as Pitt Rivers' work on Cranbourne Chase for example, have now been dated by Carbon 14 measurement, fitting some of those most careful, yet undated, excavations precisely into English history.

From the very beginning of the revolution though, many Middle Eastern archaeologists were alarmed by the crudeness and inexactitude of Carbon 14 dates, that were typically expressed, for early historical periods, with qualifications of plus or minus 150 years or so. For many Middle Eastern histories, ancient time was already counted in years and months and sometimes, even, days. By the 1970s, initial enthusiasm had waned to such a point that the careful processes of sampling that Carbon 14 requires on archaeological sites had almost vanished from Middle Eastern excavations. The effect of this was to produce what one archaeologist described as a chronological fault line, a crescent described from central Anatolia to Malta, separating northern Europe from the Middle East. To the north of this line, Carbon 14 dates reigned supreme while to the south, traditional chronologies held sway and they did not agree, a situation exacerbated by the intransigence of many scientists and archaeologists who were wedded to one system or another. Dendrochronolgy, as one of its leading exponents explained was 'superior to the disciplines of archaeology and historians'. Similar claims were made for Carbon 14, along with the suggestion that traditional chronologies might well be based upon traditional errors. Sometimes, however, it should be said, the scientists' dates beggared all historical intelligence. As François Bordes, a leading French prehistorian reportedly remarked about one scientist's dating of some important ancient material: 'You tell me 'e 'as zese radiocarbon dates, but me, I ask you so what? You tell me Louis XV 'e ride a motorcycle. Maybe 'e did, maybe 'e didn't, but me, I do not believe it.'

Inside the sound and fury of continuing debate between science and old history, a debate peripherally enlivened by the arrival of architects from Mars, exploding volcanoes and those who wish to show us that a simple adjustment of old chronology will prove the wonder of the Exodus, it is easy to forget how very useful modern science has been to archaeology. Arguments about dating now deal in centuries rather than millennia; at the very least, however, the dating revolution has produced a healthy awareness of the fragility of our traditional histories.

'A couple of years? a couple of centuries? or even, by more than a millennium?', one thing is for sure; scientific dating has removed archaeology from Rasmus Nyerup's universe altogether. Altamira Cave was painted, so Carbon 14 tells us, around 30,000 years BP. Similarly, Carmel's Carbon 14 dates for the Natufian period range from 12950 ± 150 year BP to 1068 ± 190 year BP, reflecting the time that momentous culture lived upon that site, giving it real depth and space. Similarly, we know that Lartet's Magdelanian Culture lasted some 6000 years, ending around 8750 BP. There are some new and most momentous birthdays, too: 'There is little doubt today,' the eminent Israeli archaeologist Ofer Bar-Yosef could confidently assert in a lecture at Cambridge University in 1998, 'that the emergence of Anatomically Modern Humans, took place some 300,000–100,000 years ago in sub-Saharan Africa'. That such a grand statement can be made at all, is ultimately due to Libby's clever observations. Since the bomb went off, all of human history has been placed in real time.

Leakey's Laetoli: 1976
Walking Out of Africa

BELOW: *Kenyan archaeologists Mary and Louis Leakey sorting finds at Olduvai Gorge in 1959. The patriarchs of generations of anthropologists and archaeologists, the Leakeys have since established and enlarged their revolutionary contention that humanity had come out of Africa and not Asia as*

previous archaeological discoveries had indicated. Enthusiastic populariser and fundraiser, Louis Leakey transformed the investigation of early man from a narrow scientific discipline to an area of wide popular interest. He and his wife Mary also excavated many of the most important prehistoric finds ever made.

SINCE THE EARLY 1970s, Potassium-Argon dating has revolutionised archaeological understanding of human evolution, showing, amongst other things, that the ancestors of humankind walked out of Africa 1.8 million ago and then spread out around the world. Underlining this fact, several other dating methods have established that many worldwide varieties of flint tools, that to this day are often identified by their original French place names, were made far earlier in Africa and the Middle East than anywhere else on earth. The common nineteenth-century assumption that European prehistory was the prehistory of the world has been proved wrong.

One of the most extraordinary discoveries of African archaeology was made in 1976 when the archaeologist Mary Leakey uncovered the world's oldest footprints, some seventy of them, that Potassium-Argon dating shows were made 3.6 million years ago. They are the traces of three people striding easily away from an erupting volcano – the same volcano whose falling ash preserved their footprints as they dried, hard as cement, in a shower of rain. The largest of the three had led the way, with a smaller person following in exactly the same footprints, and a child running lightly at their sides. These individuals lived long before flint tools were ever made; a pre-human species then, with adults standing some five feet tall. Although African skeletons of similar age hint at their physical type, it is now believed there were a great number of sub-species involved in the evolution of modern humankind, not a simple family tree of monkeys turning into men, no simple, single evolutionary line from savage to society, as nineteenth-century archaeologists assumed.

Perceptions of the course and pattern of human evolution have also undergone great change since Henry Christy's day. Following the discovery of the Laetoli footprints, for example, present-day archaeologists have observed that walking upright in groups seems to have preceded tool-making and therefore the final development of the human brain, thus bringing into question the old concepts of the separate development of human identity and human form. That these fleeing beings had taken to walking upright at all, others have observed, may have been due to African forests drying out, thus forcing our *ci-devant* predecessors to walk on the ground. Walking upright, the archaeologists have added, would have greatly aided the survival of their species in a time of global warming: a brain at the top of the body being better placed to serve as a radiator to help control body heat; the enlarging buttocks serving as an extra fat supply in time of hardship. Other archaeologists have observed that walking upright would have hidden the sex organs, provoked a crisis in species reproduction and prompted the evolution of a secondary system of sexual signalling – increased hairlessness, enlarging breasts and penises, to advertise the reproductive message. This transformation of the beginning of the sexual act into an act of the imagination then gave birth to metaphor and self-awareness, perhaps even, to language itself.

If these footprints had been found in Europe in the nineteenth century, archaeologists would have certainly portrayed them as the markings of a family group, a male hunter moving fearfully away from a roaring mountain god, with his savage naked mate following up behind him, and their innocent offspring skipping along beside them both. Just as the nineteenth-century explanations of our beginnings were a part of a contemporary Western fascination with human difference, with the races of the world, with the relationship of savagery and civilisation so then, today's explanations tend to reflect the interests of our present worldwide culture.

Nice: 1880–1980
Dining Out With the Past

HALF A MILLION YEARS AGO, the Mediterranean coastline was some seventy feet higher than it is today. In 1958, at Nice, a prehistoric beach was discovered high up on a hillside known as Terra Amata, above the city's nineteenth-century harbour. A few years later, with the hillside scheduled for redevelopment, local archaeologists undertook to excavate and plan this ancient environment before it was obliterated. To their great surprise, amongst the debris of that ancient beach, they found the traces of a prehistoric hunting lodge, Europe's oldest building; a seaside settlement where the continent's earliest known inhabitants had come to pass the summer months.

Complex processes of analysis enabled the archaeologists to reconstruct the ways of living of these ancient beings. They had come down to the sea in springtime, building shelters of tree branches, some thirty feet long and half as wide, piling rocks along their sides to keep out the cold north wind. They hunted rhino, elephant and deer. They cooked with fire. They made large choppers from local limestone and smaller sharper tools of flint and quartz. And they collected oysters and mussels from the sea.

Although archaeologists are uncertain whether these seasiders should be called 'humans' or 'hominids,' in some ways, we are not so very different from them. These first Europeans, after all, chose a still-popular resort for their summers, and ate much of the same food and indulged in many of the same pleasures that Edward, Prince of Wales would enjoy in the 1890s at the Hotel Negresco on the Promenade des Anglais, just a few hundred yards and a half and million years away from the shelter of Terra Amata. Two centuries of archaeology have joined us back again to our most distant predecessors. Thanks to archaeology, we no longer see ourselves as the offspring of Adam and Eve, set down perfect to rule God's earth, but as part and product of a venerable world-wide ecosystem.

For a century and more, archaeologists have usually described the path from Terra Amata to the Hotel Negresco in terms of Darwinian evolution and human 'progress' – as pseudo-histories dominated by descriptions of ever-more efficient methods of food production, medicine, weapons and the like. Now, however, there is a slow-growing realisation that our ancient ancestors were not involved in a kind of process of invention and development that would inevitably lead to the foundation of the modern world; that they were neither sillier nor more savage than us but simply different. One tantalising promise then, that this new archaeology holds, is that it will lead us to a genuinely novel past, uncover something of the skills and sensitivities of our ancestors who gathered shellfish on that ancient beach, and show us different ways of being to any that we can presently imagine.

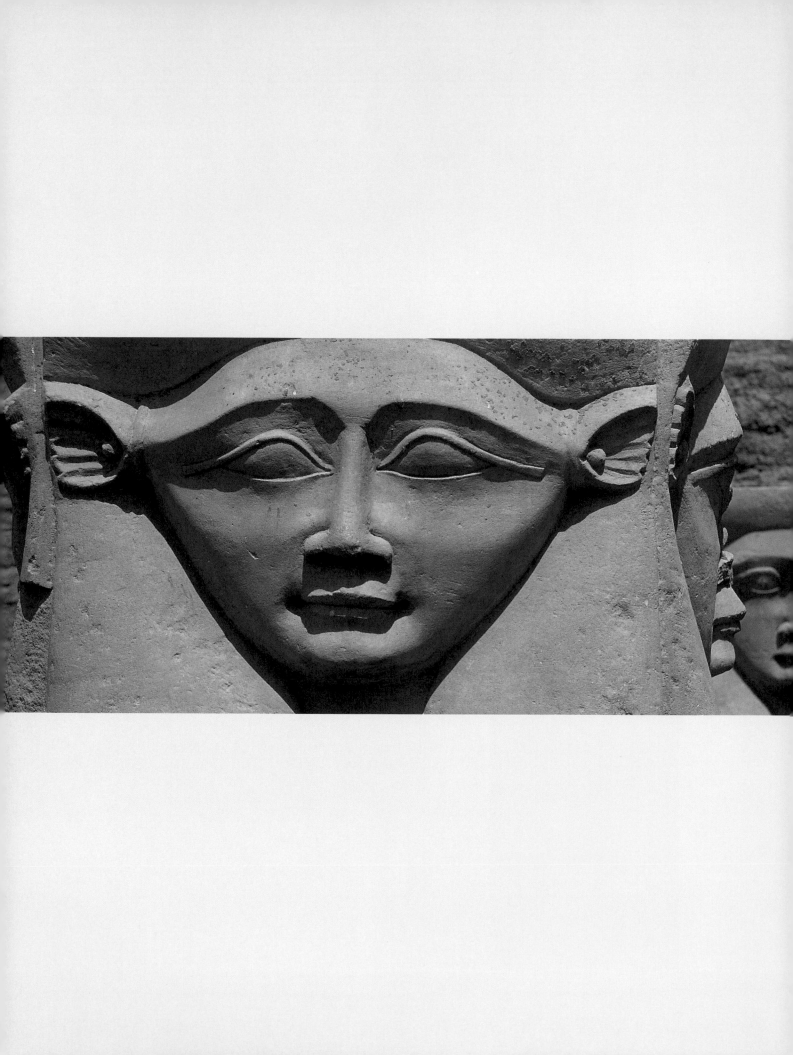

PART II

The Treasure Seekers

The Valley of the Kings: 1922
Into Aladdin's Cave

'Let me try and tell the story of it all. It will not be easy, for the dramatic suddenness of the initial discovery left me in a dazed condition…This was to be our final season in the Valley of the Kings…season after season had drawn a blank…only an excavator knows how desperately depressing that can be…yet hardly had we set hoe to ground in our last despairing effort than we made a discovery that far exceeded our wildest dreams…

Our years of patient labour were to be rewarded…It was a thrilling moment for an excavator. Alone, save for my native workmen…anything, literally anything, might lie beyond that passage, and it needed all my self control to keep from breaking down the doorway… [*some weeks later*] With trembling hands I made a tiny breach in the upper left hand corner… At first I could see nothing, the hot air escaping from the chamber causing the candle flame to flicker, but presently, as my eyes grew accustomed to the light, details of the room within emerged slowly from the mist, strange animals, statues, and gold – everywhere the glint of gold. For the moment – an eternity it must have seemed to the others standing by – I was struck dumb with amazement, and when Lord Carnarvon, unable to stand the suspense any longer, inquired anxiously, "Can you see anything?" it was all I could do to get out the words, "Yes, wonderful things." '

HOWARD CARTER – *The Tomb of Tutankhamen*, VOL I, LONDON 1923

EDITED BY A NOVELIST FRIEND, Carter's bestseller tells us very little about the realities of the discovery of the world's most famous tomb, and it is difficult now to see the truth behind the legends. All we have is a *Boy's Own* tale with a stock set of characters, such as novelists like Théophile Gautier and Rider Haggard had developed many years before. It was what the public wanted, of course, a narrative like a standard detective story, but hardly an account of what had happened. Archaeology had been overcome by a blaze of treasure; the actors in the drama speak in clichéd half-truths, and even modern experts have never managed to break away from them; indeed they often use such writings as if they were the scientific work of archaeologists.

Traces of the truth remain. There are, for example, Carter's own notes and records of his work before he found the tomb. The years of careful entries in his fine, leather-bound archaeological daybook of work in the Royal Valley stop, quite literally, in mid-sentence: 'November 2, 1922, found entrance to the tomb of…' By this very amputation, we sense the moment that changed his life forever; the moment at which archaeology gave way to fiction. Was the description of the discovery of the tomb written long after this dislocation, really as Carter describes it? Was it, in truth, the successful conclusion to a treasure hunt? Almost certainly, it was not.

By 1922, Carter had worked in the Valley of the Kings for more than twenty years. Close study of his earlier excavation records show that, for much of that time, he was not trenching the little valley, frantically searching for hidden tombs as his bestseller implies, but studying and clearing known tombs, for an archaeological history of the Valley and its tombs, one that he would never write. His notes show though, that this history was so broad in scientific scope, and so unusual that generations of armchair archaeologists have since plundered his unpublished writings for theses of their own.

Since 1902, excavations in the Valley of the Kings had been financed by rich amateur archaeologists overseen and controlled by junior professionals, amongst them the young

BELOW: *Today, the outer coffin still lies in the burial chamber, holding within it the bones of the young king, swathed in cotton wool and entirely dismembered by Carter and his team as they cut the golden treasures away from the bitumen-encrusted mummy.*

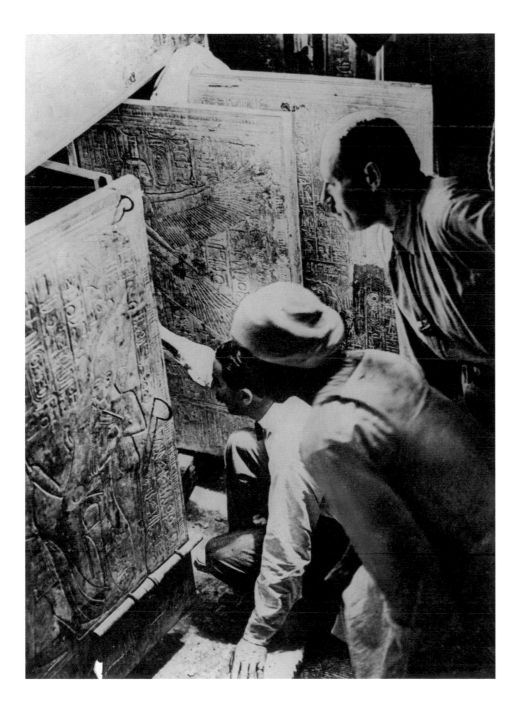

LEFT: *The set-piece opening on 3 January 1924 of the shrines that surrounded Tutankhamun's sarcophagus, most carefully lit by Harry Burton, the photographer who documented all of Carter's work. Carter is crouching on one knee, his arm holding the door of the fourth and innermost shrine. Behind him stands an anonymous Egyptian foreman and John Callender, an engineer who lived locally and provided Carter with help and expertise in the first years of the work.*

Howard Carter. By 1917, when Lord Carnarvon took up the concession, these excavations had long been part of Upper Egypt's winter season. Generally speaking, the professional archaeologists were expected to provide a 'tomb a year' for the delectation of their employers and their guests. Celebratory dinners were organised in the excavation house after a successful tomb opening and British administrators and foreign diplomats were happy to attend. Not only was the whole thing fascinating but such archaeological enterprises were listed by the British Administration as a vital economic resource of under-developed Upper Egypt.

Archaeologists like Carter were expected to supply expert information at such occasions. An excellent raconteur, Carter had a whole patter of stories; stories of séances and mummy curses, of rows of white camels carrying treasure from lost tombs, all designed as after-dinner tales. Apart from their retelling in an unfinished fragment of autobiography, they never intruded into Carter's archaeological material.

Not surprisingly, the archaeologists often stage-managed the 'discovery' of tombs and buried antiquities in the Valley for their employers and their guests – people who would themselves have recognised the event for what it was – a formal archaeological entertainment. The whereabouts of the rediscovered tombs were often known to workmen employed in previous work in the Valley, who were rewarded for their information. Until Carter's stint with Carnarvon in the Royal Valley, the sites of most excavations there were largely determined by a handful of very knowledgeable local foremen, who possessed information often handed down from workers on earlier excavations.

Most of the tombs found in those years had already been entered and even part-robbed by workmen, who were often unsupervised in their day-to-day activities. Sometimes the work gangs were already discussing and even celebrating the new treasure before the archaeologists had released the news of its discovery! It is quite astonishing today to read the words of

Europeans who seemed to believe that local knowledge of such treasure was due to a 'native sensitivity to gold' and not to the previous week's judicious spadework! Small valuable objects such as the mummies' jewels were taken, the larger tell-tale pieces being left for the archaeologists and their employers. In the decades before Carnarvon's excavations, there was hardly a discovery amongst the royal tombs of Thebes that was not preceded by objects from the 'unknown' tomb appearing on the art market – and sometimes Howard Carter and Carnarvon were actively involved in their resale. This constant pilfering though, was never acknowledged in the grandiose archaeological publications of the era; it would after all, have made the expeditions appear slap-dash and inexpert.

Here then, is much of the truth behind the myth of 'ancient tomb robbery' to which the archaeologists of those days were so keen to attribute the destruction of the treasures of the royal tombs of Thebes. In reality, a great many of these 'ancient thieves' were poor modern labourers working quite unsupervised for inexperienced foreign archaeologists employed to find a tomb a year. Though there were indeed a few robberies in antiquity, and these are well recorded in the ancient records, the great grand royal tombs, the open monuments of the Valley of the Kings, were not emptied by ancient robbers but by bureaucrats and priests. A myriad of inscriptions tell us that most of the royal tombs in the Valley of the Kings were officially emptied when the pharaohs abandoned Thebes around 1000 BC. Up until that time, however, most of these royal tombs had been subject to constant guarding and inspection. Indeed, the ancient texts most carefully inform us that when burglaries had taken place within these tombs they were repaired and carefully resealed. Only the smaller tombs were completely hidden and thus intact until the archaeologists arrived.

Carter's own excavation notes and plans point to the fact that he had uncovered the top of the steps that led to Tutankhamun's tomb in an earlier season of excavation. Experience would have told him that the tell-tale step belonged to a small tomb from the time of Tutankhamun; another almost identical staircase lay some thirty feet away which had led to a small tomb with a puzzling burial and a modest treasure of that period. Just as Carter had previously reburied some antiquities he had found in the Royal Valley so that Carnarvon and his daughter could 'excavate them with their own hands' when they came on their holidays, in all probability Carter reburied this new set of limestone steps for a similar 'discovery' on a rainy day, such as might occur when Carnarvon's interest in excavating flagged. After several seasons of slender results due to Carter's increasing interest in studying and surveying open royal tombs, the rainy day duly dawned and the gambling Earl proposed to finish with Egyptian excavation altogether.

So sure was Carter of his buried tomb, however, that he offered to pay for the forthcoming excavation from his own pocket, if Carnarvon, the concession holder would agree. Not surprisingly, at this point, the astute Earl thought it a better gamble to continue on his own account! So Howard Carter left for Thebes to start his famous final season. In

ABOVE: *As Carter worked through Tutankhamun's tomb in a ritual of archaeological recording, he undid the elaborate rites of the ancient priests who, three and a half thousand years before, had prayerfully disposed the treasure round the tomb. The wooden hieroglyph, which represents a human backbone and provided the mummy with strength, was placed at the side of the royal sarcophagus as part of the elaborate ritual that served to make order from the chaotic event of death.*

Cairo he bought a golden bird, he said, to help him find a golden tomb. At Luxor, in the Valley of the Kings, on the first full day of work and with just a handful of workmen, he found the famous sixteen steps; soon after, the sealed doorway to the tomb of Tutankhamun. Even before he had uncovered the sixteen steps, however, he had asked a friend, an engineer and not an archaeologist, to come to the Valley to help him with this apparently modest excavation, something the experienced Carter had never done before.

That Carter and Carnarvon had made a clandestine tour of the golden burial chamber before they announced its discovery is only to be expected. Many excavators had made fools of themselves by inviting dignitaries to grand tomb openings which proved to be a flop. Carnarvon was far too canny to expose himself to such a situation.

The 'robbers' hole' that Carter and Carnarvon made to inspect the burial chamber, the hole that had been opened and resealed 'probably by Ramesside inspectors' according to Carnarvon, served to kill two birds with one stone. First it enabled them to make an initial assessment of the size and contents of the tomb, second, the 'robbers' hole' provided secure evidence of ancient robbery – and this was vital if they were ever to be awarded some of the treasures from the tomb. For the standard excavation agreement of the day between the Egyptian Service of Antiquities and foreign archaeologists, stated that if an ancient tomb was found that had never been disturbed since the time of burial, the entire contents should remain in Egypt as an example of a complete ancient burial. If, however, the tomb had been robbed in antiquity and was not therefore, intact, then its excavators were entitled to a half share of the remaining contents. All permit holders in the Valley of the Kings, including Carnarvon himself, had benefited from the terms of this agreement – after all, most of the tombs they found had indeed been plundered!

From the very first days of its discovery, both Carter and Carnarvon were talking to museums to whom they had previously sold antiquities – especially the British Museum and the Metropolitan in New York – about the possible acquisition of objects from the tomb. The Metropolitan Museum also was keen to be involved in the long work of clearance and conservation that Tutankhamun's tomb so obviously required. For a major museum to move their expedition director, Arthur Mace, two first-class draftsmen and the best photographer in Egypt from a fruitful and expensive dig at the Egyptian pyramids and send them south to Tutankhamun's tomb to assist the work of Howard Carter was an act of philanthropy without precedence in archaeology. There was no reason to assume, of course, that they should not receive a lion's share of the treasure, especially as they had had a long and fruitful relationship with Carnarvon and Carter in the past.

So the officials of the Egyptian Service of Antiquities were faced with the prospect of the greatest ever treasure found in Egypt being excavated by archaeologists who were also important dealers in antiquities – and worse, they were being aided by their clients! No

ABOVE: *Howard Carter's house on the so-called 'Hill of Flies' in western Thebes, built a few hundred yards away from the area where, forty years before, Pitt Rivers had found the tell-tale flints that proved the genuine antiquity of the European Stone Age. Planned and built by Carter in the years before the First World War, and occupied by him and his team during the excavation of the tomb of Tutankhamun, the old house has been in continuous use by archaeologists ever since.*

ABOVE: *Part of the constant flood of visitors who stood in the hot sun of the Valley of the Kings throughout the 1920s and marvelled at the treasures coming from the tomb of Tutankhamun — the renaissance of Europe's popular love affair with archaeology that had begun some fifty years before, with Schliemann's reports of his search for ancient Troy.*

RIGHT: *The vast white space at the centre of the royal valley. Even today, as the evening comes and its visitors leave, the ancient burial ground holds something of its sacred past.*

wonder Carter and Carnarvon were so interested in the matter of tomb robbery; keen too, to keep their own adventure in the tomb unknown, so as not to muddy the water. Even so, in the bitter rows and recriminations that followed the opening of the tomb, Carter was indeed accused, though probably unjustly, of taking treasure from the tomb. Was Tut's tomb really robbed, then? And was the robbery, or robberies, ancient or modern? One thing is certain. Such arguments gave the government of Egypt and its servants a perfect opportunity to bind Carter and Carnarvon in legal tape. Following Carnarvon's death, after a lengthy Cairo court battle, all rights to the treasures were conceded to the Cairo Museum.

Another thing is certain too. After he found Tut's treasure, Carter dedicated the remainder of his professional life to its preservation. Following Carnarvon's death, he does not seem to have been concerned where the treasure ended up, he was simply interested in its conservation. That perhaps, is why this great conservationist was never knighted for his extraordinary services to archaeology. 'Had Carter been to the right school,' said an obituary by a contemporary English archaeologist 'he would have made a first-class human being.'

When he first found the tomb, Carter could hardly have realised that his lifetime's span of working in the Valley of the Kings would be so distorted by the spell of treasure seeking, an occupation far older than the science that has so often followed in its footsteps. Yet the opening of that little tomb became a grand event, a world sensation, as much a social and theatric happening as an event of archaeology. The miracle is that under the circumstances, Carter always kept such punctilious records of his labour, and that so many of the ancient treasures, some of them as fragile as a butterfly, are there today for us to marvel at.

Innsbruck: 1567
The Road to Tutankhamun

BEFORE ARCHAEOLOGY, NOTIONS OF THE PAST were held in ancient manuscripts, in standing ruins and treasures that were found within the earth. Tutankhamun's curse was but the last of a long line of ominous alchemies that viewed such buried hoards, the contents of tombs and pagan temples, both as a source of danger and potential power. Here are the beginnings of treasure hunting, that passion for the past that is the darker side of archaeology.

Even the ancient Egyptians collected relics from more ancient times and thought them valuable. Greeks gathered the library of Alexandria so that all the knowledge of the world would be held inside the city. In medieval Siena, when a statue of Venus by the ancient Greek Lysippus was unearthed, the city's elders first held a feast in its honour, then had it smashed to fragments that were buried in the fields of their eternal enemies, the Florentines, to bring ill-luck. In medieval Poland too, pottery from ancient grave fields was bound in gold and placed on Christian altars. Other relics, the bones of prehistoric animals, exquisite coral, and pagan idols were carefully collected by French nobles like the Duc de Berry.

Such bizarre collections were held in strong rooms like the *wunderkammer*, the wonder chamber, of Schloss Ambras, close to Innsbruck in Upper Austria. A rare survival, a unique Renaissance treasure chest, it was designed in the sixteenth century especially to hold the Duke of Tyrol's magpie collections. Both a marvel and an entertainment, set somewhere between the *National Enquirer* and the British Crown Jewels, such curiosities, such *mirabilia*, did not just enrich or entertain, but held a power in them. The collection of the dukes of Tyrol held relics as rare and various as Montezuma's feathered crowns and Benin bronzes, superb porcelain and Samurai armour, vivid portraits of Vlad the Impaler and court dwarfs, a stuffed shark and the assorted busts of Roman emperors.

During the Renaissance, as classical style and manner saturated all the arts of Europe, many scholars came to believe that the best part of wisdom,

BELOW: *Dreams of a land where lemon trees bloom. A chariot of unicorns and a view of magical Rome painted on a castle wall high in the Austrian Alps, at Schloss Ambras, outside Innsbruck. The view shows the Rome of medieval pilgrim visitors, the slender pyramid marking the area where, it was believed, St Peter had been martyred in the reign of the wicked Emperor Nero.*

Den grosten schatz hat er allein
Von silber gold vnnd edel stein
Von perlein gut auch köstlich gwat
Als nie kein fürsten ward bekannt
Dauon zu gotes dienst vnnd eer
Vil geben hat vnd gibt noch mer

LEFT: *Hidden away amongst Dürer's great architectural fantasy, a graphic celebration of the wisdom of the so-called 'scholar emperor', known as the* Triumphal Arch of Maximilian I, *this small panel offers a window into the emperor's private collection of treasures and curiosities, one of Europe's so-called* wunder-kammer — *the ancestors of modern European museums. Woodcut by Kölderer and Dürer, 1515–17.*

BELOW: *Behind their charming frescoes, the halls of the Imperial castle of Schloss Ambras once held one of Europe's most extraordinary treasure chambers.*

with all of its potential power, was born at Rome, the centre of the Christian universe. In 1580–81, the French essayist, Michel Eyquem de Montaigne, travelled to the Eternal City from Bordeaux. He felt that he was going home, for Montaigne tells us that he knew the affairs of Rome 'before I knew those of my own house. I knew the Capitol and its position before I knew the Louvre, and the Tiber before the Seine. I have meditated more on the condition and fortunes of Lucullus, Metellus and Scipio than I have about many of our own men'. Such sentiments would be echoed by nationals of every European country for the next three and a half centuries.

Rome held the standing ruins of that mythic, ancient world whose writings were the education of all literate Europeans. Rome held the home of the ancient emperors, the greatest that the world had seen; men whose very images it seemed, whose very statues bestowed nobility and power. Rome then, above all others was blessed with the ruins of the Roman past and by Montaigne's day, every prince and nobleman of Christendom wanted pieces of this literary vision for himself.

Hadrian's Villa, Rome: Statues for Home

COLLECTORS HAD VISITED ROME from the northlands since the sixteenth century and admired the collections of ancient art gathered by the cardinals and popes. Some, such as the Earl of Arundel, had made their own galleries of ancient art at home, inside their northern houses. To walk amongst such celebrated ancient figures, from naked Venuses to portraits of Plato and Augustus 'standing as it were in their own persons' as an early admirer wrote, 'mixes past ages with the present,' and it became the ambition of many British aristocrats on the Grand Tour, to buy some of these figures and commune with them inside their own houses.

The finest ancient statues and some of the most famous and most influential human images the world has ever seen, were housed and exhibited within the Vatican at Rome, and had been since the days of Michelangelo. Clearly these could not be carted off to Norfolk or Yorkshire. Regarded as treasures in their own right as soon as they were excavated, it was usually extremely difficult to buy good statues and take them home. Throughout the eighteenth century, however, as the Grand Tour grew in popularity and waves of foreigners with gold in their pockets came to see the Eternal City for themselves, many cardinals and artists set up as sculpture dealers.

By far the most powerful of these men and the most influential was Cardinal Alessandro Albani. Designed as a grandiose sculpture gallery, his palace held one of the greatest collections of antique sculpture in Rome. Moreover, his Prussian secretary, Johann Joachim Winckelmann, a connoisseur and a father of Western art history, was a famous scholar, a Europe-wide celebrity in his own right. Together they became as vital a part of the fine art business as Duveen and Berenson were in the 1920s.

A real connoisseur who knew everyone in Rome, Albani enabled purchasers to export their (usually inferior) purchases with little trouble from the authorities. He also operated a large sculpture studio of his own, which 'improved' and 'repaired' all manner of sculptures. Winckelmann was an archaeologist in the older sense of that word; a learned antiquarian who had written fundamental works on the ancient world. Winckelmann alone invented the veneration, the worship almost, of Greek art as a living, breathing thing, a vision that had immediate effect. Goethe, for example, remarked that 'Winckelmann is like Columbus, not

ABOVE: *J. J. Winckelmann, the founder of classical archaeology posed by an unknown German portraitist amongst the ancient architecture of the Roman campagna. He is pointing, surely, to one of his own books, great classics of art and archaeology, either* Reflections on the Painting and Sculpture of the Greeks, *which was first published in 1755, or his magnum opus,* A History of Ancient Art, *which followed it some nine years later.*

yet having discovered the new world, but inspired by a premonition of what is to come'.

By this he meant that Winckelmann had never seen the land of Greece at first hand nor any of its statues. He had, however, seen Roman copies of the long-lost Greek originals and studied classical texts that described the lost statues in terms of adulation. Romans doted on the Greek arts, and employed the greatest Greek sculptors of the day; they also plundered many of its finest products and took them to Rome.

With a vast act of the imagination, best described, perhaps in retrospect, as a fervent homoerotic vision of the past, Winckelmann launched Greek art upon the public of the Western world and gave it an ethos that is with us to this day. In one celebrated passage he proclaimed that 'the only way for us to become great is to imitate the Greeks' and then pursued his vision by writing vividly of the ancient sculptures as if they were living beings. All this gave an extraordinary impetus to archaeology, as Goethe put it, 'One learns nothing new when reading Winckelmann, but one becomes a new man!'. Above all, Winckelmann proclaimed that Greek sculpture had one special quality 'eine edle Einfalt und eine stille Grösse — a noble simplicity and serene grandeur'. Winckelmann's phrase became the watchword and the style of an entire age, the well-spring of both neoclassicism and German classical archaeology.

The rich English on their cultural holidays would give fortunes for such literary creations, and many of them were fooled completely by Albani and his contemporaries, as the galleries of northern Europe show us still today. 'The British are in Rome,' a correspondent writes, 'and buy everything. Thank goodness they haven't got an eye.' Not all tourists though, were quite so silly; there was always a demand for fine pieces fresh from the earth.

All excavation inside Rome, however, had been controlled since the days of Raphael, who had worked with the popes to safeguard the relics of the antique city. Outside Rome though, the great ruins in the beautiful Campagna landscapes were eagerly explored. Amongst these, the grandest and most splendid was Hadrian's Villa, one of the great treasure mines of renaissance Italy where some of Europe's most celebrated ancient statues were excavated, mapped and measured by Italy's finest antiquarians. The excavators of Hadrian's Villa, however, were obliged to give just a third of their finds to the pope.

Set on a pleasant plain below the heights of the town of Tivoli, its green lawns and lakes set within ruined walls and balustrading, the remains of Hadrian's Villa became the inspiration of a hundred English gardens. Strolling eighteenth-century gentlemen dreamed of excavating splendid statues and taking them back to the north. In the eighteenth century, Tivoli and the plain below, all filled with ruined palaces and temples, with half-buried statues and crumbling mosaics, became a European Valley of the Kings.

ABOVE: Charles Townley's Library at 7 Park Street, Westminster *by Johann Zoffany. Townley's celebrated collection of classic art, much of which was purchased by the British Museum in 1805, was gathered in and around Rome in the last quarter of the seventeenth century. Some of these statues seem to have come from excavations at Hadrian's Villa; some are fakes; others were smuggled out of Italy as soon as they were found, in defiance of a papal ban on the exportation of antiquities.*

Elgin and the Acropolis: 1803 Statues for England

I N 1751 TWO ENGLISHMEN, James Stuart and Nicholas Revett, travelled to Athens to draw its ancient monuments. In those days, Athens was a village, a walled city of a thousand houses bounded by a wall; its population was half Greek, a quarter Turk, the remainder Jews, Albanians and slaves. Above the village stood the rock of the Acropolis, crowned by a medieval Italian fortress built around the ancient monuments and occupied by the provincial Turkish governor. The Parthenon, the city's grandest temple that stood at the centre of this rock, had been devastated in a siege some seventy years before when a stray grenade from an invading Venetian army landed in a Turkish powder store inside it. Since that time, a small mosque and minaret had been built at an angle on the temple's shattered pavements, replacing the Christian church that had stood there for more than a thousand years. A cluster of official buildings filled the hilltop – the residence of the Turkish governor, a rose garden and harem, kitchens, barracks and the houses of officials, all in a maze of lanes.

Dressed in Turkish costume, aided by Italian architects that they had engaged at Rome, Stuart and Revett sat and drew the ancient monuments for four whole years. The first volume of their *Antiquities of Athens Measured and Delineated* appeared seven years after their return, under

RIGHT: *The house of Louis Fauvel, the French Consul at Athens in the first decades of the nineteenth century, built on the site of the Agora, under the fortified rock of the Acropolis. Fauvel had plans to take the sculptures of the Parthenon, along with many other antiquities, to France. Louis Dupré, the artist, shows us part of his haul; one of the celebrated panels of the Parthenon depicting the battle of the Lapiths and the Centaurs. Fauvel's grand scheme was thwarted by Napoleon's invasion of Egypt which, like Greece, was then part of the Ottoman Turkish Empire. With the French temporarily out of favour with the authorities of Athens, Lord Elgin's agents 'confiscated' Fauvel's ropes and tackle and used them for their own work at the temple. This splendid illustration, the frontispiece to Louis Dupré's memoir of his trip to Athens in 1819, shows the Acropolis still wearing the towers and crenellations of a medieval fortress. By the 1860s, archaeologists had stripped all this history away and built the walls afresh.*

LEFT: *The south-east corner of the Parthenon, one of the few areas of the temple pediments and friezes left intact by Elgin's agents.*

the auspices of the Society of Dilettanti, a London archaeological club greatly occupied with ancient monuments of the eastern Mediterranean. Unlike most of their contemporaries, Stuart and Revett had not drawn picturesque landscapes filled with nymphs and shepherds but the first archaeological survey of the Parthenon; drawings as precise as engineering plans with reconstructions of the ancient architecture revealing every member in its perfection, so displaying the temple's structure as if it were an engine.

Its effect was terrific. 'Athenian' Stuart's study of the Parthenon's Doric order especially, shocked London taste, where conservatives considered it 'barbaric'. Their ideal classic architecture came from Rome, had a flavour of Catholic grandeur which tended to the baroque. Many of the younger Dilettanti like 'Athenian' Stuart had rather different tastes. Somewhat republican and independent, they naturally admired strength and simplicity in

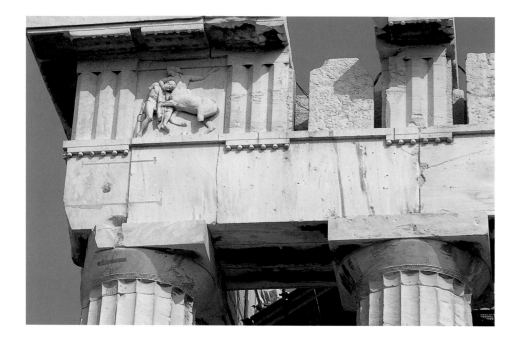

ancient architecture. Most of them were Whigs and did not like Wren or Rome one bit.

This was the first generation of European architects to divide the monuments of the past into distinct archaeological periods and styles, rather than seeing them as steps in a still-living tradition. In the eighteenth century, archaeology and architecture proceeded side by side as some of the greatest architects of the day published splendid archaeological plans of ancient palaces and temples as advertisements of their own prowess and abilities.

Unfortunately, these splendid publications also served as archaeological shopping lists. Connoisseurs were soon visiting the sites the architects had drawn so carefully, especially those far away from the vexatious archaeological restrictions of Italy. Collectors came to take monuments not measurements; above all, to search for those mysterious Greek monuments that Winckelmann's eloquence had celebrated, and which 'Athenian' Stuart had drawn for all to see. The most celebrated, the most notorious of these collectors was the British Ambassador to the Sultan in Istanbul, Lord Elgin.

Elgin had first become enthused with the abstract idea of Greek art by his architect Thomas Harrison, who had redesigned his family home in the 1790s. Harrison, a dedicated neoclassicist, had worked in Rome on schemes to house the celebrated sculptures of the Vatican and fallen entirely under Winckelmann's spell. Right from the first days of his appointment to Constantinople, Elgin conceived the idea of infusing the arts of England with sublime images from ancient Greece and petitioned Prime Minister Pitt for funds to finance a scheme to send artists to the embassy in order to collect Greek art, make casts and drawings. Although Pitt refused and Elgin was far from wealthy, he none the less determined to continue the scheme on his own account. Unwilling to pay the fees that British artists had asked for, he gathered a capable team of Italians on his way to Constantinople under the direction of the Sicilian artist Giovanni Batista Lusieri.

Elgin's plunder of the Parthenon was triggered indirectly by Napoleon's Egyptian campaign of 1799 and the subsequent victory of the British Expeditionary Force. Elgin was heavily involved in diplomatic manoeuvrings to outwit the French in Egypt, then a province of the Ottoman Empire, and when the French Fleet was destroyed in the Bay of Abukir off the coast of Egypt in 1799, he found himself in high favour at the Turkish court. After receiving the state's highest honour from the Sultan's own hands and securing a new building for his embassy and the release of the Maltese galley slaves, some of whom were British sailors, he asked for permission to visit the Parthenon of Athens, and as the Turkish letter granting permission put it: 'to remove some blocks of stone with inscriptions and figures'. So Elgin's Italians put down their pens and brushes and started to organise the removal of the surviving sections of the Parthenon sculptures.

At that time, Athens was so poor that Lusieri had to import scaffolding from the rich Greek islands. Similarly, his ropes and carts were confiscated from the French Government agent Fauvel, who, before he had been thrown into prison following the French invasion of Egypt, had also been endeavouring to take the Parthenon sculptures for France. Although Fauvel and other collectors had taken many wrecked and damaged blocks that were laying on the ground, none of the Athenians, neither the Greek mayor nor the Turkish Disdar, the military governor, would allow foreigners to touch the standing sections of the temple. Elgin's agents too, met with great hindrance, and it was not until the spring of 1801, when a second letter threatening penalty of death for any interruption was issued, that work began in earnest.

Vast scaffolds were erected at the temple's eastern end around the greatest concentration of relief, and a number of ship's windlasses were put in place to lower the huge marbles to the ground.

BELOW: *Despite its battering and scars, and present slow dissolving in the sulphurous air of Athens, the east end of the Parthenon yet remains, one of the supreme surviving beauties of antiquity.*

Even in its wreck, the Parthenon, perhaps the finest classical temple ever built, was an enormous structure, a pile of huge white marble blocks, each one exquisite in its workmanship. Until recently, when pollution has taken such a heavy toll, the surviving architecture was as fine as any in the world, its surfaces sublime. In Elgin's day, many of the temple's surviving sculptures – including the so-called metopes, rows of square panels carved in high relief – were carved on blocks integral to the building's structure. Their removal entailed severely damaging the remaining structure; it took years of work, killed Lusieri and destroyed Elgin's family fortune.

Many European antiquarians visited Elgin's gangs. One of them, Edward Clarke, a collector, indeed, a plunderer of several ancient sites was outraged by their violence: 'Some workmen, employed under Lusieri's direction, were engaged in making preparation, by means of ropes and pulleys, for taking down the metopes…We saw this fine piece of sculpture raised from its station…but part of the adjoining masonry was loosened by the machinery, and down came the fine masses of Pentelican marble, scattering their white fragments with thunderous noise among the ruins. The Disdar, seeing this, could no longer restrain his emotions and actually took his pipe from his mouth, then letting fall a tear, said in a most emphatic tone of voice: "*Telos!* (Enough! the end!)" positively declaring that nothing should induce him to consent to any further dilapidations of the building. Looking up, we saw with regret the gap that had been made, which all the ambassadors of the earth, with all the sovereigns they represent, aided by every resource that wealth and talent can now bestow, will never again repair.'

Another witness was the traveller and scholar, Edward Dodwell, a member of the Society of Dilettante: 'I had the inexpressible mortification of being present when the Parthenon was despoiled of its finest sculptures; and when some of its architectural members were thrown to the ground…instead of the picturesque beauty and high preservation in which I first saw it, it is now comparatively reduced to a state of shattered desolation.'

It seems that everyone but Elgin knew instinctively that it was wrong to smash this ancient relic that had stood as temple, church and mosque for two and a half millennia. Even the British soldiers, placed at the command of Elgin's embassy service were disgusted with their task of crating up the stones for shipment. Informing Elgin's staff of his imminent arrival at the work, Captain Thomas Lacy of the Royal Engineers wrote sarcastically: 'Congratulate me: I have at last found means to escape [my duties] and devote myself to my friends…I Embark for Athens to plunder temples and commit sacrilege, a proper finish to my diplomatic career!'

It took five years for Lusieri and his men to work their way around the temple, to denude it of the best part of its surviving art and to ship it off to London. Drawings show how the sculptures were first exhibited in London in a Park Lane attic. From the first day they were a sensation, engendering arguments on a wide variety of issues.

For many visitors it was difficult to recognise Winckelmann's 'serene harmony' in works of such energy and power. Several senior members of the Dilettante Society declared that they were poor works of art and probably Roman. The great neoclassical sculptor Antonio Canova came to view them at Park Lane however and refused Elgin's request to 'improve' and 'restore' the broken marbles, as was the usual taste of the time. Canova said that they were without parallel, broken masterpieces that no one else should ever touch again. And with his declaration, he stakes a valid claim to be the world's first modern conservator.

Very bitter arguments broke out over Elgin's offer to sell the marbles to the government

RIGHT: *At the beautiful Erechtheum, the fifth-century BC Ionic temple that stands beside the Parthenon of Athens, Lord Elgin's men removed the second sculpture from the left in this famous line of caryatids. Her modern replacement is in concrete: it is said that if you visit the galleries in the British Museum where the statue now stands, you may sometimes hear her crying for her native land. Such barbaric plundering of ancient monuments shocked all of Elgin's fellow countrymen who knew and loved the land of Greece.*

for the same sum he had expended to bring them to England. He was virtually bankrupt, the work having cost a fortune. In a biting cartoon, Cruikshank shows us John Bull's family wanting bread, and receiving stones while a fluttering flysheet advertises a fictitious book by the Earl: *Speculation, or travels in the east in search of ruinous stone fragments for John Bull* by Lord Elgin. After long debate, a government committee offered Elgin a sum for his sculpture far less than his large outlay and reluctantly he settled. England then sanctified the plunder of the Parthenon by exhibiting the stones as a national treasure, the ultimate popularisation of Winckelmann's great passion for an imagined past.

The poet, Lord Byron, who hated Elgin and his destructive work at Athens from the beginning, had ran the full gamut of poetic vindictiveness in a variety of broadsheets and poems, some so incendiary that they had caused the delay of the last shipments of the stones from Greece. His viciousness may be judged by this extraordinary couplet, written in the knowledge that Elgin had apparently contracted syphilis and lost the better part of his nose in consequence:

Noseless himself, he brings here noseless blocks
To show what time has done and what the pox.

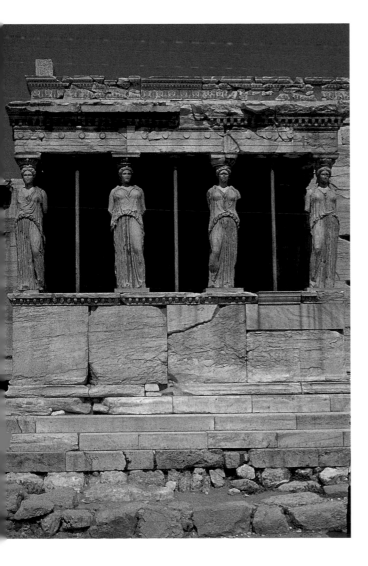

Despite the polemic, Elgin's marbles exercised vast influence on the arts of England, just as he had planned. Right around the world, indeed, Elgin's marbles became a part of the vocabulary of art, the means to an ennobling aesthetic experience, quoted by artists from Blake to Picasso. For some though, they are the sad emblems of a modern nation born of loss; for others again, the essential emblem, the prestige, of a great museum.

As to the characters in the sorry drama: Elgin died alone in poverty in France, whilst poor Lusieri, his long-suffering foreman, died in agony in Athens from a burst blood vessel. The Greeks, who despised him, found him lying in a pool of blood and said that there was a black cat sitting on his chest. Through all his years of working, Elgin had never even paid his salary.

For most people, Elgin's marbles leave a bad taste in the mouth; there are a wide variety of unresolved issues – issues concerning the legality of Elgin's, hence the British government's right of ownership and the endlessly debated problem of their return to modern Greece. Restored now, the Parthenon, a national shrine shimmering above the smog of Athens which is consuming the marble, will never hold Lord Elgin's stones again. Should the marbles then, be sent on another journey to sit in a new museum? And if they should, what of all the other 'stolen' treasures in the museums of the West? As ambiguous as the myths they represent, the marbles of the Parthenon remain a reference point, a touchstone for all archaeology.

Napoleon in Egypt: 1798
The Battle of the Pyramids

J UST AS THE BRITISH TURNED THEIR EYES TOWARDS THE EAST – so did the French. In 1798, the year before Lord Elgin left England for Istanbul, Napoleon set sail for Egypt with 36,000 men and a thousand pieces of artillery in some four hundred ships, an enormous army that, with its transport vessels and hangers-on formed a flotilla some six miles long. Napoleon's secret dream was to control the Mediterranean by colonising the countries all around it. Publicly, as his leaflets to the Egyptian people announced, he proclaimed that he was bringing liberty, equality and fraternity to a land that for centuries had been ruled by a cruel group of medieval knights – the Mamelukes.

After occupying Alexandria, 25,000 French soldiers marched quickly inland. At Cairo, the Egyptians prepared for war and their scholars read and reread the pamphlets that the

French had printed to discover the character of their enemies. Napoleon's one-page flysheets were the first documents to be printed in Egypt; he had ordered that two presses be brought with the army from France, with Arabic, Greek and French typefaces. His proclamation started in the usual way of Islamic exhortations, 'In the name of God, the merciful, the compassionate,' but then it continues with French revolutionary sentiments, 'in the name of liberty, equality and fraternity, the French Republic has come to Egypt to punish its cruel and unjust rulers…'

At first sight, the Arabic scholars did not know what to make of it. Gossip from Alexandria told that these uncouth foreigners shaved their heads but not their pubic hair and they pissed openly in the street. Who were these foreigners, and why on earth had they invaded Egypt? Careful study of their leaflet revealed the truth. The devil was in the detail, in the endings of the words, in the adjectives, in the verbs, in slips of grammar and of style. And there, they discovered that these French didn't honour God at all; that they were without honour or religion.

This then, was the huge and terrifying regiment that marched quickly past the Pyramids of Giza to do battle with the mighty Mamelukes. And as they marched, their 26-year-old commander, the grandest tourist of them all, told the half-exhausted men that four thousand years of history looked down upon their ordered columns. The prize was Cairo.

At the pyramids, they formed five equal squares of men, each one commanded by a crack general. And in this order, they moved crab-wise through the sand to Cairo. Finally, the

BELOW: *A detail from Louis François Lejeune's* Bataille des Pyramides le 21 juillet 1798. *Lejeune's marvellous painting shows Napoleon's lethal squares repulsing the charging Mameluke knights.*

OPPOSITE PAGE: *Major-General Desaix, hero of both Napoleon's Egyptian campaign and early egyptology.*

exhausted Frenchmen confronted Egypt's medieval rulers, the Mamelukes, that cruel and elegant caste, at Imbaba, a small port on the river bank opposite the great city. On contact, the French squares barely moved whilst the Mamelukes, incredible medieval visions, dressed in silk and cashmere and armed to the teeth with muskets and scimitars, rode around them like the sea beating against rocks.

The battle lasted about two hours and in the process, a quarter of the Mameluke horsemen died, along with two thousand men, and twenty-nine Frenchmen. The Mamelukes fought individually without order, and often in competition with each other while the French fought in European battle order; similar slaughters would take place on several continents over the next century. At the battle's ending, piles of Mamelukes were heaped up around the French squares, their silk and cashmere robes in flames, set alight by the gun cotton of the French muskets. In confusion, the remaining Mamelukes retreated to the waters of the Nile and more were drowned there, it was later said, than were killed by the weapons of the French. Their defeat was absolute; moreover, it had taken place under the eyes of the people of Cairo, whom they had controlled for centuries. The ageless world of Egypt had been brought to its ending by modern European order.

To the people of Cairo, the French army seemed completely dedicated, utterly fearless. Al Jabarti, a leading Islamic scholar described them thus: 'They acted as if they were following the tradition of the warriors of Mohammed – as fighters in a holy war. They never considered the number of their enemy too high, nor did they care who among them was killed. They considered anyone who fled a traitor. They faithfully obey the orders of their commanders. And they have signs and signals among themselves which they all obey. Their only shade is the hat on their head and their only mount their own two feet. Their food and drink is but a morsel and a sip, hanging under their arms. Their baggage and change of clothing hang on their backs like a pillow and when they sleep they lie on it.'

The French that day got plunder, gold and glory and old Cairo, a city of some 300,000 souls. They got another gentler gift as well; the idea of a shop that sold coffee – which the Cairenes called *cavé* – out in the street. The boulevard was born that day beside the pyramids. And so, of course, was egyptology.

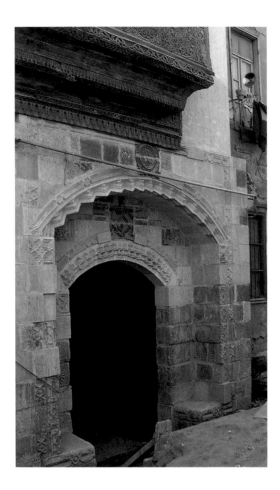

Institut d'Egypte, Cairo: 1798

At Cairo, Napoleon's officers took over the Mamelukes' grandest dwellings after their owners fled southwards up the River Nile. Three of these beauteous houses were put aside for the use of the one hundred and fifty scholars, the Scientific and Artistic Commission, that Napoleon had recruited to accompany his army. They were to examine and study every aspect of this ancient land, gathering information essential to a future French government. As one scholar suggested, with the aid of just 20,000 French settler families, France could restore the ancient land, this 'enormous garden'. Like Caesar before him, Napoleon planned to make Egypt a province of his empire.

The scholars of the Commission ranged from senior scientists of Paris, middle-aged portly academics to boys of fifteen, and included whole classes of enthusiastic youngsters, many of them from the Academy of Mines and Bridges in Paris. In Egypt, they were also planning to open mines and build bridges, design roads and irrigation schemes. There were zoologists, botanists and surgeons too, representatives of all the professions required for the good order of an eighteenth-century European government.

On 21 August 1798, in the grand dwelling known as the house of Hassan Kashef, Napoleon established an academy for his generals and his senior academics – the Institut d'Egypte.

Just as the French Army divided Egypt into military zones, so the Institut was organised in four sections; foremost in importance was the section of

LEFT: *The doorway of the Cairo house of Ibrahim Kikeyyed el Sennary, used by some of Napoleon's savants in 1799–1802, one of several Mameluke palaces requisitioned by the French to house the scholars of the Institut d'Egypte. Newly built in Napoleon's day, though in classic medieval style, one of the scholars considered such accommodations to be 'better than the Louvre'.*

BELOW LEFT: *Napoleon attending the inauguration of the Institut d'Egypte in the harem of the house of the Mameluke Hassan Kashef, on 21 August 1798. The figures of the group of men around Napoleon are miniature portraits of his general staff and senior scholars, several of whom would never see France again.*

RIGHT: *The magnificent title page of the first edition of the* Description de l'Egypte. *Bearing Napoleon's imperial monogram, celebrating the battles of his Egyptian campaign, the centrepiece shows an idealised vision of the French triumphal progress through the ancient monuments of Egypt. This first volume came off the press in 1809, some ten years after Napoleon departed Egypt. The final volume of this astonishing publishing enterprise in nineteen separate parts appeared in 1824, some three years after the Emperor's death in exile on the Atlantic island of St Helena. This was Europe's introduction to Egyptian antiquities, and the engineering training from the School of Mines and Bridges gave the plates a studied style and accuracy that archaeologists have imitated to this day.*

Political Economy. Staffed by senior generals and the most learned of Napoleon's scholars, this was intended to oversee the government of Egypt, a sort of cabinet. The other three divisions, Physics, Literature and Art, and Mathematics were staffed by groups of *savants*: surgeons, chemists, botanists, zoologists, inventors and geologists; poets, linguists, artists, architects; astronomers, surveyors and engineers. All together, the Institut would evaluate and control every aspect of the scholars' work in Egypt.

It was the first contact between the scholarship of the new and revolutionary West and the oldest nation in the world; the work of these academicians of the Institut, the *savants* of the Commission initiated Egyptian archaeology. After Nelson destroyed Napoleon's

Mediterranean fleet at the Battle of Abukir, the army in Egypt was isolated along with the scholars. Then the *savants* slowly turned their gaze away from the future to the past, and began to record the remains of ancient Egypt at ever greater length. Revolutionary zeal evaporated and notions of the new world improving ancient ways gave way to an admiration for these ancient people who had left remains of such elegance and sophistication. Egyptian archaeology was born in Egypt in this French Academy. Viewed now by foreigners with European measuring devices and machinery, old Egypt would never be the same again.

Thebes: 1798–1799. Exploring With the Army

After the Battle of the Pyramids, Napoleon struck north up the coast and into Syria hoping to open new ports of entry for the expeditionary force, after Nelson had sunk the French fleet off Alexandria. At the same time, Napoleon sent another smaller army under General Desaix south into Upper Egypt, to put down rebellion and chase the remaining Mamelukes.

Desaix had a hard, frustrating task. Supply ships from Cairo were few and far between. His three thousand men lacked bread and bullets, their uniforms were ragged, disease rife, morale low and tempers short. And they were greatly outnumbered by the surviving Mamelukes, who attacked at every opportunity. Then, after months of marching they came across the mighty ruins of the ancient temples. At Dendera, where they first saw crocodiles on the river, they also came across the great temple standing lonely in the sand. Despite their filth and hunger, officers and *savants* were moved. 'Ever since I came to Egypt,' an officer said to one of the artists, 'I have felt cheated in every way, and been depressed and ill. Dendera has cured me. What I saw today has paid me back for all my misery.'

When the ragged regiments of Frenchmen marched further south to Thebes they came across the Temple at Karnak, the mightiest of them all. 'All at once,' an officer recorded, 'without an order being given, the men formed their ranks and presented arms, to the accompaniment of the drums and the bands.' Later the artist Vivant Denon remembered 'the whole army, suddenly and with one accord, stood in amazement…and clapped their hands with delight…as if the complete conquest of Egypt were accomplished by the taking of these splendid ruins'.

In the following year, a large inscription was carved on the great doorway of the First Pylon of the temple, recording the measurements and the longitudes and latitudes of the temples that the *savants* had surveyed in Upper Egypt; a suitably scholarly tribute to the ancient people that they studied and the strength of their own extraordinary enthusiasm. All over Egypt, indeed, *savants* and soldiers were recognising the skill and sensitivities of the artists who had decorated the ancient monuments. Ancient Egypt, a great open-air museum, was slowly gaining human appreciation once again.

Five centuries before the French arrived, the great Moroccan geographer Ibn Battuta had also visited Thebes and stood amongst these same ruins. He though, tells us only of the fine pottery and strong donkeys to be seen in the nearby town of Luxor. Thebes' great temples, their statues, the bright-painted tombs go unmarked in his writings. This, of course, was not because he had not seen them, for they were the largest, brightest things in the landscape. Ibn Battuta, moreover, usually wrote enthusiastically about grand architecture. Here, in common with early Christian pilgrims in the Middle East, he simply displays a kind of pious

RIGHT: *The view from south to north across the axis of the Great Hypostyle Hall of Karnak Temple. Of all the Egyptian temples, Karnak's vast ruin fired the imagination of the French army and the pens of the accompanying scholars.*

LEFT: *One of Napoleon's* savants *making notes in the shadows of a sphinx in Karnak Temple in Egyptian Thebes. From Volume III of the* Description de l'Egypte, *which holds some fifty plates illustrating the great temple, a resource of more than a thousand separate images of its architecture and reliefs.*

BELOW LEFT: *Baron Dominique Vivant Denon, the French nobleman and scholar who survived the Revolution and Napoleon's Egyptian expedition to became director general of the museums of France. In Egypt with the army, Denon produced a splendid volume of plates that was published years before the* Description de l'Egypte *and created a wave of interest in ancient Egypt and its designs that has survived to this day. Employing his pencils and his pistols with equal verve and accuracy, renowned for his sangfroid and conviviality, Denon has become a vital part of the legend of the army's journey into Upper Egypt.*

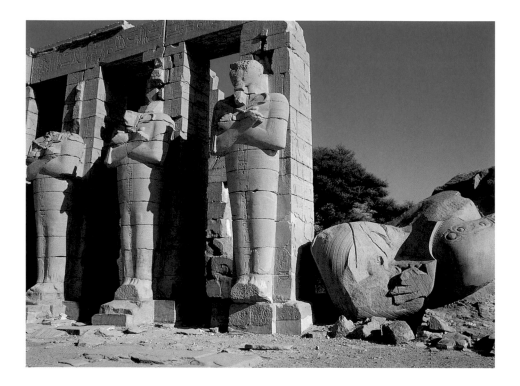

LEFT: *The fallen colossus in the Temple of the Ramesseum on the West Bank of Thebes, whose illustration by Vivant Denon inspired a London broker to pen a poor verse that, after Shelley's magnificent reformation, became the famous poem,* Ozymandias.

BELOW: *Castex, the sculptor with the Napoleonic expedition, carved his name upon the head of Ozymandias, along with that of the young Édouard de Villiers, who would later publish the first archaeological survey of the Valley of the Kings in the* Description de l'Egypte.

reticence – the same modesty that had encouraged Muslims to let pagan monuments lie in peace, an attitude which had long shielded the ruins of Thebes from all celebrity. The revolutionary French, however, had no such reticence, and had come to measure and celebrate the ancient land and, with their published plans and drawings, exhibit its ancient wonders to the Western world. And the West was entirely fascinated and has been so ever since.

Of all the monuments the wondering French visited along the Nile, those of Thebes fascinated them the most, and a small group of *savants* settled in the city for two months in August 1799 to survey and measure everything they could. Sent down the Nile with Desaix's army as part of a survey intended to increase field fertility by introducing modern irrigation, they became known as the *heiroglyphistes*.

Under-equipped, ragged, sometimes blinded by opthalmia with pus in their eyes, frequently in danger of attack, they drew and measured most of the major monuments with care and great precision, sometimes even using the lead from their bullets for pencils when supplies gave out. Two of them died of heat stroke, several were attacked and robbed, but Desaix's army supported them as best they could, providing guards and assistance for the surveyors and the artists. In fact, Desaix himself, intense revolutionary, drunk with glory and soldiering, slowly become as fascinated with the past as were the *savants*; sometimes the records of his expeditionary force seem to have the tone of a grand journey of idealists and scholars, walking through the deserts of a magic past.

Vivant Denon was the peripatetic artist whose published drawings were the first to bring the expedition's archaeological enthusiasms to Europe. This future director of the Louvre Museum was fascinated by two celebrated colossal statues standing in the plain of Thebes, the

Colossi of Memnon, that all at once seemed to be the very antithesis of European art, yet held a grandeur and a sensitivity all their own. 'These two pieces of art, which are without grace, expression, or action, have nothing which seduces the judgement; but their proportions are faultless, and this simplicity of attitude, and want of decided expression, has something of majesty and seriousness, which cannot fail to strike the beholder.'

Perhaps the *savants'* favourite temple in Egypt was the Ramesseum, the great mortuary Temple of Ramesses II. Half plundered of its stone in ancient times, the yellowed ruins were close to the green fields and still today, appear as a living version of an exquisite composition of Claude or Poussin. At the Ramesseum lay the ruins of the largest colossus of them all. Originally some sixty feet high and weighing a hundred tons, it had been broken in two as it was toppled in an earthquake, and was slowly being sliced up for use as millstones. Though the French rarely had the time or inclination to excavate the buried monuments they drew, here they cleared the great old statue, and the expedition sculptor, Castex, carved their names on the top of pharaoh's head, which lay gently on the ground.

The statue grew in European fame and legend. Just a few years later Shelley, used its image for a meditation on power and the past in *Ozymandias.*

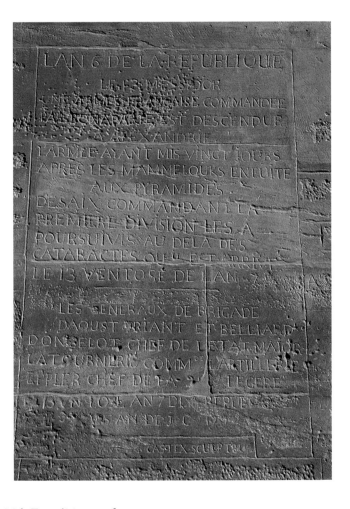

BELOW: *This inscription, proudly cut by members of the Napoleonic Army on a doorway embrasure of the great temple of Philae at Aswan, the southernmost point of their invasion, relates the whole history of Napoleon's Egyptian adventure in stirring revolutionary prose.*

> *I met a traveller from an antique land*
> *Who said: Two vast and trunkless legs of stone*
> *Stand in the desert. . .*
> *And on the pedestal these words appear:*
> *'My name is Ozymandias, king of kings:*
> *Look on my works, ye Mighty, and despair!'*
> *Nothing beside remains. Round the decay*
> *Of that colossal wreck, boundless and bare*
> *The lone and level sands stretch far away.*

By that time though, the Ramesseum, Thebes and all of Egypt had become part of a British dream as well. Three years after Nelson's navy had isolated the French in Egypt, a British Expeditionary force invaded and the *savants* and the *Armeé de Égypte* had followed Napoleon back to France. Then Lord Elgin's antiquities agent in Egypt, following in the wake of a British Expeditionary force, seized for England the collection that the French had made. He obtained too, the Rosetta Stone with its bilingual inscription that greatly aided Champollion's decipherment of hieroglyphics. For all their careful drawing of the temple's text, the *savants* had not understood a single ancient word of them!

Colonised, described, deciphered, the next forty years saw a wide variety of antiquarians and adventurers collect up the smaller treasures of this antique land and ship them off to Europe. As Napoleon's armies wandered Europe, Vivant Denon established the museum of the Louvre – the first national museum in the world – to hold their plunder, art gained in price and prestige and the international art market was born.

The Young Memnon
Belzoni at Thebes: 1817

THE MOST VIVID OF ALL OF THESE EARLY Egyptian adventurers was Giovanni Batista Belzoni, an Italian engineer from Padua, a handsome red-headed giant of a man, some six feet seven inches tall. Down and out in Cairo in 1816, after a varied career all over Europe, Belzoni was employed by the newly arrived British Consul in Egypt, Henry Salt, who had entered into partnership with well-known traveller Jean Louis Burkhardt to export a colossus from Thebes to London. Considering the poverty of Upper Egypt at the time and the sheer bulk of these statues, this was quite an enterprise, and Salt and his partner wrote a careful contract for the Italian giant.

'Mr. Belzoni is requested to prepare the necessary Implements, at Bulak [at Cairo], for the purpose of raising the head of the statue of the younger Memnon and carrying it down the Nile. He will proceed as speedily as circumstances will allow...'

'Having obtained the necessary permission to hire workmen, Mr. Belzoni will proceed direct to Thebes. He will find the head referred to on the Western side of the River opposite to Karnak, in the vicinity of a Village called Gurna, lying on the southern side of a ruined temple...To the head is still attached a portion of the shoulders, so that altogether it is of large dimensions, and will be recognised – 1st by the circumstances of its lying on its back, with the face uppermost – 2ndly by the face being quite perfect and very beautiful – 3rdly by its having on one of its shoulders a hole bored artificially, supposed to have been made

BELOW: *Belzoni's famous illustration of his heroic struggle to remove the 'Young Memnon' from the Ramesseum for its journey down the Nile and up the Thames to the British Museum. Though generations of later scholars insistently observed that the statue was not of 'Memnon' but another king, recent studies have shown that the eyes of the early travellers were more acute than the readers of the royal hieroglyphs, and that great Ramesses who built the Ramesseum Temple had, in fact reinscribed a statue of Amenhotep III – from which the name of Memnon is derived – and set it in pride of place at the centre of his temple.*

RIGHT: *Giovanni Batista Belzoni, the Paduan adventurer, sometime hydraulic engineer, showman, strongman and egyptologist, whose charm and candour shed such light upon the murky days of early excavation and collecting in the ruins of ancient Egypt.*

LOWER LEFT: The Fruits of Enterprise, *a contemporary illustrated children's book told the stories of Belzoni's Egyptian adventures:* 'Although Belzoni's chief object was not to see antiquities at that time, yet he felt desirous of visiting the famous pyramids. . . Having gratified his admiration . . .he examined several of the mausoleums, and returned to Cairo highly delighted with having seen a wonder'.

LOWER RIGHT: *'Belzoni undertook to erect a machine which would rise as much water with one ox as the machines of the country of Egypt did with four.'The failure of this enterprise lead Belzoni to consider other employment;* 'A gentleman by the name of Burkhardt, had for a long time premeditated the removal of a colossal bust, known by the name of the young Memnon. . .'

by the French for separating the fragment of the body – and 4thly from its being of a mixed blackish and reddish granite, and carved with hieroglyphics on its shoulders. It must not be mistaken for another lying in its neighbourhood, which is much mutilated.'

'Mr. Belzoni will spare no expense or trouble in getting it as speedily conveyed to the bank of the river as possible, and he will, if it be necessary, let it wait there till the River has attained sufficient height…'

Belzoni, an ingenious and inventive man, had been a renowned showman in England, and something of a celebrity in Covent Garden, designing waterfalls for operas and playing the strongman in them, on stage. This then, was another opportunity to display his skills and the bestseller he would later write about the work became his literary platform. In his book, *A Narrative of the Operations*, Belzoni tells us how he set up house with his wife Sarah and their long-suffering Irish servant inside the temple. He found the thirty-ton colossus, he says, lying face down in the sand apparently 'smiling at the thought of being taken to England'. And then he went about recruiting extra labour to help him move young Memnon out of Egypt. First he made a frame to hold the smiling statue, then the giant engineer and his men engaged in a month-long purgatory of pushing and pulling to get the colossus out of the temple and on to the ancient causeway that led down to the riverside.

Suffering nose and ear bleeds from prodigious feats of strength, and continuously battling with the agents of other avaricious consuls, the Italian strongman eventually got young Memnon safely aboard a boat for Cairo. Seventeen months later, to London's great delight, forty Royal Engineers installed the gentle granite portrait in the British Museum.

After his battle with young Memnon, Belzoni was well bitten by the antiquities bug and both he and Consul Salt decided to continue hunting for exportable antiquities. Thebes however, was filled with just such consular agents, each with his own hunting ground, each protected with armed gangs. Their shenanigans having proved embarrassing to their masters, Thebes was now divided east and west, just as Chicago was divided by gangs of gangsters. In this consular carve-up, the French and Italians got Karnak and the East Bank, Belzoni and Salt the West Bank and the ancient cemeteries including the Valley of the Kings, a lonely desert *wadi* in the west of Thebes filled with open, painted tombs of ancient pharaohs.

Belzoni, who had decided to find some more, started looking in the lonely western branch of the Royal Valley. His book tells us that in August 1817, as he was walking past the tomb of Memnon (Amenhotep III) that a young French *savant* had discovered twenty years before 'I happened to have a stick with me and on thrusting it into the holes amongst the stone, I found it to be very deep'. His gang of local workmen soon uncovered a buried doorway for his inspection and Belzoni wandered down into the warm, dark corridors of the first royal tomb he ever found, the tomb of King Ay, Tutankhamun's successor on the throne of Egypt, whose burial had been broken into in the century after his death, some fourteen centuries BC. In an age of fortune hunters seeking treasure, this ruined monument was not much of a find. But it was enough to give Belzoni a taste for buried tombs, and he proudly inscribed his name above the ancient doorway. What he really needed though, to soothe the Consul, was something valuable that he could send to England.

Two months later, Belzoni and his workmen were digging in the central Valley of the Kings, and here amongst a group of little tombs he found the remarkable painted corridor

ABOVE: *A mysterious enshrined god, an ancient image of one of the many statues placed in the great tomb at the time of the royal burial. This is one of hundreds of such images carved and painted on the walls of the tomb of Seti I in the Valley of the Kings, the tomb that Belzoni and his contemporaries regarded as the single finest monument of Egypt.*

RIGHT: *Belzoni's drawing of the burial chamber of Seti I, the only record of the position in which he discovered the famous alabaster coffin of that king, a marvellous work of ancient art, which was sold to the architect Sir John Soane. Belzoni's plate that accompanied his book, shows the coffin lying across the entrance to a subterranean passage which, to this day, has never been fully excavated. If the picture is accurate, it is likely that the coffin had been brought up into the burial chamber by the ancient priests who took Seti's mummy out of the tomb for a secret reburial in the Theban cliffs.*

of the tomb of Prince Montuhirkopeshef, a veritable masterpiece of Egyptian art. To his eternal credit, Belzoni never mutilated the tombs he found by cutting pretty fragments of their paintings from the walls as both earlier and later archaeologists would do. The problem was, he still had not found the Consul a treasure worthy enough to be taken to England.

Belzoni, however, had read the writings of the ancient Greeks who visited Thebes when the ancient temples still had their priests and gods in them. He knew that they had counted some forty tombs in the Valley of the Kings. Less than half that number were visible to Belzoni. So Consul Salt backed Belzoni's enthusiasms. Soon tomb after tomb was uncovered, congregations of mummies followed quickly on each others' heels and soon royal sarcophagi and some very pretty statues were sailing off to London.

Belzoni came into his own at Thebes. From his writings, it is clear that he understood the Royal Valley, understood its landscapes and how its limestone and shale had been shaped by ancient floods and waterfalls; understood too, how the ancient masons had used the landscape to excavate their tombs. His work indeed, shows subtleties that many scholars who would follow in his footsteps sorely lack. Other travellers who Salt sent down to Thebes have described Belzoni at this time: how his physical presence impressed his workmen; how they were treated to tours of freshly opened tombs displayed to them by Belzoni with the panache of a born showman. Then in October 1817, he made one of the great discoveries of archaeology, which is best described in his own words:

'On the 16th I recommenced my excavations in the valley of Beban el Malook [the Valley of the Kings], and pointed out the fortunate spot, which has paid me for all the trouble I took in my researches. I may call this a fortunate day, one of the best perhaps of my life...I do not mean to say, that fortune has made me rich; but she has given me that satisfaction, that extreme pleasure, which wealth cannot purchase; the pleasure of...presenting the world with a new and perfect monument of Egyptian antiquity, which can be recorded as superior to any other in point of grandeur, style, and preservation, appearing as if just finished on the day we entered it...'

'I caused the earth to be opened at the foot of a steep hill, and under a torrent, which, when it rains in the desert, pours a great quantity of water over the very spot I have caused to be dug. No one could imagine, that the ancient Egyptians would make the entrance into such an immense and superb excavation just under a torrent of water; but I had strong reasons to suppose, that there was a tomb in that place, from indications I had observed in my pursuit. The Fellahs [workmen] who were accustomed to dig were all of the opinion, that there was nothing in that spot, as the situation of this tomb differed from that of any other. I continued the work however, and the next day, the 17th, in the evening, we perceived the part of the rock that was cut, and formed the entrance. On the 18th, early in the morning, the task was resumed, and about noon the workmen reached the entrance, which was eighteen feet below the surface of the ground. The appearance indicated, that the tomb was of the first rate: but I did not expect to find such a one as it really proved to be.'

'The Fellahs advanced till they saw that it was probably a large tomb, when they protested they could go no farther, the tomb was so much choked up with large stones, which they could not get out of the passage. I descended, examined the place, pointed out to them where they might dig, and in an hour there was room enough for me to enter through a passage that the earth had left under the ceiling of the first corridor...I perceived immediately by the painting on the ceiling, and by the hieroglyphics...that this was the entrance into a large and magnificent tomb.'

The tomb is known today as that of Seti I, one of the finest in the Valley, a deep, relatively small-corridored monument that, was as perfect as the day it had been closed for the royal funeral. Its effect on its first visitors was electric.

ABOVE: *Part of the magnificent astronomical ceiling in the burial chamber of the tomb of Seti I. Considered one of the wonders of the monument, its figures were celebrated in the contemporary European pottery of Sévres and Wedgewood.*

FAR LEFT: *The face of the Goddess Isis from the entrance corridor of the Tomb of Seti I, in the Valley of the Kings. Pure, white and fresh as a flower in Belzoni's day, the goddess now glistens with the grease of human contact.*

ABOVE: *Two darkly eloquent and mysterious deities engraved upon the walls of the tomb of Seti I, in the Valley of the Kings.*

They, after all, had come to a wild and extravagantly hot desert *wadi* and there, amongst the brutal heat and boulders had been led down into the cool of a perfect masterpiece whose decorations changed dramatically in style and colour with every passing hall and corridor. The style too, precise, perfect, slightly pinched and earnest was greatly to contemporary taste. Consul Salt wrote poetry about it; his French counterpart was rendered speechless with admiration.

What to do though, with such an immovable masterpiece? Suddenly, the giant showman had an inspiration, and one that brought him fame and fortune. He would make castings of the tomb walls and some copies, and reconstruct parts of this long-lost Egyptian masterpiece in a gallery at Piccadilly, London, built for exhibitions of every sort, from the fine arts to Siamese twins and Japanese mermaids.

In 1821 in the Egyptian Galleries, Belzoni showed his casts and copies of the tomb, along

RIGHT: *The wadi in the Valley of the Kings explored by Belzoni in 1817, in which he found a succession of great tombs, including that of Seti I. The tomb's entrance is indicated by the second shadowed walkway running right, off the central path that leads to the wadi's head.*

ABOVE: *'At the end of this corridor he came to a long staircase, at the foot of which a door opened into a still longer passage. . . at the end of this passage he reached a large pit . . .as deep as our house is high. He had better take care of what he is about!' The plate and description of Belzoni's first exploration of the tomb of Seti I in the Valley of the Kings, from the* Fruits of Enterprise, *a contemporary children's book.*

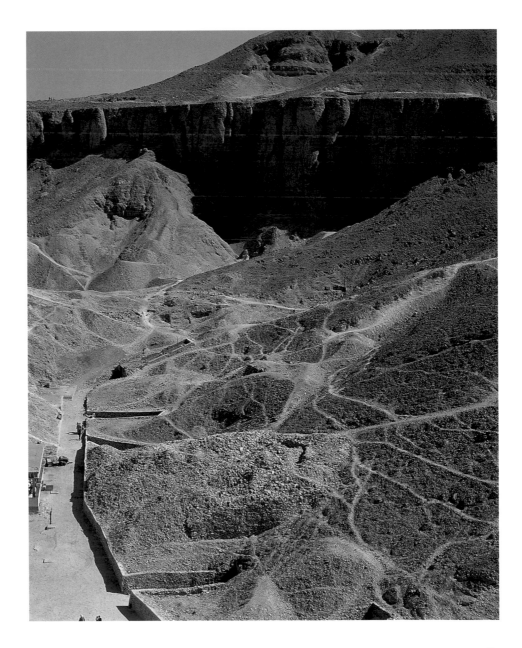

with a gigantic model. His exhibition was the sensation of the season. At its opening, Belzoni unwrapped a mummy before a distinguished audience, and *The Times* commented on the 'mechanical ingenuity and indefatigable diligence by which Mr Belzoni has been enabled thus to transport to the arena of European controversy the otherwise immovable excavations of ancient Egypt'.

Weeks later, George III graciously accepted a copy of his *Narrative of Operations*, the book of the show. Belzoni had realised what it would take others another century to understand; sometimes the treasures of Egypt reside in the imagination, not simply in the sand.

The Fruits of Enterprise. Belzoni at the Pyramids: 1819

Belzoni went north to Cairo after his Theban adventures, and there, just like everybody else, he visited the Great Pyramid at Giza and its mighty burial chamber. Ever since it was built, people had known that this vast antiquity had a tomb at its centre. Arab legend told that a caliph had once found the ancient corridors leading down to the burial chamber by quarrying a tunnel into the pyramid's north face.

The Second Pyramid though, Chephren's Pyramid, that stood behind the Great Pyramid on the Giza Plateau, was believed to be completely solid. Since the days of the Greeks and Romans, who had talked to living ancient Egyptian priests about such ancient things, no one had imagined that there might be a burial chamber or corridors inside the Second Pyramid.

Belzoni though, who by this time had opened up many a hidden royal tomb at Thebes, thought differently and decided to start an excavation to look for a hidden doorway in the same place as the entrance to the corridors of the Great Pyramid. This area on the Second Pyramid was deeply buried in rubble and sand.

In January 1818, he engaged eighty labourers and double that number of boys and girls to carry off the dirt – a system that was used, indeed, until Egypt changed its labour laws in the 1950s.

Ten days passed, during which one of his gangs dug down into the centre of the northern face through shifting sands and loose rock where Belzoni calculated, the entrance should lay. They found nothing; his work force thought that he was mad. Working on his own account and not the Consul's, Belzoni was running out of money.

So he stopped his excavation for a day, to think again about the ancient Egyptians and how they had worked. Walking past the Great Pyramid, he suddenly realised his mistake. The corridor of the Great Pyramid that led straight down from the surface of the Pyramid to the royal burial chamber entered the burial chamber, a sixty-foot-long chamber lying at the dead centre of the monument. If the Second Pyramid was the same, the doorway to the entrance corridor would not be at the centre of the northern face but half a burial chamber's length, that is, some thirty feet, to the east of centre.

ABOVE: *Belzoni's charming illustration of the Book of the Divine Cow, a scene that fills an entire chamber in Seti's tomb. The cow's great belly is also the night sky. Gods hold up the stars and heavens, and the great bark of the Sun God floats amongst the celestial bodies.*

So Belzoni and his men went back to work and after just two days, they found the doorway to the burial chamber, covered in the sand and rubble. In his book, he says that he had 'pyramidal brains'; we would say that he was thinking like an archaeologist – perhaps the first Westerner in Egypt to do so.

Belzoni was very proud of his achievements in Egypt. Above all his Theban adventures however, he was always known as the man who had opened the Second Pyramid at Giza – for that reason, his book, published in 1820, was entitled *Narrative of the operations and recent discoveries within the Pyramids, temples, tombs and excavations in Egypt and Nubia*. Widely translated and often reprinted, it remains a classic of archaeology. Lord Byron, though, did not appreciate such goings-on. Even before Belzoni's bestseller had appeared, his satirical epic, *Don Juan*, reported someone 'rummaging burgularously' around inside Cheops [sic!] Pyramid, someone who had broken Pharaoh's coffin lid; and he pictures a future given over to archaeology, worlds away from the recent romantic past, when wild lords and ladies rode through the dramatic ruins of half-buried ancient temples in the moonlit desert:

ABOVE AND RIGHT: *'Whilst Belzoni's friends went into the first pyramid. . . he seated himself on a large stone near the second pyramid, which is about the same height, and fixed his eyes on that enormous mass, which for so many centuries had baffled the conjectures of ancient and modern writers.'* The Fruits of Enterprise *account of Belzoni's progress at the Pyramids of Giza and a view of the north-western corner of the Great Pyramid today.*

> *What are the hopes of Man? Old Egypt's King*
> *Cheops erected the first pyramid*
> *And largest, thinking it was just the thing*
> *To keep his memory whole and Mummy hid*
> *But someone or other rummaging burgularously broke his coffin's lid.*
>
> *Let not a monument give you or me hopes*
> *Since not a pinch of dust is left of Cheops.*

Egypt: 1850
il Ardh Marsud: the Enchanted Land

AFTER BELZONI, THE DELUGE. Every collector, every European government wanted a piece of ancient Egypt. The most ancient past became a thing of popular interest and ownership of 'important pieces' became a matter of national prestige. At the same time, the French government bought the Venus de Milo and began excavations at Olympia in Greece; British travellers inventoried and part-ransacked virtually every country in the Middle East, Mexico, the Crimea and central Italy. At the same time, the first chair of Art History was founded at Göttingen University; now though, the professors were searching for a different sort of treasure: ancient records, ancient history.

In Egypt, the French government and the Grand Dukes of Tuscany mounted a joint expedition that produced more elegantly ponderous volumes worthy of Napoleon's scholars. This time, however, they had the advantage of understanding the inscriptions that they drew, for the leader of the expedition was Champollion, the genius who in 1822, began the decipherment of Egyptian hieroglyphic. None the less, the expedition was still interested in hard antiquities as well as literature; at Champollion's suggestion, the obelisk now at the Place de la Concorde was removed from Thebes whilst his expedition plundered tombs in the Valley of the Kings discovered a few years earlier by Belzoni, and left intact by him.

Ten years later, young Champollion was dead and Europeans were compiling histories from Egypt's standing monuments. In 1843, Richard Lepsius, one of the very greatest of egyptologists, went to Egypt to make the Kaiser's own *Description d'Egypte* known as the *Deukmaeler ans Aegypten und Aethiopieu*. The great work marks the end of the heroic period of egyptology. Lepsius laid out the framework of Egyptian history and the elements of egyptology that are still with us today. Lepsius was still interested in traditional forms of treasure, however; not gold so much, but objects and monuments illustrative of the history and culture he was building. At the end of an extraordinary expedition that took him a thousand miles up the Nile, the Prussians shipped sixty barge-loads of antiquities, some 15,000 pieces, back to Berlin. Old Egypt was being stripped and emptied of its treasures by the very men who were opening up its ancient past.

Lepsius' guide at Thebes had been a man well known to travellers, a man nicknamed Timsah (crocodile), who had been Champollion's head man in Luxor as well. Timsah had worked with antiquity collectors since Belzoni's day just as he and his successors would work with so many other Western antiquarians until the century's end, some of the ubiquitous but unsung practical experts on antiquity.

Timsah's family lived at Karnak, once the centre of the statue collectors' attentions in Upper Egypt, in the besooted upper sections of a half-buried temple, now known as the

RIGHT: *'On a large stone, at some height, by the entrance to the Pyramid of Cheops' the diary of Richard Lepsius records, 'we left an inscription five feet in breadth, and four feet in height, painted in with oil-colours;' an erudite mock-Pharaonic text honouring the birthday of the King of Prussia; 'Thus speak the servants of the King, whose name is the Sun and Rock of Prussia, Lepsius the scribe, Erbkam the architect, the brothers Weidenbach the painters, Frey the painter, Franke the former, Bonomi the sculptor, Wild the architect. Hail to the Eagle, Shelterer of the Cross, the King, the Sun and Rock of Prussia, the son of the Sun, freer of the land. Frederik William the Fourth, the Philopator, his country's father, the gracious, the favourite of wisdom and history, the guardian of the Rhine stream, chosen by Germany, the giver of life. May the highest God grant the King and his wife, the Queen Elisabeth, the life-rich one, the Philometor, her country's mother, the gracious, a fresh-springing life on earth for long, and a blessed habitation in Heaven for ever. In the year of our Saviour 1812, in the tenth month, and the fifteenth day, on the seven and fortieth birthday of His Majesty, on the pyramid of King Cheops; in the third year, the fifth month, the ninth day of the Government of his Majesty; in the year 3161 from the commencement of the Sothis period under King Menophthes.'*

Temple of Khonsu, but which in those days was simply a part of one of the little villages built against the ruined temples. The people of Karnak called this strange domain *il ardh marsud* (the Enchanted Land). It was as if from the times of the ancient High Priests of Amun through succeeding centuries of Christianity and Islam, they had held distant memories of the riches once heaped in the sanctuaries and treasuries of one of the world's greatest temples. Even the buildings were bejewelled: gold plate, faience and lapis lazuli sheathed walls and obelisks, bronze and silver shone from the vast cedar doors, and in the darkness of their shrines, the gods themselves were bright with gold.

Some villagers believed that it was still all there; that a magician had bewitched it and made it invisible. That if you were able to exorcise this spell, then all the temples' gold would shine again, and if you were agile and could escape the djinns who lived within the temples'

doorways that you could escape with treasure beyond all imagining. Once a year, they said, a ghostly procession with incense and gods and sparkling music passed through the great pillared halls carrying the golden boat of Amun and rowed again across his Sacred Lake. And then, they said, anyone could walk aboard that boat and take its treasures. No villager though, had ever made a penny from the sacred boat. Because the spirits' condition was that as you walked its ancient decks, you must not utter any word, nor thank your God or even make involuntary exclamation, or the magic boat would disappear. And, as everyone knows, all the local people love to talk.

One man though, they said, a Frenchman, was able to keep his lips shut tight and take the sacred treasure. And that is how the Cairo Museum got its gold. As they remember ancient treasure, so the villagers remember Auguste Mariette, the man who rescued Karnak from the treasure-seeking consuls and its choking dust and built a museum in Cairo to house the treasures that he found.

Mariette was born in Boulogne in 1821, one year before Champollion deciphered hieroglyphics. At the age of twenty-eight, after working on a Boulogne newspaper, he found a job at the Louvre copying Egyptian hieroglyphs; these had fascinated him from childhood, when he had had talks with a relative who had worked in Egypt with Champollion. Affable, extremely determined and completely self-assured, Mariette was sent to Egypt to search out and buy ancient texts for the museum. A year later, in the Egyptian desert, he excavated the monument that would make him famous; the story of its finding is the first great tale of Egyptian archaeology.

Making the rounds of the French community in Cairo, Mariette noticed in their gardens a number of pretty sphinxes similar in shape and size. These, he was told, came from the desert south-west of Cairo, the ancient cemetery of Sakkara. Visiting Sakkara, Mariette found more of these same sphinxes still buried in the sand and beside one of them, a stone offering table made for the god Apis, a local manifestation of a deity which was worshipped in the form of a living bull. Then came a moment of inspiration; he remembered a passage in the work of the ancient Greek traveller and historian Strabo, who had clearly walked in this same desert 2000 years before him: 'One finds a temple of Serapis in a spot so sandy that the wind causes the sand to accumulate in heaps, under which we could see many sphinxes.' Using the money that the Louvre had given him to buy papyri, discreetly, almost furtively, he says, Mariette engaged a small team of labourers to dig down the line of buried sphinxes and soon found the doorway of the temple. Writing like a good journalist, he quickly informed the French government of his scoop. As the Italians had found the buried city of Pompeii, just as it was described in ancient Roman writings, so he had found a legendary Egyptian treasure house well known from the writings of the ancient Greeks. His funds, he noted, were entirely exhausted; a further grant was indispensable.

Four years of work, sometimes digging, sometimes dynamiting, freed the galleries containing twenty-five gigantic sarcophagi that once had held the sacred Apis bulls, and splendid fragments of their burial jewellery. The real haul though, were hundreds of commemorative tablets with the names and family histories of the priests of Apis, many of which gave the date that they had been dedicated. In an age when Egyptian history was still unclear, they promised a thousand years and more of detailed, dated histories.

This was plunder though, not archaeology, as Mariette tells us: 'In approaching the entrance to the tomb of Apis, one sees to the right a somewhat large circular hole caused by the falling in of a portion of the stone work. In blowing up the debris with gunpowder, we discovered not an Apis but a human mummy. A gold mask covered its face, and jewels of every description were arranged upon its breast.' When early Christian monks had sacked and destroyed the sacred galleries, they had missed this unique burial which had been covered by an ancient rock fall. Mariette had dynamited the grave of Prince Khaemwase, favourite son of Ramesses the Great, High Priest and benefactor of the cult of Apis. Along with the treasures of the Serapeum and the tablets of the ancient priests, the princely priest's surviving jewellery was crated up and sent off to the Louvre.

The miracle of Mariette is held within the story of the next decade of his life. At thirty-six at the instigation of the French government and various businessmen, he was appointed by Said Pasha, the ruler of Egypt, to organise a state antiquities service, the first in the Middle East. Twenty-five years later, Mariette Bey died in the house beside the national museum that he had founded, the predecessor of the Cairo Museum of today, one of the world's greatest archaeological treasure houses.

Much to the chagrin of foreign governments and archaeologists. Mariette stopped foreign treasure seekers and the damaging and wholesale exportation of antiquities. Following his appointment, his first act was to obtain a royal decree outlawing all excavations in Egypt other than those of his department. For a quarter century, Mariette and his devoted staff excavated its greatest sites: Tanis, Giza, Sakkara, Meidum, Abydos, Edfu and Dendera; Karnak, Deir el Bahari and Medinet Habu, and left them cleared of rubble, reformed and landscaped for visitors.

When we visit them today, we still walk through Mariette's vision of what ancient Egypt was. This extraordinary man, who at his ruler's command, found time to write the story of Verdi's *Aida* and design the costumes of the first production as part of the celebrations of the opening of the Suez Canal, left us the vision of Egypt that is still portrayed by Hollywood and history painters.

Why though, this tremendous change of heart; why did this classic nineteenth-century European treasure hunter transform himself into the protector of ancient Egypt?

ABOVE: *Auguste Mariette Pasha, the saviour and first conservator of ancient Egypt, born at Boulogne-sur-Mer in 1821, died at his house in Cairo in 1881. After working as a teacher, journalist and textile designer, Mariette began his astonishing career in egyptology after studying the papers of a recently deceased member of his family, the artist Nestor l'Hôte, who had passed his adult life drawing the monuments of Egypt.*

Sakkara: 1854. Scenes From Daily Life

The foundations of Mariette's little expedition house still litter the Sakkara sands close by the avenue of Sphinxes. Whilst he foraged in the Serapeum, he lived there for four years; years, he remembered, he was 'compelled to spend in the Egyptian sand – but years I would never regret'. In common with a lot of northerners, Mariette was falling in love with the deserts of the Middle East.

This desert cemetery of Memphis, ancient Egypt's greatest city, was unique in all the world. It looked as if a war had been fought around the Step Pyramid that loomed above the site. The loose yellow sands were pock-marked with holes and scattered stones, the stain of ancient, decayed mud bricks smeared across the sands; debris of generations of treasure hunters sifting the earth for riches. Dismembered mummies, their torn wrappings flapping in the breeze, and fragments of ancient coffins, loomed out of the dunes.

After the adventure of the Serapeum, Mariette spent years here, uncovering ancient nobles' tombs that the local people call 'mastabas', because they were the same shape on a gigantic scale, as the little brick benches known as mastabas that they built beside their houses. Many of these tombs were already damaged beyond all recognition and famous fragments of the precious wall reliefs were already exhibited in European museums. Before Mariette though, no one had systematically examined this enormous graveyard, uncovering the secret chambers the robbers had overlooked or obscured in their hurried search for further treasure.

By the best of today's standards, Mariette was never a careful archaeologist. He often left his gangs unsupervised for weeks on end and regarded the work as merely the uncovering of buried monuments, with little thought for the wider significance of what information the earth contained.

ABOVE: *The majestic bulk of the Step Pyramid, the oldest large stone structure in Egypt, at the centre of the cemeteries of Sakkara, the burial grounds of ancient Memphis.*

LEFT: *A cow on the estates of the Vizier Ptah-hotep is milked by one of his peasants. A detail from the reliefs in a chapel of Ptah-hotep's tomb, carved in the fifth Egyptian dynasty of kings, around four and half thousand years ago, and cleared by Mariette in the 1860s. 'The house, the farm, the cattle,' he wrote, 'the fields, the harvest, everything is here represented, and by the solidity of its construction the tomb becomes truly an eternal abode.'*

One day, he later wrote, at his Sakkara house he heard the screams of his workmen reverberating across the sand and saw them in the distance, running about in all directions. 'Sheikh el Beled, Sheikh el Beled,' they were shouting. On arrival at the excavation, he found that the mud brick wall of an ancient mastaba had collapsed revealing an extraordinary sight. Standing once more in the Egyptian sunlight for the first time in forty-five dark centuries, stood a portly life-sized wooden statue whose inlaid crystal eyes regarded him with kindly, if detached disdain.

However European collectors might regard such an extraordinary work of art, Mariette had seen the effect it had had on his Egyptian workmen, local villagers who had an immediate and frightening connection with this object of the distant past. The head-man of their village – their Sheikh el Beled – greatly resembled the figure they had brought into the light; it was if the ancient statue had been waiting four thousand years to frighten them.

Mariette found large numbers of desert tombs far better preserved than that of the Sheikh el Beled's, whose ruins had largely disappeared beneath the sand. Inside these grand stone mastabas, which he cleared and recorded one by one, Mariette detected a constant architectural preoccupation. The entrance doorway of the tomb usually led into a courtyard where animals had been slaughtered to nourish the dead. A deep grave shaft led down from here to a burial chamber with a stone sarcophagus. Above, beyond the courtyard were funerary chapels and storage rooms for the priests who served the dead. Stone carvings, representing doors, promised to connect the chapels to the world of the dead. At the foot of these false doors were the offering altars. As the estate's offerings were laid on the altars, the two worlds, the living and the dead, met. And all around the false doors of the chapels were pictures of the life that the departed had left behind; the good life of Egyptian noblemen. Small rooms filled with life-like statues like the Sheikh el Beled looked out on the living from the darkness of death through small slits cut in the stone walls of the tomb.

No one had ever completely cleared such monuments before, preferring to plunder odd walls as they appeared in the consuming sands. Row upon row, cemetery upon cemetery, Mariette though, brought them to the light and opened them for exhibition. Many of these courtiers' tombs contained rare scenes of everyday life, scenes that seemed to bring the distant past alive, a past still mirrored in village life in Egypt. Masterpieces, some of them of such surpassing liveliness and beauty that the ancient artists who had made them were proud enough of their labours to inscribe their names in hieroglyphs on the tomb wall. Mariette even found that one of these ancient sculptors had left his pot of outline paint behind; he found it dried out, still standing on a stone shelf in the tomb. The hieroglyphs of some of these monuments were

ABOVE: *The Sakkara cemeteries viewed from the south. Mariette spent years here, uncovering ancient nobles' tombs.*

ABOVE: *Nile fishermen on the wall of a chapel in the tomb of the nobleman Ptah-hotep at Sakkara pull in their nets. 'There is nothing mournful here, nothing of death,' Mariette observed about these scenes he excavated, 'the deceased seems to be in his home: he receives relatives and the people of his household. . .'*

LEFT: *The architectural climax in all of the great tombs of Sakkara is a central hall, with altars for food offerings and so-called 'false doors' which in this instance, in the tomb of the nobleman Mereruka, holds a statue of the owner. One of the finest monuments at Sakkara, Mereruka's tomb was opened and cleaned by Mariette's successor.*

of such beauty that egyptologists still employ them as the finest exemplars of their type. Tombs such as those of the nobles Tiy and Ptah-hotep were celebrated and illustrated in countless histories of art and architecture. Thus these ancient Egyptian nobles and their families, servants and estates all lived again.

In all these monuments, Mariette found profound contact between the ancient past and contemporary Egypt. Not only could his workmen relate to the statues and the scenes inside these ancient tombs, but sometimes they could also tell the visiting scholars precisely what activities the ancient artists were portraying; the ancient scenes of daily life were those to be seen every day in the living villages of Sakkara. Slowly, Mariette came to realise the profound connection between the ancient art and the land in which it was made. Those ancient things had their reality in the land; they reflected daily life in the ancient world, a daily life that still endured in Egypt. A connection that was lost forever when the warm stones of Egypt were shipped to the cold museums of the north.

Dahabiya: Mariette Upon the Nile

Over the years, Mariette's boat became a familiar sight on the Nile, drifting from Aswan to Cairo, supervising the work of the *Départment des Antiquités* in tombs and temples, work overseen by a trusted, inner group of foremen and assistants.

One day, he was sailing to a dig at Thebes that had discovered the jewellery and golden coffin of an ancient queen, which the provincial ruler, the Mudir of Kena, had plundered for his harem. As chance would have it, Mariette's boat encountered the Mudir's barge upon the river, so Mariette stopped and boarded it and with his own hands, took back the ancient gold. Informing Said Pasha of his exploits, Egypt's ruler was so impressed that he promised Mariette a museum for his growing collections and Queen Ah-hotep's splendid jewels are now amongst the greatest treasures of the Cairo Museum.

Years after his exploits on the river, in the Paris Exhibition of 1867, where Mariette exhibited some of his excavations' greatest finds, the French Empress Eugénie, a keen antiquarian, pointedly asked the new Egyptian ruler Ismail, the Khedive, Said Pasha's son, for the same ancient jewellery as a present. Ismail could hardly refuse such a request directly so the subtle man replied, 'There is a man more powerful in my kingdom than myself' and he gestured towards Mariette, who had no hesitation in refusing to let his treasure leave Egypt for the Louvre. Mariette preferred to give such worthies beautiful and precious fakes which he designed and had made up in Cairo workshops. He was a skilled designer and draftsman, and it was easy for him to simply copy precious things from temple and tomb walls. Today, several great museums still exhibit some of Mariette's confabulations. Now, of course, after a century and a half they are antiques as well, and with their own romantic histories and past!

Mariette's momentous change from treasure seeker to archaeologist came not a moment too soon. The mid-nineteenth century saw the opening up of ancient Egypt, a boom both in tourism and in the trade in antiquities. Thanks to Mariette's famous and much publicised restorations, the monuments were filling up with visitors and he was appalled at the mauling they were suffering; 'more damage has been done in the Sakkara tombs within the last ten years,' he wrote, 'than in the previous 4400 years of their existence'. In typically trenchant style he published a lengthy list of names culled from graffiti scrawled on the monuments under the title of *A List of Imbeciles*, yet this was a problem that even Mariette could never solve, and it is with us still today.

ABOVE: *The* dahabiya *rented by the photographer Francis Frith for his journey down the Nile in the winter of 1856–7. The top photograph shows one of the last of these great touring boats of the nineteenth century now beached at Luxor in Upper Egypt, awaiting a refit.*

By the 1870s the grand, slow sailing boats like Mariette's, known as *dahabiyas*, had become the favourite transportation of wealthy tourists. Some foreign egyptologists owned their own, with libraries set all around the cabins in the stern. James Wilbour, an affable New York lawyer in perpetual exile after the Tamany Hall scandal, spent many years on his *Seven Hathors*, drifting on the Nile in a haze of scholarship and sightseeing. And not only did the rich keep their libraries and mistresses on their boats — they also stored illegal collections of antiquities deep down in the hold. Sometimes though, the purchased past became an inconvenience. Having bought the mummy of a Theban pharaoh, two English ladies, the Misses Brocklehursts, sunk the 'dear departed' as they called him, when the cabins of their *dahabiya* began to fill up with a vile odour. Although buying and exporting antiquities became a game for archaeologists and princes, it was never again practised on the scale seen in the days before Mariette and his *Service*.

The railways too, also threatened the ancient world of Upper Egypt. At Luxor, it is said that ancient coffins were collected up to fire the engines' boilers. Part of the Berlin Museum's superb collection of panel paintings was gathered by a German count who spent some weeks scrambling over the fuel tenders in Luxor station, rescuing the best pieces that remained.

Mariette loved the slow progress of the Nile, and from the decks of his boat he witnessed and recorded the gradual passing of the ancient way of life, the breaking of the

BELOW: *Sitting atop a Sakkara mastaba in the course of its excavation in the 1860s, Mariette Pasha admires his workmens' discoveries. Some of the statues that they brought him, masterpieces of ancient art, are amongst the greatest treasures of the Cairo Museum.*

BELOW AND RIGHT: *Before and after. Taken in the last years before the enormous monument was excavated by the order of Mariette, Frith's photograph (below) of the great temple of Hathor at Dendera in Upper Egypt shows it still buried in the debris of the ancient town that once surrounded it*

Undertaken by forced labour and controlled by assistants who have left us little more than their first names, such titanic enterprises ensured that these monuments were not quarried for their stone, as had already happened to several other temples in the first years of Egypt's industrialisation.

'ancient silence' as his friend Pierre Loti called it. In his day, as in the time of the pharaohs, there were still papyrus swamps along the river banks and hippopotamus and crocodiles as well, although these were quickly killed off by European hunters and by the steamboats that he loathed. 'Everything is comfortable on them,' he wrote, referring to the lethal steamboats, 'and at regular intervals the tombs and temples are admired in the company of a dragoman and fellow travellers whom one has never seen before.' Larger than life, passionate, romantic, individual, our brave new world with its mass tourism would not have suited Mariette.

Mariette Presents the Past

In the 1850s, most of the great Egyptian temples were choked to their roofs with ancient sand and dirt and modern village houses. Some were used as warehouses, stables or barracks. Most of the ancient cemeteries were rubbish heaps of broken half-buried tombs and ancient tomb furnishings. Under Mariette's supervision, vast forced labour gangs of thousands upon thousands of peasants dug out most of the monuments of ancient Egypt that we know today. In this process — a hasty and completely random business quite unlike modern archaeology — Mariette created the landscapes, the ambience around the temples that still exists today.

Mariette left France when the first works of state conservation of ancient monuments in the world — the restoration of Vézelay Abbey followed by Notre Dame Cathedral and Carcassone Castle — were being undertaken by the architect Violet-le-Duc under the direction of the writer Prosper Merimée, a state inspector of the recently formed *Commission des Monuments Historiques*. Mariette surely knew about this innovative work; even so, his own pioneering labours, excavating and preserving the temples of Egypt in the face of 'the greed of peasants and the covetousness of Europeans' as he puts it, were remarkably precocious.

A local, and more immediate impulse to state conservation was first provided a quarter

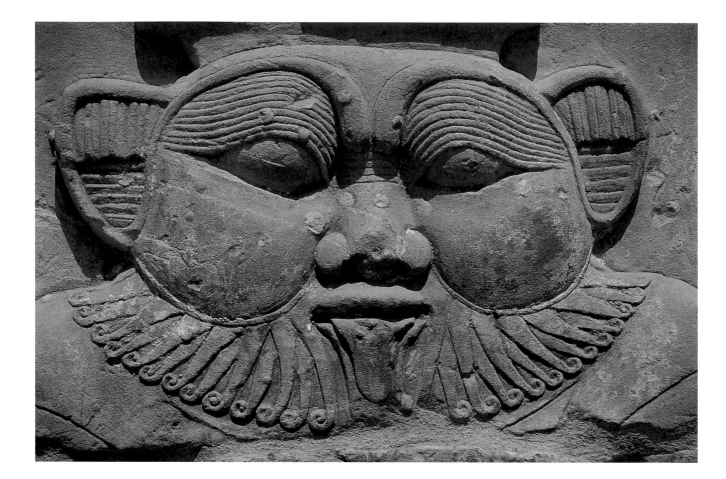

of a century earlier in the long petition addressed by Champollion to the Viceroy of Egypt, Mohammed Ali Pasha. In this, the first of many such, Champollion begged that the wholesale destruction of ancient monuments then underway – temples were being demolished to serve as factory foundations and river barrages – should stop.

Mariette though, was not simply a restorer of antiquity. He published good plans of the monuments he excavated and elaborate copies of the vast numbers of the inscriptions that he found – many of them still vital parts of our picture of ancient Egypt (this, despite the fact that many were printed on paper which, due to its method of manufacture, has entirely dissolved, so that now only facsimiles remain). Mariette was completely fascinated by the monuments that he excavated and very anxious to understand their purposes. Although his archaeology remained primitive to the end, his publications, even now, contain extraordinary insight.

The great Temple at Dendera, Mariette observes, is a Greek synthesis of the most ancient cults and rituals, its mutilations due to the 'misguided enthusiasm' of early Christian converts. The building, he explains, is not a church for services with ancient congregations, nor was it a place for divination, nor magic oracles or confessions, but the ritual starting-point of great religious processions that, moving in tandem round the year, linked Egypt to the cosmic processes of generation and regeneration. The temples indeed, were like machines, each room, each group of rooms, from those designated for the preparation of sacred perfumes, to stores that contained the ritual objects used in the

ABOVE: *A splendid image of the dwarf God Bes, from an unknown temple at Dendera. A cheerful divinity who often carried a tambourine, Bes protected women from danger during childbirth.*

ABOVE: *Frith's photograph shows Edfu Temple in Upper Egypt, as it had been for many centuries. As Mariette observed, 'the modern village had invaded the temple, its terraces being covered with dwellings, stables, storehouses and rubbish of every kind'.*

processions, were designed to accommodate the endless rites and ritual. To Mariette, these vast Greco-Roman structures seemed to be an elaborate recording and encoding of the most ancient Egyptian rituals, as if their designers were preserving the past from attack. His views have been refined perhaps, but never really superseded.

As he excavated at Abydos, the ancient sanctuary of Osiris, great god of the dead, the local workmen were amazed when he unerringly located ancient buildings underneath the sand that they had never known existed. 'I've been here thirty years.' exclaimed a peasant, 'and never seen all this before.'

'I've been here three thousand years,' smiled sprightly Mariette.

Mariette Bey: 1821–1881

Mariette died from the effects of diabetes at sixty in 1881 at his house in Cairo, an elegant Turkish villa set in jasmine-scented gardens inhabited by tame desert antelopes, just a few hundred yards from his present tomb, beside the grand museum which he never saw. The small museum that Said Pasha first gave him had been a deserted warehouse down by the riverside, set between the royal stables and a tramway depot near what is today the Cairo TV tower. Now, that little building with its mock-Pharaonic entrance like a modern tourist shop exists only in sepia photographs that show its small rooms crammed with the masterpieces that we still see today shining under the spotlights of international travelling exhibitions all around the world. It was the first national museum in the Middle East

LEFT: *Over the years, Mariette's Egyptian Museum was filled to its very roof with precious antiquities. This photograph shows a treasure trove of royal mummies and their coffins brought from Thebes in 1881, the year of Mariette's death. Just a few years earlier, an unusually high Nile had flooded out the museum and scarcely had order been restored when Mariette was struck down by diabetes.*

The key element in Mariette's change of heart from European collector to nationalist curator was his realisation that, for their proper conservation and understanding, ancient monuments should be kept in their original environment and not mined and dispersed by foreigners for display as fragments in far-away museums.

In his last hours, delirious, Mariette saw a vision of a new museum for his antiquities, for his was sorely overcrowded and yearly threatened by the river's flood. His successor, Gaston Maspero, vividly recalled the last hours: 'In the delirium of his death-agony, Mariette saw rising before him the ideal museum which he had coveted all his life; during one half-hour, the evening before his death, he imagined that he saw his dream realised, and the incoherent words which fell from his lips revealed to those who were present the intensity of this last joy.'

Twenty years later, the present grand museum was built exactly as he would have wished and Mariette's tomb, an ancient Egyptian sarcophagus, but made in Europe, was placed beside its entrance. His statue is surrounded by busts of Egyptian archaeologists who followed him into the *Service*.

Today Mariette's praises are not much sung by most modern egyptologists – yet perhaps, he was the greatest of them all. In his lifetime, Egyptian archaeology changed from a dashing adventure in the desert to an academic discipline in a foreign country, with glittering prizes all of its own. It was no longer the promise of the sparkling jewels of pharaohs that set the archaeological pulse tingling, but the hint of inspiration for an idea, a theory, that might earn you academic promotion, and that was best hunted down inside a library.

After Mariette, many of the greatest egyptologists did not visit Egypt very often, and many of those who did, did not like it very much. Once they were excavated,

RIGHT: *Built at the turn of the century, the Cairo Museum is one of the world's great treasure houses, a monument both to ancient Egypt and to the archaeologists who brought it back into the light again.*

BELOW: *Mariette's tomb and statue now stand beside this great museum. Cast in bronze, the great man's simple epitaph faces his vast sarcophagus of Swiss granite, carved in the manner of the pharaonic tombs that Mariette had excavated beside the Pyramids of Giza.*

measured and described, once their inscriptions had been drawn, translated and published, the great standing monuments of Egypt in which Mariette had spent his life, were of little importance to them. In the wider world, however, that most ancient dream of gold remained; from Napoleon, and earlier, from medieval times, indeed to Indiana Jones. And that perhaps is why poor Howard Carter, an essentially decent man who found a treasure so large, so vulgarly impressive, that even the dullest egyptologist could hardly fail to be thrilled by it, was so engulfed by envy, argument and scandal, as he struggled to conserve the treasures that he had found in Tutankhamun's tomb. That he succeeded, you may see in Cairo. Much of that treasure would be ruined now, were it not for Carter, and half of Tutankhamun's gold at least, would be in England and the USA, were it not for Mariette and his successors at the Cairo Museum. And that ultimately, is due to the belief of the *Service des Antiquities*, that Egyptian antiquities should stay in Egypt.

So nowadays people have to come to Egypt to see the world's most famous ancient treasure. Golden objects in antique cases still lit by the light of the Egyptian sun. And to their great surprise, at the centre of it all, they find the calm mask, the gloves, the combs, the underclothing and the little toys of a young man smiling at us all from beyond an ancient grave, an alien eternity. As you gaze upon the golden features of that young man who died so very long ago, there is a real shock of recognition; and in that simple contact is the greatest treasure of them all.

PART III

Digging by the Book

Heinrich Schliemann: 1822–1890
At the Tomb of Indiana Jones

THE TOMB OF THE ORIGINAL INDIANA JONES is in Athens, Greece, in Central Cemetery number I, a sunny pile set on the side of a solemn hill. 'I cover Heinrich Schliemann' reads its inscription 'whose repute is great; he laboured much for us, him you should emulate'. A scruffy, awkward little chap, not obviously made for stardom, Heinrich Schliemann turned himself into archaeology's original mythic hero, a man who, in the 1870s, made archaeology seem so exciting that children and adults too, suddenly wanted to be archaeologists as well as train drivers. His very name was a watchword for adventure all over Europe. The original Indiana Jones was a small sallow man with a bulbous, balding head. The British archaeologist, Sir Arthur Evans, remembered Schliemann as having 'very foreign glasses, who seemed to peer deep into the ground…a veritable Columbus of archaeology, whose tombs and treasures opened up eras of the past that the public had not even dreamed of'.

At the same time though, fellow Germans, professional excavators, called him half mad and openly derided him and his excavations; even the epitaph on his tomb was declared to be bad Greek. Although he is sometimes labelled a liar and a cheat, and his discoveries claimed as fraudulent and partly faked, in many ways, archaeology began with this passionate little man who was said to have made love to his young wife on site 'in an excess of antiquarian delight' when he found what he thought was King Agamemnon's gold.

If Indiana Jones' existence was inspired by war movies and the Saturday morning pictures, then Heinrich Schliemann's was, in turn, inspired by the great classical texts, especially the epic poetry of Homer describing the Trojan Wars. His tomb is covered in its images: Artemis and Athena; Greek ships; the death of Patroclus; Electra and Orestes. There are reliefs of Schliemann too on his tomb, a kind of marble movie of his life mixed in with the scenes from Homer. One of them shows the archaeologist with his wife Sophie. The key to Schliemann and his success is the book that he is holding in his hand; a marble Schliemann holding a marble Homer – his great inspiration. Schliemann's invention of the heroic archaeologist was but part of the same imagination that also inspired his archaeology.

Like classic Homer, Heinrich Schliemann cast his life in an heroic mould and indeed, it is a classic nineteenth-century tale. Born in 1822 in the family farmhouse of a poor German pastor, Schliemann became the Moscow

BELOW: *The new image of the successful archaeologist, a world away from the dusty antiquarianism of old Europe. A confident bourgeois Schliemann, the discoverer of Troy with Sophie, his pretty young wife, dressed for an Athenian evening promenade of the 1870s. A splendid portrait by the Belgian artist Eugene Brooerrmann.*

ABOVE: *The tomb of the original Indiana Jones! The Schliemann family tomb in the main cemetery of Athens, designed by Ernst Ziller, Schliemann's architect friend who also designed his Athenian house and first suggested that he should excavate at Troy.*

representative of Schröder's merchant bank at the tender age of twenty-four; at twenty-eight he was bankrolled by one of the Rothschild banks to purchase gold dust from the miners of the California Gold Rush; at forty, after cornering the world indigo market and making a fortune from explosives and the Crimean War, he sold up and was left with a yearly income of what today would be about a quarter of a million pounds sterling a year.

Moving to Athens and taking a second wife, a Greek woman some twenty years his junior, he devoted half of his substantial income to archaeology. So successful was he that when he died, the king of Greece stood vigil by his coffin and all of Athens came to the cemetery to see him laid in his tomb. Quoting the speech that Homer puts in the mouth of beauteous Helen as she bids farewell to Hector going off to certain death, Sophie said these words over his coffin: 'Twenty years are come and gone. . .my tears flow both for you and for my unhappy self.' Confidentially, to a friend, she said that her husband's death seemed to her to be an awakening from a long, long dream. Schliemann's life was indeed, a carefully constructed fairy story.

Ruthless business man, naive historian, born publicist, Schliemann was completely equipped to bring his childhood fantasies alive and fill the world with tales of heroes; a real-life Indiana Jones. And in the process, Schliemann found great treasures and millennia of unknown history. He set the West's archaeological imagination turning. Most archaeological fictions after all, still start with a man with a dream and determination winning out against all odds, proving the fuddy-duddies they were wrong: Schliemann invented that story, just as he also invented his own strange life.

Excavating Homer. Schliemann at Troy: 1871

In October 1871, Schliemann came to the bleak plain of the Turkish Troad, south of Istanbul, with his wife Sophie, seven camels loaded with equipment and a volume of Homer's *Iliad*. He planned to find the legendary city of ancient Troy – the city which his beloved Homer had described in such eerily realistic detail. For nine long and bloody years, tells Homer, the mightiest warriors of most ancient Greece besieged the city of Troy. Homer's tales of their warrior code of conduct and chivalry would influence everyone from Alexander the Great to the British Grenadiers.

Schliemann was forty-seven years old. Ten years earlier he had retired from his business career to dig for Homer's heroes, first writing a thesis on the subject as a 'mature' millionaire student at two northern European universities, then touring the Mediterranean sites traditionally linked to the cities of Homer's *Iliad*. He had visited the Troad two years before his expedition, and written a book on the location of ancient Troy that rejected the usual view that it had stood upon the hill of Ballidagh, at the centre of the plain. Schliemann based his arguments, as he would always do, upon a literal interpretation of the ancient words. Homer had described Troy as situated by two springs, one hot, one cold, just as earlier travellers had found at Ballidagh. Thorough Schliemann, however, had found a total of thirty-four springs around the hill, both hot and cold, and further noticed that although Homer had described Troy as being the equivalent of three miles from the sea, Ballidagh was eight, and that the ancient coastline had not changed. And how, he asked, could Homer's mighty Achilles have fought and killed poor Hector on the plain below Ballidagh, where neither the people on the hill above nor the Greek armies below on the sloping plain would have had a clear view of the combat?

After consulting local farmers, including one who was an amateur archaeologist who had himself excavated on the plain, Schliemann chose another lower mound called Hissarlik, 'the towers', a little north of Ballidagh, just three miles from the coast. This, he noted with approval, was bounded by two small rivers, one fast, one slow. Here he felt, Homer's heroes could have seen Troy's towering walls above the flat-plained battlefield, just as the Greeks could from the beaches where they set up their boats, as Homer describes.

Schliemann's first expedition on the Hill of Hissarlik took place over three years, from 1870 to 1873. The first season, employing just a few workers, he began the excavation of a vast trench across and through the mound. He had guessed that Homer's city lay well beneath the Roman remains sprinkled on the top of Hissarlik, somewhere near the level of the plain. Progress was slow that first year, the heat and dust intense, the great old hill confusing in its ruins, piled one upon the other. The local food, too, was poor; old friends at Schröder's Bank lightened Schliemann's lot with crates of canned corned beef and peaches, tongue, beer and cheese.

The second season saw Schliemann better organised. This time, Schröder's sent him some of England's finest pickaxes and wheelbarrows, which, the archaeologist observed, greatly aided progress. Eccentric Schliemann seems to have had a particular regard for Albion – for many years he sent his washing from Athens back to England to be laundered. All the while, however, inside his trenches, Schliemann was doing something that no one had ever done before, but which is now the very heart of New and Old World archaeology. He was digging up a type of hill that, ever since Schliemann's time, archaeologists have called by the Arab name of 'tell' – that is, a man-made hill made up of the ruins of ancient dwellings, built one upon the another, for millennia upon millennia. There are tens of thousands of such tells in the Middle East – a few of them are dug now, by dedicated teams of experts over entire lifetimes. All Schliemann had were Schröder's pickaxes, Homer and a quick, clear brain.

Crafty negotiations with the local farmers brought increased productivity; huge trenches were cut swiftly through the ancient mound, through city after city, deep down into a past that no one had ever seen before. Schliemann carefully recorded the changes in the broken pottery he found in every layer, and drew all the jewellery and copper implements they uncovered as well. He also planned and measured the stone walls that were revealed, before dismantling them to dig down deeper in the tell. Unfortunately, he completely missed the softer house walls of mud brick where Homer's heroes would have lived; they were buried in the dust of ages in the mound and went unnoticed.

In Schliemann's day though, no one had ever done such a thing before: no one knew anything of dirt archaeology in the Middle East; no one could read the sides of the deep trenches he was cutting and recognise tell-tale changes in the earth's colours and textures, changes you might only see in different angles of light. Such small changes, if excavated carefully and followed out across the excavation site, allow modern archaeologists to map real ancient living spaces once again, to walk carefully on the most fragile ancient floors, and to re-create, through analysis of animal bones, pollens and other spare remains, how the ancient people who once inhabited them had lived.

BELOW: *The great central trench excavated by Schliemann during his first years of working on the Hill of Hissarlik, in his search for ancient Troy. The stone walls that lie across the bottom of the cut are the foundations of ancient houses of the Early Bronze Age, that is, around 2900–2450 BC, about the same age as the great Egyptian Pyramids. In the last few years, the Troia project of the University of Tübingen has restored Schliemann's trench as an archaeological monument in its own right.*

Schliemann though, tore deep into ancient Troy, found high walls of a great fortress which, he thought, were Homer's 'topless towers of Ilium'. Built in these walls were huge stone ramps and gateways, one of which he thought was the very Scaean Gate where Greek Helen, the face that launched a thousand ships, had once looked down upon the army of her angry husband and his friends. 'They were excellent speakers,' says Homer 'these Trojan elders, sitting there on the tower like cicadas perched in the wood chirping delightfully. When they saw Helen coming to the tower, they lowered their voices. "Who on earth," they asked one another, "could blame the Trojan and Greek men at arms for suffering so long for such a woman's sake"…'

In 1873, close to the bottom of a wall beside this Scaean Gate, Schliemann made archaeology's first grand discovery – an event that he immediately recast for public consumption by reporting his find in articles in *The Times* of London and whose fame in consequence spread right around the world. Here was the other side of Schliemann's personality. Though his archaeological reports are sober to the point of tedium, he also aimed at popular acceptance of his theories, through newspapers and public lectures. And these especially, aroused the ire and envy of many academic archaeologists.

What then, had Schliemann really found on that day, when he claimed he had found the treasure of the Trojan king? In the side of an earth-filled trench, he had found a golden treasure; an anonymous, extremely ancient uninscribed treasure of some 9000 pieces of pure gold, in an ancient rotted chest. Schliemann proposed that the treasure had been thrown down and abandoned by the Trojans as they hastily fled from the sack of Troy by the Greek armies. Schliemann excavated the treasure by himself after calling an early breakfast break for his workmen. In the California Gold Rush he had seen at first hand what effect the yellow metal could have on people.

In *Troy and its Remains*, Schliemann recorded that Sophie, his dear wife, a native of Athens

ABOVE: *The first photograph of Schliemann's Trojan treasure, published by him in 1874 as part of his report on his excavations. After Sophie Schliemann appeared in a German fashion magazine wearing some of the jewellery pictured on the top shelf of this photograph, it became famous as the 'Jewels of Helen'. Since its capture by the Soviets in World War Two and its recent disinterment from the basements of Moscow's Pushkin Museum, this jewellery has regained its romantic pedigree. Despite Schliemann's detractors who describe this treasure as a fake, most archaeologists believe it to be a genuinely ancient collection of disparate products — just as one would expect to find in a wealthy city, set on a major trade route between East and West, between Europe and the ancient East.*

who had the warmest appreciation of the poet Homer, had stood by his side as he had cut the treasure from the ashy earth and gathered it up in her shawl. One of Schliemann's letters, written to a British archaeologist admits that this was not true; Sophie had been at home in Athens. To make things worse, Schliemann illegally removed the treasure from his excavation and sent it off to Athens, breaking the rules of a hard-won contract with the Ottoman bureaucracy. Very Indiana Jones perhaps, but not the way of modern archaeologists.

Above all else though, the reason why so many of his archaeological contemporaries considered Schliemann to be unbalanced was that consensus held that the literary past, from Homer to the Bible, was just a literary creation. Schliemann though, had taken the ancient words as gospel truth and made excavations to trace out the stories that they told. Later, when at the height of his fame, Schliemann was offered the chance to excavate a rich Etruscan cemetery, one filled with gold, fine tombs and the promise of much more, he rejected the offer, saying that there was nothing there to prove. Schliemann, the first archaeologist to use old books as guides to excavation, was also the first archaeologist to excavate to a predetermined agenda — an attitude decades ahead of his time.

Despite his dubious swashbuckling, indeed perhaps, in part because of it, Schliemann set Troy and archaeology squarely in the contemporary nineteenth-century consciousness of Europe. Using Homer's ancient texts, archaeology's first hero had found a brand-new past for us. From Madrid to Moscow, there was not an educated person for whom the *Iliad* did not live in their imaginations. Schliemann had suddenly brought those ancient stories back to life and set those majestic heroes walking on the earth again. And so, if Schliemann wrote his tale as it should have been rather than as it really was, then this perhaps was but another manifestation of the same fierce imagination that had sent this merchant banker to a lonely Turkish plain to excavate an ancient poem.

Schliemann at Mycenae: 1876. The Masks of Agamemnon

Following his theft of the treasure of Troy, Schliemann was banned from further excavations in Turkey, and the Ottoman administration sued Schliemann in Athens for its return. It took two years to arrive at a settlement in which Schliemann paid the Turkish government a huge sum and kept the Trojan gold for himself. A photograph of the period shows a pensive Sophie wearing the ancient jewellery.

Throughout this lengthy litigation, Schliemann had looked at sites in Italy and Greece suitable for excavation and, after flitting hither and thither, had eventually settled upon the ancient fortress city of Mycenae, the city of Homer's Agamemnon, husband of Clytemnestra, Helen's sister. Not surprisingly, the Greek government authority, mindful of the Trojan scandal and litigation, set Schliemann stringent conditions for his work. Mycenae was regarded as one of the archaeological wonders of the world. However, despite his contracts and agreements, and true to his own fashion, Schliemann would take very little notice of anyone except the ancient authors.

His principal guide to Mycenae was not Homer, but Pausanius, a Greek traveller of the third century BC, who compiled a large, erudite guidebook to the monuments of Greece, largely from personal observation, from information offered by contemporary guides to the monuments and from older reference works in libraries. Pausanius had travelled at the absolute peak of Greek prosperity before civil war, invasion and the Romans robbed it of its glitter, when all the monuments and statuary though perhaps a little old and ivy-covered, were still alive with priests and holiness.

As Schliemann rode through the plain which stands in front of the ancient fortress, he rode back into ancient times, moving through literary landscapes, identifying every stream, hillock and ruin, until at last he rode with the ancient rulers into the city he had come to excavate, that well-built city whose broad streets were rich in gold and whose family histories embodied an oriental mix of incest, murder, blood and gold so beloved of the nineteenth century.

Pausanius tells that the murdered Agamemnon, killed by his wife and her lover when he returns from Troy, as Homer and so many other ancient writers told, lay buried by the city walls, along with many members of his family and his faithful charioteer. Going once more against archaeological opinion, which held that ancient graves were always outside the city gates, Schliemann took the old words and the ruins he saw at face value, and started to excavate inside the high standing walls of the fortress itself. Schliemann literally dug his way into ancient Mycenae, cutting down through the earth and rock that half-blocked the

BELOW: One of the golden masks that Schliemann excavated from the Grave Circle in the fortress of Mycenae in southern Greece. 'The wrinkles to the right and left above the mouth,' writes Schliemann, 'can leave no doubt that we have here the portrait of a man of more advanced age. The forehead is very large and so are the eyes. . .in this mask is preserved part of the skull of the man whose face it covered. . . The five bodies of this fourth tomb were literally smothered in jewels.'

great gateway to the city, with its two lions set high above its mighty lintel stones. It was August and very, very hot and dusty, but Schliemann's inner eye saw the ancient purple cloth that Homer says was spilled out in welcome on the pavements of Mycenae to welcome Agamemnon home, a dark omen of his blood that would soon be spilled on those same stones.

While Schliemann ran hither and thither, starting small excavations, digging holes, demolishing 'Roman' walls to see what lay underneath, Sophie fended off the wrath of Panagiotes Stamatakes, the government's appointed archaeologist and officer of the Greek Archaeological Society. The Schliemanns had bitter daily arguments with long-suffering Stamatakes, who was not the least overwhelmed by the wealth and celebrity of the eccentric German and his formidable Greek wife.

After digging through the great Lion Gate, and clearing a 'gate-keeper's lodge' and another large stone building set beside it which he labelled a 'granary', Schliemann came to a flat, almost circular area of earth that was held in its position on the hillside by a semi-circular section of the city wall. From here, high up on the fortress walls, Schliemann could look right across the magnificent Plain of Argos, Homer's 'horse-feeding Argos', brown now in late autumn; and here at the walls he started, against all odds, to look for tombs.

Almost immediately, his gangs began to excavate antiquities. Not just pieces of the distinctive pottery that Schliemann had already found, and which he knew to be older than the classical monuments of Greece, but simple monuments of cut stones, some with drawings on them. Beneath a swirl of spiral decoration, one block showed a warrior, a man in an ancient chariot like those that Homer's heroes rode around the walls of Troy. Quickly digging into deeper levels, at some ten feet down in the soft red earth close by the city walls,

LEFT: *The Lion Gate of Mycenae, the famous entrance of the Bronze Age fortress, cleared by Schliemann on his way to the Grave Circle, which is to the right of the doorway beyond the Lion Arch.*

OPPOSITE ABOVE: *'In the Treasury, in which Mrs Schliemann is excavating, we work with thirty labourers and two horse carts, and find the very greatest difficulty in removing the hundreds of huge wrought stones which have fallen from the Vault.' Schliemann's Mycenae Diary, 30 September 1876. Now regarded as a tomb rather than a treasury, the so-called Tomb of Clytemnestra, whose door Sophie guards, yielded just seven round beads and a short piece of copper wire. It is one of a large group of similarly monumental circular and ingeniously vaulted structures that are dated to the Late Bronze Age.*

OPPOSITE BELOW: *The plain of Argos in southern Greece, dominated by the walls of the Citadel of Mycenae. 'The situation of Mycenae,' observed Schliemann, 'is beautifully described by Homer . . .in all antiquity, the plain was celebrated for the breeding of horses, and Homer, seven times in the Illiad, praises its splendid horse-pasture grounds. . .the epithet very thirsty,' he adds, 'which Homer gives to the Plain of Argos, agrees perfectly with its present condition . . .' The great Grave Circle discovered by Schliemann fills the foreground of the picture.*

Schliemann came across a deep rectangle of dry stone walling, which he took to be a grave shaft; he identified some ash and some small fragments of gold and ivory that his men dug out of it, as the remains of cremations, the usual mode of funeral for Homer's heroes.

Two months had passed, however, since he had ridden to Mycenae; the winter rains had started and Schliemann's local work force, some seventy-odd farmers, were carting away mud. Groundwater slowly seeped into the shaft. Undaunted – despite his appearance, Schliemann was physically tough – he moved his work gang several yards back from the walls where the soil lying on the bedrock of the hill drained quickly down towards the other shaft. Here he could dig deeper than before. First he moved two large stone slabs he thought were tombstones. Beneath them, partly built on the steep slope of the living rock, they found another dry stone shaft; then at a depth of twenty-five feet, a thin layer of pebbles and white clay which, though Schliemann did not know it, was the collapsed remnants of an ancient roof. And underneath they found a treasure.

Three large men were buried in the shaft, their heads towards the east, lying three feet apart. Between them, they were decorated with fifteen crowns of thin sheet gold. All around their skeletons lay silver cups and wine jars, various ornaments, a mass of glass, sharp knives of black obsidian and two small clay figurines that, Schliemann later wrote, had delighted him the most – this because he thought, erroneously, that they were evidence of the worship of a goddess at Mycenae which he fancied he had also found at Troy.

After clearing the shaft, Schliemann now turned his gang's attentions some yards to the south. Once again they moved some large 'grave stones' and began to dig. And right away, they found another, smaller shaft and at the bottom of the shaft another treasure. Three women, buried in the same position as the men, 'laden with jewels', with two small children carefully wrapped in thick gold sheet beside them. As well as copious gold jewellery and two golden crowns, these women also had golden discs sewn on to their vanished costumes. Schliemann found some seven hundred discs, all superbly decorated with a dozen different patterns. There were great pins too, to hold their vanished robes, and toilette boxes, such as the women of many ancient cultures used. It was a veritable blaze of gold. Schliemann continued with his excavation.

Schliemann soon found the mouth of another burial shaft close by the enclosing wall, again beneath heavy stones. This was the largest shaft of all. Here, wrote Schliemann, he found five men – two of these skeletons, in fact, were women – and their burials were even richer than the others. Amongst a mass of wine cups made of faience, pottery and precious metal, was one in solid gold shaped like a lion's head, another in silver, a superb image of a bull's head. Here too, were clothing discs again, and heavy bracelets and signet rings exquisitely engraved with scenes of war and hunting. And – echoes of a truly Trojan past – there were no fewer than fifty-six long swords made of bronze and some superb small daggers too, beautifully inlaid with scenes of hunting. For the first time, there were face masks as well, three of them cut from heavy golden sheet that seemed to have been pressed roughly over the dead faces of the three men to make eerie impressions. After clearing another smaller shaft containing a single burial, a man with crown and sword, knives and pottery, Schliemann turned his attention

LEFT: *Viewed from the southwest, the Grave Circle showing the open shafts that held the golden burials excavated by the Schliemanns. The double ring of stones was reset after Schliemann's day by later archaeologists. The bellying-out of the city wall visible in the upper left hand corner of the picture, shows that the Bronze Age architects shaped their rampart to accommodate the Grave Circle, which had originally laid outside the walls of an earlier and smaller fortress. Schliemann's belief that the royal graves had been constructed inside the walls was wrong; his find therefore, was wonderfully serendipitous.*

back to the first shaft lying close by, which had by then dried out.

After such an extraordinary blaze of gold, it is difficult to imagine anything more impressive waiting to be found, yet everyone later agreed that this would be the climax of this wondrous three-week excavation. Three massive men rested at the bottom of this grave shaft, lying as were all the other burials, on a thin bed of small pebbles. Here amidst a mass of treasures were two more face masks, one of them much finer and much better made than those that they had already found. To his amazement, Schliemann uncovered a face beneath this mask. Yet, just as he gazed down upon his Trojan hero in the flesh, it dissolved, as he put it 'on being exposed to the air', the first time perhaps that this distressingly common archaeological event had ever been noted.

The second central burial proved to be in a similarly fragile condition to the first. The third though, beneath a simpler golden mask that bears a distinct resemblance to Colonel Blimp, still had a perfect face and head, as well as part of a torso. And neither crumbled into dust. There was no hair, Schliemann says, but both eyes were still visible and the mouth, a grinning rictus, displayed thirty-two beautiful teeth. Like all good archaeologists, Schliemann maintained a veritable mania for counting, measuring and weighing everything. After having the corpse carefully drawn and painted, Schliemann called in a local chemist to aid its preservation, which was accomplished with a thick glaze of gum arabic dissolved in alcohol.

Throughout the three-week period of opening the golden tombs, Schliemann had been sending off reports to an increasingly excited international press. Now he sent a public telegram to the king of Greece as well. Not one that began 'Today I have gazed upon the face of Agamemnon' as later legend has it, but one joyfully announcing that he had discovered the 'tombs which tradition, echoed by Pausanius, has designated as the sepulchres of Agamemnon, Cassandra, Eurmedon

BELOW: *Hexagonal box of sycamore wood covered in decorated gold plates. Excavated by Schliemann from the Grave Circle at Mycenae, archaeologists can now date this by its designs to around 1550 BC.*

and all their companions'. In all, he had found nineteen souls inside the Grave Circle, sharing some thirty-five pounds of golden ornament between them. Schliemann also fancied that the human head and golden covering mask were those of Agamemnon — though popular belief had given the title to the other more splendid mask from the same grave shaft. In eight weeks, Schliemann transformed his dispatches to *The Times* of London into a weighty illustrated book, *Mycenae; a Narrative of Research and Discovery*. It quickly became not merely a bestseller, but the first archaeological sensation.

Many academic archaeologists, however, were unimpressed. Even when visiting Schliemann whilst he was still excavating at Mycenæ some professors had made fun of him behind his back. Later when the treasure was first exhibited, the great German archaeologist Ernst Curtius, the excavator at Olympia, declared the tombs to be of the Byzantine period and of a poor and local quality! Yet another leading German archaeologist publicly labelled him 'half-mad,' a sentiment many were happy to endorse. Schliemann though, who always gave as good as he got in such barbed transactions and indulged in feuds of great longevity, was well aware that despite his brave announcements, many of his public statements were still waiting for their proof. As he dug according to a programme, with the eye of a scholar, rather than that of a treasure seeker, Schliemann always understood the intrinsic significance of what he found, even if he could not explain it to the satisfaction of the establishment. After he had returned from Mycenae and someone questioned the authenticity of 'Agamemnon's Mask,' he exclaimed impatiently, 'So this is not Agamemnon; so these are not his ornaments. All right, let's call him Schulze!'

What then, would we call this Schulze today? If nothing else, Curtius' earlier observation, at once tetchy and confused, shows just how novel Schliemann's finds were for academic archaeologists. Just as Schliemann claimed, they were evidence of a culture that had flourished long before the ages of classical Greece. Schliemann called it Pelasgian; today we call it the Greek Bronze Age and make a broad distinction between the earlier cultures of Crete and the later cultures of Mycenae. In Schliemann's Grave Circle, objects from both cultures seem to have been anciently mixed. Traditionalist scholars are still delighted though, to note that Schliemann had been wrong in his interpretation of Pausanius. His shaft graves, which are now dated to 1600–1500 BC first lay outside the city walls; they were encompassed by new city walls in about 1300 BC, which were especially curved to hold them. At this time too, the shaft graves were surrounded by rings of cut stone — the unique so-called Grave Circle of Mycenae — and buried under a heavy filling of earth in which Schliemann's 'grave stones' were set as altars. Some of these stones had holes in them to permit the oil of offering to seep down to the gold-rich graves beneath.

Another grave was found inside the Grave Circle after Schliemann left. True to form, he had stopped work when he had found five royal graves, because Pausanius seemed to him to imply that the graves were five in number. Stamatakes though, did not share Schliemann's faith in ancient prose and following the comments of a surveyor that Schliemann had sent to Mycenae to map the excavations, he excavated a space inside the doorway of the Grave Circle and found another golden grave.

Today, all this treasure is displayed with the contents of another set of graves found further down the hill. Between them, they form a great glittering mass, confronting visitors as they enter the National Museum of Greece, the gold flashing and trembling as the crowds push all round it. Ever the businessman, at the end of his famous telegram to the king of Greece, Schliemann wrote these prophetic words: 'These treasures alone will fill a great

ABOVE: *A detail of a golden breastplate excavated by Schliemann at Mycenae showing a typical so-called 'running-scroll' design that decorated jewellery, armour and the gravestones of the Grave Circle and which may be provisionally dated to the sixteenth century BC.*

museum, the most wonderful in the world, and for centuries to come thousands of foreigners will flock to Greece to see them…God grant that they may become the cornerstone of an immense national wealth.'

Iliou Melathron – The Palace of Troy

In the year after finishing his season at Mycenae, Schliemann bought a plot of land on the main street of Athens at the very centre of the city, where he planned to build a house for Sophie and their growing family. An old friend was commissioned to design the house, the architect Ernst Ziller, who years earlier had first told Schliemann about the archaeological excitements of the Troad. He designed and built a grandiose Roman *palazzo* for his friend, all marble and vaulted arcades, and designed its grand furnishings as well. Schliemann named the mansion *Iliou Melathron* – the Palace of Troy – and, with his usual energy, set about designing interiors for it that were a visual diary of his career in archaeology. They made what is perhaps the world's most extraordinary memorial to archaeology.

Even the railings in the street, Schliemann decided, should display ancient images of Athena's wise owl, and swastikas too, that Schliemann had found as decoration on so many Trojan pots. Like many polymaths with an extraordinary memory, he was deeply fascinated by pattern and its changes and transformation around the world. Once inside, the front door of the mansion opened onto a curving marble staircase under which stood a copy of a fine relief of Apollo brought from Troy. The public rooms upstairs were decorated in the style of a Pompeian house, a style echoed even in the splendid glazed, mahogany screen doors. This was a sort of echo of Schliemann's first exposure to archaeology, in the great buried cities all around the Bay of Naples. Each public room, however, is entered through a grand doorway made in the style of the celebrated beehive tombs of the Greek bronze ages – Schliemann's Pelasgians. Sophie had excavated one of these at Mycenae while her husband had concentrated on the shaft graves.

All the mansion's floors, made to Schliemann's orders by families of Italian mosaic artists brought especially to Athens, are elaborately decorated with patterns from his archaeological notebooks: the circular gold discs from the shaft tombs with their sharp patterns, cuttle fish, leaves and bees; and images of Trojan pottery too, with its distinctive double-handled vases; and the small sculptures that Schliemann fancied demonstrated the worship of the same god at both Troy and Mycenae.

In the first years, to their guests' amazement, display cases in the hall showed off the Trojan treasures, as did Sophie herself on occasion, at the grandest galas. In Athens, in a new country with a young Danish king, Iliou Melathron was one of the grandest private houses in the city. Yet Schliemann lived in his dark red Pompeian study and did not often choose to socialise. Most mornings he was up at four, riding to Piraeus for a swim in the sea, an invaluable aid to health, as he so frequently advised his wife. By six he was back and working in his study, most days writing determinedly in a series of vast notebooks, in a wide variety of languages that he learned one after the other. He habitually answered letters in the language of the nationality of the recipient; he could also recite most classical texts from memory, as well as the Koran and much Persian poetry too. Culled from the classics, a variety of moral exhortations decorated many walls. And in the dining room, his daily diet of nourishing foods, were carefully painted by the same Italian artists who also made a splendid series of archaeological scenes on the ceilings. Here there are *putti* playing the roles of

ABOVE: *One of a large number of golden disks excavated by Schliemann from the shaft graves at Mycenae which were sewn onto the womens' burial robes in the classic ancient Middle Eastern way. Such pretty patterns were used by Schliemann in his house at Athens. With an eye for a bargain, he imported a group of Sicilian mosaic artists who copied them in the designs of the mosaic floors*

BELOW: *Schliemann's daybooks from his excavation at Troy provided many of the designs used in the decorations of his house at Athens. This page shows two rows of spindle whorls, designs that especially interested Schliemann, as they did other archaeologists of his day who were interested in tracing the migrations of ancient peoples through the ancient world.*

Schliemann and Sophie, excavating Mycenae and Troy, measuring and drawing, writing and, with black pince-nez, reading, inevitably, the works of Homer.

Over the years, naturally, Schliemann's attentions returned again to the windy Hill of Hissarlik, as he realised that many questions yet remained unanswered. In his own words, here heavily paraphrased: 'By my excavations on the Hill of Hissarlik, I supposed that I had settled the Trojan question forever. I thought I had proved that the small town, the third in succession from the virgin soil, must necessarily be the Troy of the legend immortalised by Homer. But I became sceptical. . .'

'Yet the tradition of all antiquity regarding the war of Troy was quite unanimous, and to this overwhelming testimony, a further proof has been added by the ten treasures of gold ornaments which I found in my excavations on Hissarlik. I therefore resolved upon continuing the excavations, to clear up the mystery, and to settle finally the important Trojan question.'

This then, was work that Heinrich Schliemman pursued until the ending of his life, travelling from his Athenian palace to the windy Hill of Hissarlik, to re-examine and extend his previous excavations.

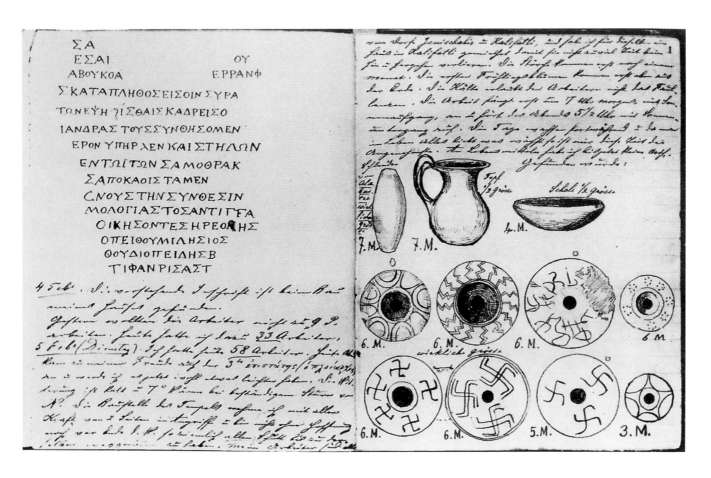

Return to Troy: 1889

In 1889, aged sixty-eight, very deaf and, as can be seen in photographs, displaying obvious signs of suffering from years of acute pain within his ears, Schliemann returned to Troy for the last time in his life. Nearly twenty years of celebrated excavations in Egypt, Greece and the Islands, a second campaign at Troy itself and other sites around the Troad had sown deep doubts within him about the excavations that had first brought him fame. Mycenae especially, along with several other of his Greek excavations had revealed the relics of a splendid ancient civilisation with distinctive pottery, characteristic jewellery and armaments; seemingly the very accoutrements of the Greeks who besieged Homer's Troy. Yet he had found none of these distinctive things within the walls of Troy.

Troy indeed, still appeared to be a city completely by itself, and had remained so even after Schliemann's 1882 excavations with a young German archaeologist, Willhelm Dörpfeld. A most careful man, Dörpfeld had been trained by the German excavators of Olympia, some of the finest working archaeologists in the world. In his book *Troja*, which describes that season's work, Schliemann lists a number of small excavations undertaken right across the Troad, including the hill of Ballidagh which, before Schliemann's work on Hissarlik, was widely regarded to be the ancient hill of Troy. As Schliemann pursued a characteristically erratic course across the landscape pursued by Ottoman intelligence officers, Dörpfeld carefully surveyed the surviving mounds of Hissarlik and Schliemann's earlier excavations and was able to distinguish and map seven separate cities, one above the other. Schliemann gratefully accepted Dörpfeld's information and in *Troja* forcefully argued that the second oldest of Dörpfeld's cities was the city of the Trojan Wars. Even as you read his words, however, you feel that Schliemann is arguing against his own self-doubts.

On his return in 1889, Schliemann called a conference of scholars at Hissarlik to reopen the whole issue once again. By this time many of his old adversaries had come to see that, whatever his personality or competence, Schliemann had indeed found unique monuments of great age and significance. Yet Schliemann himself was not satisfied with Troy and its relationship to Greece and when the conference was concluded, he began to dig again. Dörpfeld was working with him, continuing his detailed survey of the strata and ruins of the mound. Schliemann though, following his nose as usual, took a large gang of workmen off to dig above the Scaean Gate in unknown territory which seemed to him to be in a similar proximity to the gate as the golden Grave Circle had been to the Lion Gate at Mycenae.

Once again, the old archaeologist's instincts brought him good fortune. Not gold, just two large rectangular rooms of stone and some broken potsherds. These potsherds though, were different from anything else that he had found at Troy; but he knew the type well, from many Greek sites he had excavated. It was, as he called it, Pelasgian, and of the same type and design that is seen pictured in the Valley of the Kings in Egypt, in the tomb of Ramesses III which he knew, was dated to approximately 1200–1100 BC. It was the pottery of 'Agamemnon's Mycenae'.

At last, Schliemann had connected Troy to Homer's Greece and even provided them with dates! What Schliemann had excavated in 1889 in fact, was part of Dörpfeld's sixth Trojan city and lay, for the most part, well outside the area of Schliemann's original excavations. Schliemann's golden treasures had been found in Dörpfeld's second city. Clearly this showed that Schliemann's original assumption that Homer's Troy would be found in the lower and earliest levels of the tell had been wrong. Troy, it was now proved, was far more ancient than the age of Homer's heroes (in fact, we know it to be a millennium older). This showed of course, that the Trojan treasures that Schliemann first found, were also of a far earlier date than the age of Homer's heroes, and all his years of argument had been in error. At the same time, the discovery that Troy VI was contemporary with the graves he found at Mycenae must surely have thrilled him, for he had always worried that Troy II, the city of his treasure and the 'Scaean Gate', was far too small for such a celebrated fortress city; he once described it, somewhat disappointedly, as being 'no bigger than Trafalgar Square'. Now at last, he knew that a larger city, suitable for Trojan heroes, lay under the unexcavated portions of the mound and in a few years he could excavate them.

A few months later, Schliemann died, alone and in great pain, collapsing in a square in Naples after a visit to Pompeii, the first excavation that he had ever seen three decades before. He had not written about the new discoveries at Troy, but before he left there for the last time, he told Dörpfeld that he recognised that he had been mistaken in his identification of Homer's city. Just two or three more seasons' work, he added, should establish Homer's Troy beyond all doubt! That, of course, gives the lie to those modern critics who claim him to have been nothing more than a cheat. Mixed with the dubious ethics of nineteenth-century entrepreneurship and a strong dash of naiveté common in such tyros, Schliemann also had the curiosity of a scientist, an archaeologist searching for the truth.

LEFT: 'Plan of Homeric Troy,' one of many such maps that Schliemann published. This example, the result of a survey of the Hill of Hissarlik undertaken in 1883, shows Schliemann slowly beginning to adopt the standard archaeological practices of the day.

Dating Schliemann: Flinders Petrie and Mycenae

L ATE IN DECEMBER 1890, as Schliemann lay dying in the Grand Hotel at Naples, a young British archaeologist, Flinders Petrie, was completing two long seasons in the pyramid fields south of Cairo, excavating mostly desert cemeteries and ancient villages of many different periods of Egyptian history. The sites were very rich; Schliemann himself had visited Petrie's camp early in the work and marvelled at the fragmentary ancient manuscripts of Homer which some of the Roman inhabitants of the area had taken with them to their graves.

Petrie had been especially excited by the non-Egyptian material that he found at some of his sites, including large quantities of painted pottery which he knew was similar to that which Schliemann had found at Mycenae and other sites in Greece. Straight away, he recognised their significance for archaeology in other countries: 'It really seems as if we have got here one of the great prizes, the contemporary remains of the Western races in their earliest contacts with Egypt: an historical plum.' A year later, on his way from Egypt to England, Petrie visited Greece, travelling to Mycenae and many other sites where Schliemann had excavated, examining the pottery collections of the British School in Athens (one of a half dozen national archaeological institutes already resident in Greece) whose director Ernest Gardner, Petrie himself had trained on earlier expeditions.

By this time, a broad chronology of ancient Egyptian dynasties had been established beyond all reasonable doubt, thanks to the surviving hieroglyphic king lists made by ancient Egyptian scribes and the meticulous studies of nineteenth-century egyptologists. Petrie could ascribe many of the ancient buildings from which he had excavated Greek pots to specific dynasties and sometimes even individual kings. Knowing the date of the Egyptian building and finding Greek pottery within it meant that he now held the key to the chronology of Bronze Age Greece.

What Petrie did in Greece was to compare the types of dated pottery that he had found in Egypt with those undated pots from Mycenae and other Greek sites, and this he did with phenomenal accuracy and clarity. As Gardner sat and watched him working in the library of the British School, Petrie drew up a table of dates for many of the finest monuments of prehistoric Greece. In two articles for the *Journal of the Hellenic Society*, he laid out the order and approximate dating of the Greek Bronze Age, and so added a millennium and more to European history. Though there were, and indeed still are, continuous and bitter arguments about the dates of individual pharaohs and their dynasties, and the division of pottery styles by time and type, Petrie's basic framework still remains.

The rough dates that Schliemann had earlier ascribed to Mycenaen pottery following his observations in the tombs of Thebes, had not convinced the archaeological establishment. Now though, Petrie's virtuoso display, based on hard-won archaeological evidence, had convinced this same establishment of the authenticity of those vast eras of Greek history that Schliemann had excavated and publicised for so many contentious years. This would surely have made Schliemann very happy. His ideas, if not his personality, had at last become part of the academic archaeological establishment; the cultures that he unearthed at Troy and Greece are now amongst the most studied periods in archaeology.

And yet, and yet; the central premise of Schliemann's work, that ancient literature can provide archaeology with a guide to the past, is far from proven. How do old books like Homer, filled with gods and mighty warriors fit into the realities of the archaeological past?

Today at Troy, a huge wooden horse erected by the National Tourist Board greets visitors who have come to see the ancient site. It is a reproduction of the statue, which as Homer tells, was secretly filled with Greek warriors and taken unknowingly into Troy, causing the downfall of the city when the warriors inside opened the gates to the Greek armies on the plain. Yet the truth remains that no ancient inscription bearing the name of Troy has ever been found upon the hill of Hissarlik. The best argument archaeologists can make for Hissarlik is of exclusion: it's the best bet; if this is not Troy, where on earth could Homer's fabled city be? So we come full circle, back to the arguments of some of Schliemann's adversaries; why does a work of literature require locating on the real earth?

Such arguments are not of merely academic interest. Schliemann's tremendous success immediately provoked a host of imitators all around the world. If Homer's heroes and their cities could be excavated, then why not the locations described in other ancient books as well: El Dorado, Pliny's villa by the Tiber or the city of Atlantis? Above all else though, with its insistence upon historic place and time, with the very dates of Western history counted from the birth of Jesus Christ, many Christian archaeologists turned straight towards the Holy Land for archaeological evidence of Jesus and the ancient worlds that held the Bible's stories. And there, once more, the brilliant Flinders Petrie played a key role in the story.

ABOVE: *Petrie in his early thirties, when he had already undertaken his ground-breaking survey of the Pyramids of Giza and excavated the oldest Greek colony ever found in the Egyptian Delta.*

Petrie at Tell el Hesi: 1890. Excavating Palestine

In a few phenomenal years, Petrie not only provided an historical framework for the Greek Bronze Age, but ancient Palestinian history too. In a dazzling solo expedition to an unknown tell, he placed the Old Testament squarely within scientific Middle Eastern history. And in doing that, he connected the words and images of the Bible – the modern world's most influential book – with archaeology.

In March 1890, Petrie closed his excavations at the pyramids, took a steamer up to Palestine and was soon walking the dusty tracks south of Jerusalem with two camels, a driver and his Egyptian cook. He was there at the invitation of the Palestine Excavation Fund, a London society established in 1865 for surveying and mapping the Holy Land. A few years earlier, they had asked him to undertake the excavation of a tell in Palestine in an attempt to establish a broad framework for the history of ancient Palestine. No one had ever done such a thing before. At thirty-seven though, Petrie was well equipped for such a pioneering task. At the height of his considerable powers, with ten years of excavations behind him, he had accepted the Fund's offer because he thought it would help him to better understand some of the foreign pottery that he was continually uncovering in Egypt. After looking at a variety of tells and ruins in the desert plains south of Jerusalem, Petrie settled at the remote mound of Tell el Hesi, just north of Gaza.

When Schliemann first walked the Hill of Hissarlik, he had sensed the presence of his Trojan heroes in the very dust. As Petrie walked lonely Tell el Hesi, however, he was not even certain of its ancient name. Yet he also knew that each stratum, every human habitation level of this utterly anonymous hill could be accurately dated by the pottery it held. Although later armchair archaeologists took Petrie's maps of Tell el Hesi and placed within them the reigns of Solomon and David, the books of Chronicles and Kings, as far as Petrie was concerned, all Tell el Hesi offered was the archaeological opportunity of gaining a first outline of Palestinian archaeology.

RIGHT: *The great mound of Tell el Hesi, the first archaeological site to be scientifically examined in the Holy Land, bisected by Petrie's excavation. The reeds in the foreground are growing in the bed of the River Hesi, whose waters had eroded the side of the tell, bringing its stratigraphy into the sunlight, and enabling Petrie to examine the strata of the tell with a minimum of effort.*

LEFT: *At an ancient Egyptian site of known date, Petrie excavated the Greek Bronze Age pottery seen to the left, and so provided Schliemann's world-famous Mycenaean excavations, where similar pottery had been excavated, with an archaeologically established date of around 1500 BC.*

EASTERN FACE OF TELL HESY.
1:600

Consummate, cunning and with a first-class eye for field archaeology, Petrie saw that Tell el Hesi offered immediate access to the interior of an ancient city. At Troy, such a cut into the past had cost Schliemann massive amounts of time and money. Tell el Hesi, on the other hand, stood over a small rush-filled stream, the River Hesi, which had eroded a great part of the tell, cutting a cliff through an enormous succession of strata, a cliff some sixty feet in height. At the beginning of the work, Petrie simply climbed up and down the parts of the tell that had been eroded by the river, prizing pieces of pottery from the strata in the cliff face with his penknife; this would become the first excavation in the Middle East whose strata would be dated as the work progressed.

At the top of the tell, in the later strata, were well-known types of foreign pottery made in well-known historical periods; Greek ceramics of types he had already excavated in Egypt, and on top, as you would expect, the pottery of the Roman Empire. At the bottom of the tell, however, beside the river, in its first layers of human habitation, Petrie found a type of pottery he had never seen before; large, thick pots and jugs, sometimes spouted and with crude handles, of dark coarse clay. Inventing a biblical terminology of his own, Petrie dubbed this pottery 'Amorite' after one of the generations of Noah, a tribe who lived in Palestine before the coming of the Israelites. Today it is considered to belong to the periods of Early and Middle Bronze Age Palestine.

High above these levels, in later strata, Petrie found those types of pottery that he had already excavated in Egypt, and that Schliemann had found in Greece and Troy. These he divided into two main groups – 'Phoenician' and 'Aegean' – the latter including that of the Greek Bronze Age, the former being, so he proposed, the contemporary indigenous pottery of the Levant. From his Egyptian excavations, Petrie knew that these two pottery types came from Egyptian excavations dating from between 2000 to 1200 BC. Not only did this prove that the 'Amorite' pottery below was dated to the third millennium BC, but also allowed him to apply dates to the more common locally produced ware, which he split into two sub-types naming them 'Early' and 'Middle Jewish'.

A tiny piece of this 'Phoenician' pottery had a scrap of an inscription on it written out in letters that are now known as Proto-Canaanite, a hieroglyphic-derived script that was an ancestor of Hebrew, Greek and Latin. It was the first time that this script had ever been found in an archaeological, and therefore datable context. Petrie had dated an ancestor of the language of the Bible and the modern West.

Above the levels containing the 'Phoenician' and 'Aegean' wares, Petrie first found evidence

ABOVE: *Petrie's section of the mound of Tell el Hesi, published in 1890: the first map ever made showing the superimposed ancient cities buried in a tell. Allied to Petrie's drawings of the pottery from the strata of this tell, this section long served as a basic time chart for later biblical archaeologists.*

RIGHT: *Some five years after excavating Tell el Hesi, whilst digging royal temples at Egyptian Thebes, Flinders Petrie found the first mention of the name of Israel in ancient records outside the pages of the Bible. In this drawing – Petrie's own record of the relevant part of the hieroglyphic text – the name of Israel fills the right side of the central line.*

of fire and destruction, then a stratum of pure sand laid down when Tell el Hesi had been uninhabited. Above this natural deposit, he found a distinctive and very different type of pottery which Petrie, again adopting biblical inspiration, called 'Jewish' and dated between the time of David and the Book of Kings, that is, between 1000 and approximately 650 BC, just beneath the Greek pottery.

All this while, Petrie and his cook lived in tents. At night, he killed deadly black scorpions that crawled from the snake-infested mound into his bed linen. River Hesi proved to be polluted and Petrie was forced to have his drinking water brought on donkeys from a spring six miles away. Even this, he tells, was green and salty, its 'taste and colour almost too much, soup, fish and greens in one'. As the expedition came to its end, he was attacked and robbed upon the lonely plain, sustaining a broken windpipe that made his voice husky for the rest of his life. 'The life of an excavator is not of the easiest,' he once observed.

After his solo survey, Petrie took 'thirty thirsty Muslims, each with a woman or girl to carry their basket' and set them working at different levels on the eroded side of the tell, burrowing deep into the mound, following walls and floor levels. In just six weeks he produced the first archaeological map ever made of a tell, showing all the architecture he had found, mostly mud brick walls of various periods, set into the strata, which he dated from the pottery.

Amongst other things, Petrie's genius lay in the vast amount of information, shapes and colours he could hold in his memory, then process as data with all the crushing logic of a computer. Few other archaeologists of his time could have begun to match his mental capacity. But this was a person, probably that most unfashionable thing, a genius, who performed complex multiplication by 'imagining a slide rule' in his head.

As was his habit, the excavation report on Tell el Hesi was published in book form within a year. It emphasised to archaeologists around the world the tremendous value of pottery in understanding and dating stratigraphic excavations. It had also given structure and form to the archaeology of Palestine, the strata of the tell were like the pages of a book; the hunt for the earthly remains of the kingdom of God was on. Yet in Petrie's terms, in scientific terms, Israel still did not exist as an archaeological entity simply because no archaeologists had ever found its name upon any ancient record outside the pages of the Bible — and as a science, archaeology cannot simply trust a book alone, whoever its author.

The Land of Abraham
Excavating Iraq

SINCE THE HEADY DAYS OF PETRIE'S EARLY excavations, the ancient Israelites, the people of the Old Testament, have been almost as difficult for archaeologists to find as Homer's Trojan heroes. Ancient Mesopotamia (today's Iraq) the home of biblical Abraham, the land of scarlet Babylon and of the Hebrew Exile had attracted archaeologists even before Schliemann had started work at Troy. Just as it had been the region on which Byron's Assyrians had descended like wolves on the fold, his cohorts all gleaming in silver and gold, so throughout the nineteenth century, assorted Europeans had followed in their footsteps; consuls and crooks, merchants and adventurers, linguists and archaeologists; most of them intent on taking whatever relics of the past they could back to the museums of Western Europe.

The most competent part of the archaeology of these adventurers is on a par with Schliemann's early work at Troy; the greater part, however, was more like what one archaeologist has described as 'digging for potatoes'. In 1899, however, the German government began its excavations at Babylon, north of Baghdad, one of the world's greatest excavations, with lavish funding and first-class archaeologists; the work lasted eighteen years until the outbreak of the First World War. Indeed, it is said that the last Germans left their work with the sound of gunfire in their ears, the surrounding Arab tribesmen having sided with the Allies.

Robert Koldewey, the expedition leader, was an experienced archaeologist who had worked for many years in Sicily and Greece. At Babylon he introduced the concept of stratigraphic excavation into Mesopotamia, setting standards that would dominate the field for decades. The sheer scale of the excavations was enormous, vast triumphal highways,

ABOVE: *The fearsome walls of Babylon, the mighty city of the biblical Exile, brought back into light again by the Deutsches Orient Gesellschaft under the direction of archaeologist Robert Koldewey in a dazzling decade of excavation before the First World War.*

enormous civic architectures were extracted from the ancient dust and even, Koldewey suggested, the ruins of the Hanging Gardens, one of the Seven Wonders of the ancient world. After many years of restoration, the mighty gates of Babylon, packed away in 649 wooden crates, rose again in Berlin's Vorderasiatisches Museum and became one of the wonders of the world's museums.

As they dug deep into the dusty hill of Babylon for eighteen long years, many of those archaeologists must surely have expected to find some relic of ancient Israel amongst the many tons of dry, dark dust. Even the august offices of the Deutsches Orient Gesellschaft, an archaeological agency in Berlin, would have trembled at such news, for like no other find in archaeology, the slightest trace of a biblical character found in excavation stirs public interest in archaeology as nothing else on earth. Such relics never materialised, however, or at least, no one realised that they had until years later. Buried in the tens of thousands of ancient texts that Koldewey shipped from Babylon to Berlin, an ancient receipt was translated recording the issuing of oil to Jehoiachin, King of Judah. The Second Book of Kings *exactly* amplifies this same story, telling that this same king and a few courtiers lived out their lives in Babylon and found favour at its court. Many years later, when this remarkable fragment was deciphered and recognised for what it was — a rare link between dirt archaeology and the pages of the Bible — Koldewey's expedition had long since finished its work and the expedition no longer required the wine of such remarkable publicity.

After the First World War, Iraq was no longer under Turkish domination, German influence had waned and British archaeology was paramount. Numbers of youthful archaeologists, attracted by careers of colonial excitement, were recruited from the major universities to excavate the ancient cities littering the plain to the south of Baghdad. Amongst them, Leonard Woolley, later Sir Leonard, achieved popular success, excavating golden treasures from Tell el Mukkayer that, like Schliemann's find in Turkey and Greece, held the attention of the world for a season. In strata dating to the third millennium BC, Woolley found the extraordinary and unique grave of a noble lady. What made her tomb sensational, however, was not her golden burial treasures, but the fact that her court had been immured alongside her in a vast mass grave. Christened the 'Death Pit' by Woolley, the haul of treasure was extraordinary; chariots and statues plaited with gold, fine cups and jewellery, musical instruments and furniture. These treasures, that could only have come from a sophisticated and extravagant court, put most ancient Mesopotamia which until that time had been the haunt of specialist antiquarians, on the popular archaeological map.

In all of this, Woolley's greatest achievement was not the location of this great treasure, but its successful excavation. Buried at a considerable depth, most of the objects in the 'Death Pit' were of gold foil on wooden bases that had entirely rotted away. Digging fragile foil from hard mud was a difficult enough exercise in itself; recovering the forms that they had

ABOVE: *An ancient harp from the burial of a Sumerian queen at Ur in south Iraq, dating around 3100 BC. Working in the desert with little assistance, Leonard Woolley excavated and conserved a vast cemetery of regal tombs containing hundreds of unique and nigmatic burials, rich in gold.*

BELOW: *From the disposition of a few mud bricks and ruined walls in the suburbs of ancient Ur, Woolley made this reconstruction of a 4000-year-old house. That he named it 'a house from the time of Abraham,' has since given the surviving fragmentary structures in the desert of Iraq the status of semi-holy relics.*

once covered was a remarkable achievement that translated into galleries of glittering objects, the treasures of an ancient court. Had Woolley not been a most brilliant and practical craftsman, able to work with the simplest of materials under the most difficult of circumstances, one of the world's great archaeological treasures would have been reduced to pretty scraps of ancient gold.

Despite the considerable successes of their archaeologists, British museums were never as generous with their funds as their German equivalents and Woolley, 'noting,' as he put it 'the want of pence that vexes excavations,' played the Bible card. Tell el Mukkayer had been one of the great cities of most ancient Mesopotamia, one of the centres of Sumerian culture. In all likelihood, its ancient name was Ur, the city in which Abraham was born and where he started his journey along that long arc down to Egypt and up again, to Hebron in Canaan. Dating the span of Abraham's life by traditional biblical scholarship to around 1800–1200 BC Woolley labelled a plan of a middle-class house of that period with the label 'house of the time of Abraham' which swiftly became translated to 'the house of Abraham' and has remained so to this day, even promising to become a place of pilgrimage.

In later excavations, at the deepest levels of human habitation at Tell el Mukkayer, Woolley came across a tell-tale band of silt amongst the strata left by human habitation. This, he claimed, was certainly the biblical flood on whose waters Noah's ark had travelled.

A pious man of absolute integrity, Woolley was finding biblical connections throughout his excavations on the tell and like Schliemann he believed that the words of the Bible reflected physical truths that could be verified by digging in the ancient earth. The real truth though, is that neither Ur nor Abraham's house nor the Bible's flood can be placed at Tell el Mukkayer beyond reasonable scientific doubt. As General Pitt Rivers would have said, the evidence would never 'stand up in a court of law'. Like Palestine itself, ancient Mesopotamia had been partly mapped out in the image of the Bible's stories, and the relics of the Bible's stories are believed because a great part of our society wants them to be true.

What numerous excavations throughout the Fertile Crescent have decisively shown, however, especially with the decipherment of thousands upon thousands of ancient texts, is the precision of the Old Testament's descriptions of that ancient world. The first chapters of the Bible are partly set in the genuine environment of the most ancient East, as archaeology and ancient texts continually confirm. The writers of those passages from the Bible knew that ancient world far better than we ever can.

The irony in all of this for archaeologists is that the great treasures of the Death Pit, Woolley's *magnum opus* in a long and distinguished career, are not nearly as well known today as 'Ur of the Chaldees', the 'house of Abraham' and the 'City of the Flood'.

Once in Royal David's City
Excavating Jerusalem

WHAT THOUGH, OF BIBLICAL JERUSALEM? No archaeologist has ever had to refind the city; armies have fought over its possession for 4000 years and more. No one has ever excavated on the Holy Mount where the vanished Temple of the Jews once stood, built on the rock, where Abraham offered Isaac in sacrifice, and where the Prophet Mohammed began his ascent into heaven. Uninvited archaeology here means war. Before the Arab-Israeli War of 1967, the archaeological picture of ancient Jerusalem had to be painstakingly assembled from small and often deep excavations in odd little spaces, such as basements or gardens, left unoccupied inside the walls of the tight-packed medieval city. The most intensive programme of such excavations took place in the 1960s, before the Arab-Israeli conflict and was conducted by Kathleen Kenyon, a distinguished British archaeologist who had worked in Palestine for decades.

Outside the city walls, however, yet still close to the Temple Mount, the situation was different. Though partly covered in modern dwellings, the valleys and slopes all around the

RIGHT: *The modern Arab village of Silwan faces the Israeli archaeological site on the so-called 'City of David'. Part-excavated in the 1920s and 1950s by British archaeologists, whose work was amplified and enlarged by Israeli excavations in 1978–82 under Yigal Shiloh, the high walls in the foreground have proved to be part of a Late Bronze Age fortress. At the foot of this wall, a small house of the seventh century BC was excavated that contained clay sealings bearing the Hebrew name of a scribe who may be the same person as a scribe mentioned in the biblical book of Jeremiah.*

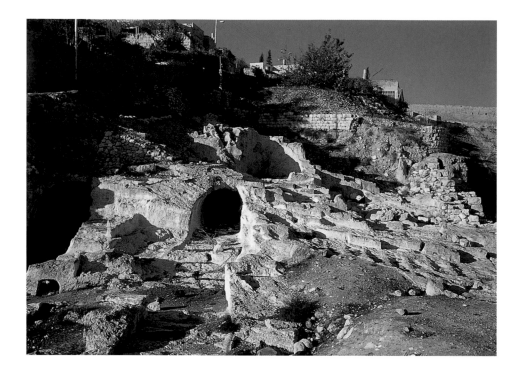

LEFT: *Deep-vaulted tombs on the so-called 'City of David,' part-cut away by later Roman quarrymen. If King David and his successors ever lived on this little hill, these tombs, of typical Israelite type but with grand dimensions, may well have been their final resting-places.*

Arab village of Silwan offered space for excavation. Here, there is archaeological evidence of Bronze Age dwellings at Jerusalem, the oldest-known evidence of habitation at the city. Here too, the Old Testament tells, is the rocky spur of the south-east hill below the Temple Mount where King David built his house. Not surprisingly, excavation started here as early as the 1870s, with French priests and British Army officers. In the 1960s Kenyon's teams worked in and around the same area, dotting it with archaeological squares and trenches. These appeared to show that the reality of Iron-Age Jerusalem – that is, according to biblical chronology, the Jerusalem of David and the later kings of Israel – was that the area had been a modest sector of the city with poor houses, a high terrace running along the spur's top ridge, and a Canaanite, 'heathen' shrine set inside a little cave cut further down the slope.

These were certainly not the relics of Hollywood's Biblical imaginings. Nor indeed, was there any archaeological evidence of David's palace, nor of any other of the Bible's kings. Yet at the same time, Kenyon's excavations on this rocky spur also showed that in the Iron Age, the topography of this modest hilltop town was very similar in its geography to many of the settings of the Bible's stories of David and the later kings. Stories about high walls and towers and fortresses, and even stories of seduction. Stand on a rooftop there today, in the cool shadowed evening and you could still peep down into your neighbour's bathroom, just as David did, according to the prophet Samuel.

> 2 SAMUEL 11, 2. *And it came to pass in an eveningtide, that David arose from off his bed, and walked upon the roof of the king's house: and from the roof he saw a woman washing herself; and the woman was very beautiful to look upon.*
> 3 *And David sent and enquired after the woman. And one said, Is not this Bathsheba, the daughter of Eliam, the wife of Uriah the Hittite?*
> 4 *And David sent messengers, and took her; and she came in unto him, and he lay with her.*

Small town stuff though, especially when some irreverent Bible scholars have suggested that the word 'david' is merely a local word for 'commandant' and archaeologists have noted that in history, if not the Bible, the Hittites had vanished centuries before biblical King David's time.

The Six-Day War of 1967 brought great destruction to the Holy City. Hasty clearances inside the Jewish Quarter and by the west wall of the Temple Mount, previously called the Wailing Wall, caused further gashes in the city's medieval fabric. With demolition, excavation and rebuilding following in quick succession, archaeologists were provided with several windows on to the ancient city. Their work completely changed all earlier pictures of it. In the ruins of the Jewish Quarter, the Israeli archaeologist Nahman Avigad, excavated an enormous Iron Age city wall – securely dated by pottery – and quite the equal of any known from other Iron Age hill-fort cities of the Levant.

Other excavations inside the city also showed further fragments of similarly massive walls and doorways too; there was a broader spread of Iron Age habitation than Kenyon had supposed. It was now an archaeological possibility, as the Bible implies, that Old Testament Jerusalem had been a large imposing city set beside its temple. A variety of theories soon arose on how this city had grown and spread across Jerusalem's many hills

These discoveries have had extraordinary repercussions – a measure of the powerful effect of combining archaeology and faith. In 1978, excavation began again in Kenyon's old stamping grounds on the southern spur below the Temple Mount, renamed now 'the City of David'. Further excavations were undertaken in and between Kenyon's excavations. In an area above the Canaanite shrine, these new archaeologists uncovered the burnt ruins of the house of a scribe, who had sealed his long-lost correspondence with stamps bearing inscriptions in archaic Hebrew. The style of writing showed that this scribe had lived in the time, the Bible tells us, of the Book of Kings. There was nothing though, to link this scribe to the Bible stories. Indeed, it should be noted that to this day, neither King David nor Solomon, his glorious son, have any archaeological existence whatsoever; they only live in faith and legend.

Although the young archaeologist, Yigal Shiloh, who did this work sadly died of cancer (a direct result, some Jerusalem religious fundamentalists uncharitably asserted, of his tampering with his ancestors) his work continues. The hill, however, now looks very different. An Arab village twenty years ago, most of the houses are now inhabited by Israeli settlers, and much of the rest has been transformed into a sort of urban park with bright new terracing and ornamental olive groves. While a great part of Kenyon's deep trenches, including the Canaanite shrine, have been refilled and covered over, the ancient scribe's house now forms the centrepiece of an archaeological display, with railings and buttressing painted in Israel's national colours. Sometimes soldiers come here, stack their guns and swear solemn oaths. The trilingual labels that explain the complex archaeology of the site have been disfigured; the sections written in Arabic and Hebrew describing the archaeology of the house of the Israelite scribe have been vandalised, scratched and struck in anger.

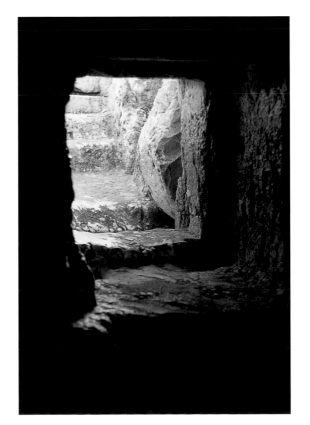

BELOW: *The doorway of the tomb of Queen Helena of Adiabene, in north Jerusalem. A convert to Judaism in the decades after Jesus' crucifixion, Queen Helena's tomb dramatically displays a rolling stone, the same closing device and one common in the cemeteries of Jerusalem of that time which the New Testament tells us, also closed the tomb of Christ.*

In the year before the First World War, French archaeologist Raymond Weill excavated a series of ancient tunnels cut deep in the grey limestone of the rocky spur at the far end of this same contentious hill. Stone benches in the tunnels showed them to be tombs. In recent years, many similar vaults have been found in the hills around Jerusalem, although they are of much smaller sizes. If biblical David and Solomon had really built their palaces on this 'City of David', then these grey tunnels could well have been their burial vaults.

Such Iron Age tombs were family vaults. Fresh burials were first laid on the stone benches shaped like narrow beds. Later, when another funeral took place, the bones of the previous burials were simply pushed to the back of the vault to join the bones of other family members – this, quite literally explaining the biblical euphemism of being 'gathered to the ancestors'. One of these undisturbed burials contained a Hebrew text on a sheet of silver dated palaeographically to the eighth century BC; it is similar to a prayer in the Old Testament. This text is the oldest Hebrew inscription yet found at Jerusalem. Most of these tombs though, were never rich in worldly goods, containing just jewels and trinkets of such ordinary Levantine style that no archaeologist would raise an eyebrow if they had been excavated in Syria, southern Turkey or the Lebanon.

There is nothing distinctive then, in the material culture of ancient Jerusalem; all archaeology can deduce is that these tombs were the modest burials of families who lived on a crossroads between the larger and more powerful contemporary civilisations in Egypt, Syria and Iraq. Only the Old Testament distinguishes Iron Age Jerusalem as a special place; that careful compilation of songs and stories, prayers and meditations, histories and legends written over millennia, the single greatest product of a modest material culture that, so its people came to believe, held the ear of the Lord of all Creation.

ABOVE: *Following the Six-Day War of 1967, Israeli archaeologists excavated large sections of the ancient city that they had captured from the Jordanian Army, both inside and outside the city walls. The foundations of the wall to the right of the picture are those of the platform of Herod's Temple. In front of them, Israeli archaeologists excavated the ruins of a variety of ancient buildings, most prominently, the extensive ruins of an early Arab palace. The white sunlit area in a corner at the far end of this wall proved to be a portion of the staircase built in the days of Herod the Great and was widely used by visitors to the temple in the time of Christ.*

RIGHT: *The Dome of the Rock, Jerusalem. Built by the caliphs in the first centuries of Islam, this superb monument, the final fruit of the architecture of the ancient Mediterranean world, bears a moving text inviting the three religions of the city to unite in the worship of the single God of Islam.*

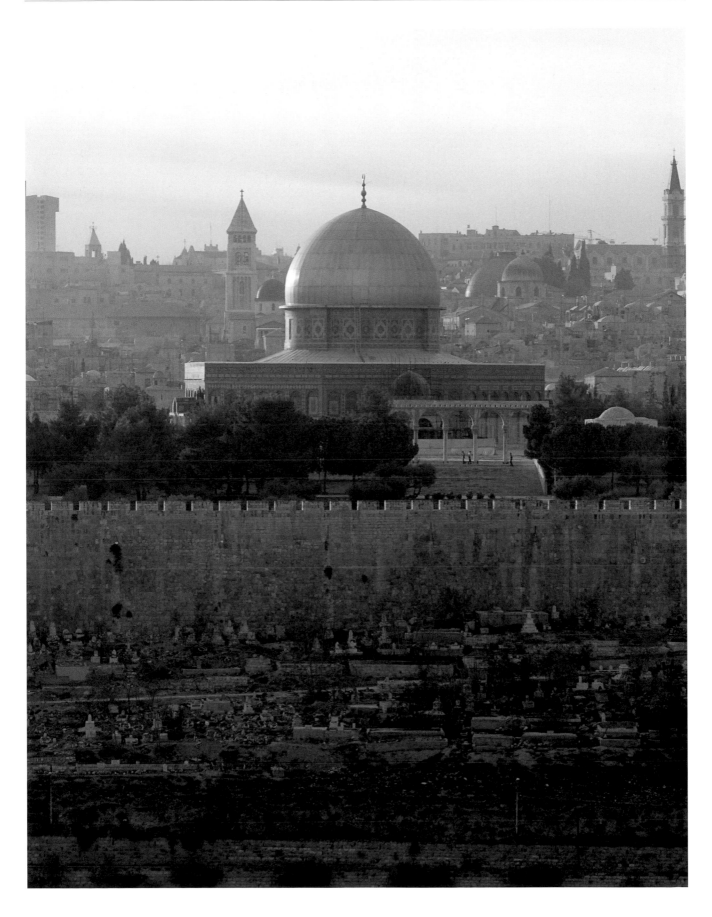

Bethesda: 1951
A Place of Miracles

IF KING DAVID AND SOLOMON ARE STILL UNKNOWN to archaeology, what hope for Jesus, a humble country carpenter and peripatetic preacher who, the Bible tells us, wrote only upon sand? Despite the fact that Christian archaeologists have long since proved that the Via Dolorosa – the road between Pilate's palace and the tomb of Christ studded with the stations of the cross – was not the ancient road by which condemned prisoners of Jerusalem were led away to execution, the medieval route is still the traditional way of pilgrims, sanctified by prayer and sword and many centuries. It is a sacred landscape fashioned in the image of the Bible. What though, has archaeology to tell us of Jesus' Jerusalem, that hallowed, literary city that still haunts the West's imagination?

> JOHN 5: 2–9. *Now there is at Jerusalem by the sheep market a pool, which is called in the*
> *Hebrew tongue Bethesda, having five porches.*
> *In these lay a great multitude of impotent folk, of blind, halt, withered, waiting*
> *for the moving of the water.*
> *For an angel went down at a certain season into the pool, and troubled the water: whosoever*
> *then first after the troubling of the water stepped in was made whole*
> *of whatsoever disease he had.*
> *And a certain man was there, which had an infirmity thirty and eight years.*
> *When Jesus saw him lie, and knew that he had been now a long time in that case,*
> *he saith unto him, Wilt thou be made whole?*
> *The impotent man answered him, Sir, I have no man, when the water is troubled,*
> *to put me into the pool: but while I am coming, another steppeth down before me.*
> *Jesus saith unto him, Rise, take up thy bed, and walk.*
> *And immediately the man was made whole, and took up his bed, and walked. . .*

In 1951, archaeologists from the Dominican École Biblique began their excavations beside the crusader church of St Anne at Jerusalem by demolishing a number of small sheds and houses, so exposing walls of several unknown ancient buildings. St Anne's Church in old Jerusalem was the traditional site of the birthplace of Mary, the mother of Jesus and stands behind the first Stations of the traditional Via Dolorosa, the Way of the Cross.

Seventy years earlier, when St Anne's was under restoration, enormous stone walls had been excavated close to the church, and were found to begin deep in the ground. Archaeologists agreed that the stone work of these walls was of a type common at

ABOVE: *The eleventh-century Crusader church of St Anne at Jerusalem which houses and protects the traditional site of the childhood home of Mary, mother of Christ. The sunlit column base in the foreground of the picture is part of the ruins of an enormous Byzantine church, built some six centuries before St Anne's, which covered the traditional site of Bethesda, where Jesus performed a miracle of healing.*

Jerusalem in the second century BC; the huge wall, it was soon understood, was part of a system of pools and reservoirs which served the nearby temple. With its constant regime of offerings, the temple required large amounts of water for the ritual preparation of sacrifices. And indeed, further excavation uncovered portions of two deeply buried ancient pools, which a large, deep trench revealed, the vast stone wall had dammed and divided. Further soundings showed the extent of these ancient reservoirs; irregular rectangles, the larger of the two was almost 200 feet along its longest side, the smaller almost 180 feet. The excavation of such elaborate arrangements for water conservation had long been a common finding in archaeology in the Holy City. From its very beginnings, the hill-top city had to carefully conserve the products of its springs and winter rains, damming them in pools and cisterns and distributing their contents in elaborate underground conduits.

The Dominican excavations of 1951 discovered that some of the ancient walls they had exposed by demolition stood on the top of the huge stone dam; one of them, the ruin of a crusader chapel was perhaps part of the twelfth-century monastery of St Anne's where several crusader queens had lived out the last years of their lives. To the fathers' great surprise, they then found that this chapel had been built inside the ruins of another church, a vast Byzantine basilica of the fifth century, almost 150 feet in length. Astonishingly, and quite uniquely, the Byzantines had built their great church suspended in the air, its west end and entrance doorways standing high above the water cisterns, with vast swinging arches and the great stone wall supporting it some fifty feet above the bottom of the ancient pools. A church that seemed to float above the shimmering water of the pools.

Why such vast expense and elaborate construction? Continuing their excavations in the shadows of the Byzantine foundations, beneath the church's eastern end, the fathers found the scant remains of an ancient temple, a healing sanctuary of the god Aesclepius. Dating to the second century AD, this temple had been sufficiently famous in the Roman city of that time to make an appearance on its coins, represented as a typical little Roman temple. Here too, the fathers found fragmentary small carvings made of marble: *ex votos*, testimonials of the sick, little symbols of their illnesses and offerings to the gods who cured them, such as are commonly found by archaeologists on similar sites throughout the Roman Empire. Deeper yet, beneath the temple floor, the fathers found the ruins of an older, simpler healing shrine; it held five small ritual baths with stairways leading down into the healing waters situated round a small central piazza. A place, where for centuries, the sick had came to meet and to be cured. The Byzantines had built their church precisely on a pagan hospital beside a pool. Right away the fathers were reminded of John's story of Jesus visiting Bethesda; for those five plastered baths were certainly in use in Jesus' time.

Many of the details of John's story fitted well with this place. The 'troubled' water moving when the healing spirit manifested itself, a well-known phenomenon at Roman healing temples, was activated here by an occasional spring which ran erratically at the little sanctuary, and ran red, from natural iron oxides in the water dissolved from the surrounding rock. The man's complaint to Jesus that he could not reach the healing waters was also borne out by the architecture of the five small shrines, whose steps are steep and curved. Even Jesus' command to 'Rise, take up thy bed, and walk' is not only a biblical phrase but as archaeologists had often found, was part of a common form of healing in the Greek and Roman world. Sometimes *ex votos* took the form of stones or other objects that had been successfully lifted by the paralysed, then dedicated to the god, a tradition that is still common today in many Christian sanctuaries, where offerings of beds and crutches or silver *ex votos* stand testimony to answered prayers.

The excavations even seemed to solve a major puzzle of the Bible story. John's Gospel describes the pool of Bethesda as having five porches, information that hardly corresponds with the excavated archaeological remains of the provincial Roman Empire, when pools shaped in the pattern of pentagons are unknown. Take St Anne's two great pools as a single unit divided by the huge stone wall and you have a rectangle with five sides, with five porches as the Gospel says.

Was this Bethesda? Did Jesus visit the pagan sanctuary,

BELOW: *Part of the second-century AD ruins of a sanctuary of Aesclepius, the traditional Greek god of healing. The traditional name of Aesclepius' sanctuaries, 'The House of Mercy,' may also be reflected in the Hebrew word Bethesda — the name that the site now bears. Such Greek healing sanctuaries were often erected on traditional sites that were anciently connected with hospitals and healing. In this instance perhaps, the place where the Bible tells us, Jesus performed a miraculous cure.*

ABOVE: *Two Dominican fathers, Vincent and Abel surveying the fabric of the Holy Sepulchre in the years before the First World War. Many Christian archaeologists such as Louis Vincent have dedicated their lives to archaeology and conservation in the Holy Land and left us an extraordinary legacy of a century and more of careful excavation records. Though much of this work has served to disprove many of the sites traditionally venerated as the holy places of the Bible, a remarkable picture of real-life Roman Palestine has also emerged to underline the basic accuracy of most of the New Testament's topography.*

now behind St Anne's, to heal the sick? The notion seems sensible enough, a hospital is a reasonable enough place to find people who are ill and the White Friars who administer St Anne's have claimed this explanation to be the truth.

Some Franciscan archaeologists, however, from the Roman Catholic office that oversees the Holy Land, protest that the Lord would never have visited such a pagan place. The Dominican Fathers, on the other hand, who excavated the healing shrines are more circumspect, preferring to address traditional literary arguments about the Gospel, discussing the possible meanings of the word 'Bethesda' and the like. They propose the site simply as a possibility, that it could be Bethesda. None of this debate bothers an increasing number of pilgrims who come to the ruins to pray and sing and, by the laying on of hands, experience the most ancient type of healing.

Writings of the early church show that the traditional site of Bethesda and Jesus' miracle beside St Anne's was also known to them. Visited and venerated for centuries, with the bed of the 'impotent man' prominently displayed, it functioned as a place of healing. By the fourth century AD though, a hundred years or so before the Byzantines built their vast church, a bishop was warning that the healing grotto, then in use for at least six centuries, was a wicked pagan place. If the astonishing Byzantine church so carefully and so elaborately fitted above a pagan grotto had indeed been intended to mark Jesus' miracle at Bethesda, then it had enclosed a holy Christian site and obliterated a pagan sanctuary at a single stroke!

There are of course, too many 'ifs' in all of this for archaeology; too much ambiguity and too few facts. What the excavations by St Anne's have shown, however, and underlined for us, is the extraordinary precision of the New Testament's descriptions of Jesus' Palestine. Other excavations in Nazareth and Galilee and Bethlehem and at Jerusalem, all confirmed the extraordinary accuracy of detail in the New Testament's description of early first-century Palestine. Whoever wrote the Gospels had intimate knowledge of the land of Jesus' life and times.

Does archaeology then, prove the book?

Would the excavation of the Berlin Wall prove the existence of James Bond? Of course not. It would though, confirm that James Bond's author knew and understood something of the landscapes of the Cold War, and that might well help future archaeologists as they sieve through the strata of the twentieth century. Only the most circular of arguments, however, would pretend that it had proven the physical existence of the hero.

None the less, after a century and a half of excavation, a tension, an expectation, has grown up around the Gospels and archaeology. This is utterly irreconcilable; one cannot prove the other because they are two entirely different entities: the New Testament is a narrative, not an archaeological report. Its rich circumstantial detail which archaeology continually confirms is the very antithesis of its tales of miracles and the stories about the Son of God, narratives that bend and break the laws of science. And that, surely is the point; just when archaeology, when fact and faith appear to move together they always slide apart: their resolution invites a leap of faith.

The Burden of Proof

ALK THROUGH THE SPLENDID GALLERIES of Jerusalem's Rockefeller Museum and the careful rows of contrasting, catalogued, anonymous pots provide a very different history of the Holy Land than does the Bible. What information does the archaeological past provide for us, beneath its labels? Very few stories; archaeologists excavate data. Hardly ever do they find evidence of ancient individual narratives. The greater part of the archaeological past adds up to random assemblages of buried and broken objects; at best they represent a series of fragmented snapshots of bits of ancient peoples' lives, people usually, with no names or histories.

And what of Jesus in all of this; what should science be expected to provide for us concerning his life and times? Quite simply, if any traces of this particular itinerant preacher were found in excavation it would be a statistical miracle of archaeology; the name of the Roman provincial governor, the powerful Pontius Pilate, is preserved but once in all of Palestine. Yet it would be wrong to think of the science of archaeology and belief in the Bible simply as a collision of faith and stony science. Like faith, archaeology has its own belief systems that often change more rapidly than theology; systems that make their own distinctive narratives.

In Palestine, it all began at Tell el Hesi. For thirty years or so after Petrie's pioneering six-week dig on that tell, archaeologists in Palestine used his dating systems and his labels, 'Amorite' and 'Early', 'Middle' and 'Late Jewish'. Soon though, the pots became the names of periods of history that with their strata and their evidence of destruction, abandonment and plenty, enabled archaeologists to write pseudo-historical narratives from their excavations, as if they were retelling written ancient histories.

Most archaeologists, however, were unhappy with Petrie's 'Early' and 'Middle Jewish' labels. Virtually all archaeologists working in the Holy Land look to the Bible, and the Bible tells that Israel took the Holy Land from the Canaanites. Better then, it seemed to them, to call the two ceramic types not 'Jewish' but 'Canaanite', a change that appeared to place the arrival of Israel in its Promised Land. Slowly, with the Bible's aid, the archaeological narrative was growing. Looking further afield, to tie Palestine closer into ancient history, some archaeologists also imported foreign terminologies into ancient Palestine. And all the time, as is their wont, archaeologists argued about their respective dates.

Following the First World War, Palestine became a British Mandate and a Department of Antiquities was established whose director was John Garstang, one of Petrie's pupils. He convened a meeting with three other eminent archaeologists: a French Dominican, an American professor and an English vicar. Together they decided that the archaeology of the

Holy Land should adopt the anonymous, less loaded terminology long used in Europe, that of Thomsen's Iron, Bronze and Stone Age, with suitable subdivisions of Early, Middle and Late, yet subdivided further by numbers and by letters. Now you could excavate a pot in Palestine of the Early Bronze Age, section four, subsection a, or EB IV a, in short. The system was soon adopted in the Rockefeller Museum where innocent visitors looking for pottery from the age of David or Jesus were suitably nonplussed; this after all was science, not theology.

Slowly, however, there emerged another problem. The excavated past was not as pat as scientific system seemed to imply. In an age before mass production, the potters who had obligingly supplied these sequences sometimes varied their output. A vast proliferation of letters and numbers began to grow around the pretty pots. Archaeologists spent longer arguing about changing their classifications than they did in excavation. Palestinian archaeology was divided into different schools, each with its own labelling systems. Many archaeologists observed that the Three Age System was itself too blunt a tool with which to unpick the complexities of the Holy Land. Neither did it differentiate between the Bronze Ages of Egypt, Syria and Palestine, which were, obviously entirely different cultures.

Following the Arab-Israeli Wars, control over archaeology in the Holy Land largely passed to Israel, whose archaeologists wished neither to use the old labels of the British Mandate, nor the simplicities of Petrie. Proposals were made to return to local terminologies and that Thomsen's Three Age System be abandoned. Although ancient Israel was not well attested in the archaeological record, and although Solomon and David have no archaeological existence at all, such terms became commonplace again. A system was proposed in which the Bronze Age became the Canaanite Age, and the Iron Age became the Israelite Age 'to faithfully reflect,' it was asserted, 'the two most significant periods in the history of this country (ie. modern Israel) within the Near Eastern and biblical milieu' – a system accepted by those sympathetic to the politics of modern Israel, yet rejected by those who noted that even the Bible told that the Israelites had only held the high ground in their Holy Land, and to dub the cultures of the seaside plains as 'Israelite' was to abolish the ancient history of the modern Palestinians – the descendants of the Canaanites. Whether it describes material progress, like Thomsen's Three Age System, or biblical divisions such as Canaanite and Israelite, archaeology somehow makes its own narratives from the silent past.

Just like faith then, archaeology has its own built-in belief systems that change as rapidly as theology. The difference is that these changes are not argued out in churches in the name of God, but in universities and government departments, and for a wide variety of causes.

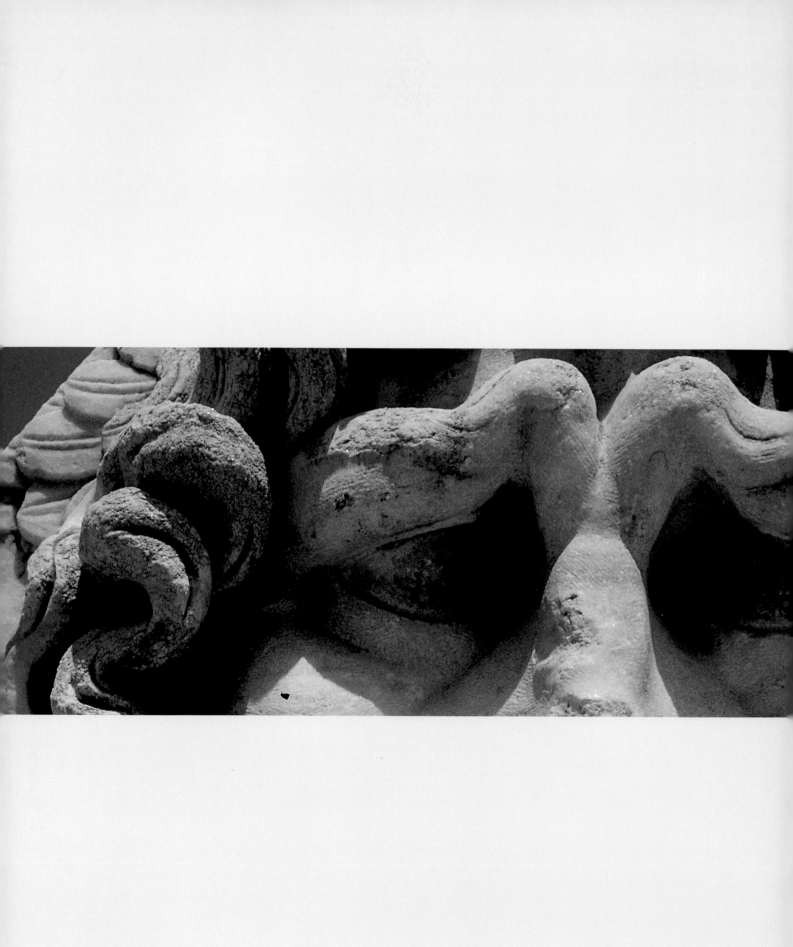

PART IV

Looking for the One Beginning

✳ Pyramids in the Jungle. Stevens and Catherwood at Palenque ✳
✳ Il Zócolo. Mexico City: 1792. An Unwanted Past ✳
✳ Explaining Civilisation. Tylor and Christy in Mexico: 1856 ✳
✳ Petrie at Nagada: 1894. Egypt and the Dawn of History ✳
✳ Sumer and the Dawn of History ✳
✳ Breasted and the Rockefellers. Chicago and the Ancient Orient ✳
✳ Henri Frankfort, Bonded Brick and Senator McCarthy ✳
✳ Mars Attacks? Pacal and Tutankhamun ✳
✳ American Firsts. The Valley of Oaxaca: 1966–81 ✳

Pyramids in the Jungle. Stevens and Catherwood at Palenque: 1839

I N JUNE 1839, A LITTLE GROUP OF MEN — AN ENGLISHMAN, a North American and their guides and bearers — were cutting their slow way through the jungles of South Mexico. They had been travelling for months and were searching now for the legendary city of Palenque. They had already found many ruined cities in the rainforests and over the next two years, they would find many more. 'Cities,' the North American Stevens, would later write, 'like shattered barks in a green ocean, their masts gone, their names lost, their crews perished and none to tell from whence they came.'

John Lloyd Stevens, from New Jersey, was a clever, widely travelled extrovert, a best-selling author with a passion for archaeology. The Englishman, Frederick Catherwood was a much quieter person, a moderately successful architect and a brilliant draftsman who had spent some fifteen years planning and drawing the monuments of ancient Egypt and the Holy Land. They had met in Leicester Square in London, where Catherwood had set up a 360° painting of the city of Jerusalem, a popular Victorian entertainment called a Panorama, the nineteenth-century version of the IMAX cinema. Despite their different temperaments, Stevens and Catherwood had much in common. Both had spent long years in the Middle

LEFT: *The central area of the ancient jungle city of Palenque, cleared now of the enveloping forest the Mayans called the 'great sea'. The pyramid on the left of the picture holds the tomb believed to be that of Pacal, a sixth-century Mayan ruler of Palenque, who governed when the vast city was at its height.*

PREVIOUS PAGE: *The furrowed brow of Apollo from a sculpture at his temple at Didyma on the western coast of Turkey. One of the wonders of the Greek world, Apollo's temple has been uncovered and restored over the past century by French and German archaeologists.*

ABOVE: *Catherwood's grand lithograph of the so-called 'House of the Governor,' at the Mayan city of Uxmal. Catherwood twice collapsed from malarial fever whilst he was at Uxmal; on one occasion Stevens found him unconscious by his easel. This drawing was made on their return to that city, after their first trip had been abandoned due to illness.*

East amongst its ancient monuments, and both had experienced the discomforts and dangers of exotic exploration. In days when lengthy travel books were widely popular and lithography the preferred means of book illustration, such an experienced combination of a successful writer and a brilliant draftsman was a publisher's dream

It was Catherwood who had first shown Stevens a book on the Central American jungle cities. From the beginning, both men were intrigued and set their sights on Yucatan, that perpendicular peninsula framing the southern end of the Bay of Mexico. Over the next few years, from 1836, when Catherwood first visited New York and renewed their friendship, they carefully planned an elaborate Central American expedition, both as a pleasure and as a business venture. They would write large books together, collect what antiquities they could and purchase ancient buildings to ship to New York for public exhibition.

On their arrival at Palenque, they set up house in the building that is called the Palace. They had already realised, of course, that these ancient buildings were so vast and so complex that their removal to America was well beyond their means. None the less, when given the opportunity to purchase a jungle city, Stevens had bought the vast ruins of the City of Copán from its owner for just $50 US, the archaeological bargain of all time. These cities looked very different then than they do today. In 1839, like every other monument, the Palace of Palenque was smothered in the engulfing rainforest which, as Stevens wrote, 'needed cutting at every fresh trip of the visitor'.

High in the stuccoed white vaults of the Palace, Stevens and Catherwood saw the sooty graffiti of earlier travellers, one of whom they had known; he had been hacked to death in the previous year whilst asleep in his hammock. Life in the rainforest was hard, and the unpredictable and frightened tribesmen were not their only hazard. As Stevens scribbled away and Catherwood measured and drew the temples, it rained constantly and was very hot. After a few weeks in the Palace all their possessions were mildewed and rusted. Even their matches did not work; Stevens tells us that he caught fireflies in a jar to light his desk at night. They both had malarial fevers too, and were bitten by blood-sucking ticks. On top of this, Stevens' feet were attacked by chiggers, burrowing insect larvae that he had to cut out with a knife. Poisoned and unable to walk, he was forced to retreat to the relative comforts of San Domingo, a nearby town. On his return he found Catherwood still at work, 'gaunt, lame and swollen-faced, with his left arm hanging by his side'. The desperate journey though, was to continue for ten more months before a near-lethal bout of fever forced them to abandon the adventure and retreat by steamer to New York, where Stevens wrote the most famous of all his books. *Incidents of Travel; in Central America, Chiapas and Yucatan* is a dreamlike mix of archaeology and the prose of pure adventure set with grim officials and jovial priests in shining jungles. And always on this epic journey, they were accompanied by willing

ABOVE: *The sprawling building, the so-called 'palace' at Palenque, that accommodated Stevens and Catherwood and so many other early visitors, to that jungle city.*

BELOW:: *A small anonymous pyramid at Palenque, cleaned of the surrounding forest that still engulfs the greater part of this ancient city.*

Mayan Indians who took these two frail foreigners to the long-lost cities and carried them on their backs when they were fevered, bruised or simply just exhausted. In the following year, Stevens and Catherwood made a further trip into the dripping forests. All in all, in these two adventures between 1839 and 1842, they visited nearly a hundred lost Mayan sites, including fourteen major ancient cities. It was the first time that the Central American past had been observed in a serious and modern-minded way. In a series of splendidly illustrated books, they showed their researches to the world and Mayan archaeology was born.

From the beginning, the single biggest question that these cities raised was this; who on earth had made these pyramids and palaces in the jungle? When had they been built? Where had their owners come from? Where had they gone?

As to their origins, at the beginning of their work, Stevens and Catherwood were independently 'struck by a comparison with Egypt'. After a time, however, they saw that the people pictured in the ancient monuments shared much with the indigenous people of the rainforest with whom they were in daily contact, from physical characteristics to religious observances. The monuments, Stevens and Catherwood concluded, were built by the 'ancestors of the present inhabitants'.

As to their age, Stevens simply noted that they were 'probably' older than the Spanish conquest of Mexico of 1519, though by how much, no one had any idea. Many people who read Stevens and Catherwood's books were unconvinced by their observations. In the nineteenth century, few people really believed that native jungle dwellers — 'savages' — could ever have built such marvels. Not surprisingly, the sceptics' answers to the questions of origin and age were traditionally European.

People proposed that the jungle cities were relics of travellers who had come to the New World from the Old; the Lost Tribes of Israel perhaps, or boatloads of ancient Egyptians with the plans for making pyramids. And such opinions still have currency today of course, inspiring a raft of pseudo-scholarship from von Däniken's theories about visitations from outer space to a wide variety of New Age speculation. Despite the fact that these crackpot theories are usually created in ignorance of historical fact, their origins, the basic theory of the diffusion of ancient knowledge, goes back to the very roots of scientific archaeology. When, a century or more ago, archaeologists first posed such questions, they too were looking for the 'one beginning' of all the civilisations on the earth.

BELOW: *One of the rare reliefs that still survives in the temples of Palenque. Protected from ancient times by the architecture and foliage, many of these reliefs were destroyed in fires lit by early travellers to free the monuments from the profusion of the jungle.*

RIGHT: *'Idol at Copán,' the first magnificent plate, one of twenty-five, in an album published by Catherwood and printed by his old friend Owen Jones. Thirteen of these great stelae still stood in the centre of the Mayan city of Copán, which Stevens, with an eye for a bargain, had bought in its entirety, for just $50. 'Copán may be called the City of Idols,' writes Catherwood. 'It stands on the bank of a river, and was surrounded by walls; that on the riverside is still, in places, from sixty to ninety feet in height. The remains of a vast temple, or collection of sacred edifices, lie scattered about, together with innumerable fragments of mutilated ornaments and statues.'*

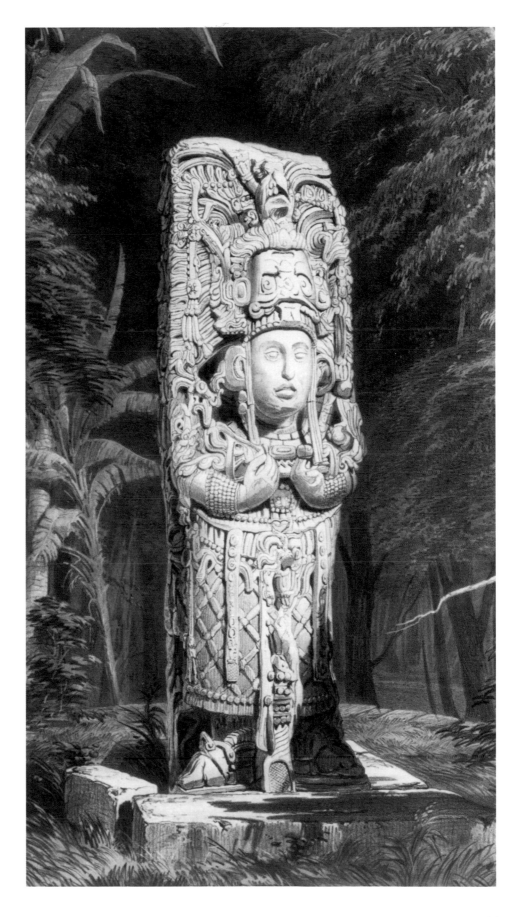

Il Zócolo, Mexico City: 1792
An Unwanted Past

T WO VAST, CARVED BLOCKS OF STONE came to light in 1792, as new drains were being excavated in the main square of Mexico City, called the Zócolo. They were an epitome of the public image that the Aztecs had left for us. One was a clever, circular diagram, a subtle yearly calendar as intricate as clockwork; the other was a colossus representing a decapitated goddess with two snakes for a face and a necklace of human skulls. The two stones, weighty survivors from a frightening past, caused an immediate sensation. The scholar who first studied them, claimed them as most ancient relics of the nation, explaining their significance and purposes by reference to the centuries-old texts of Christian missionaries who, in the wake of conquistador Hernan Cortés' invasion in the sixteenth century, had worked for the Spanish church in Mexico and recorded pagan customs. The civic authorities, however, viewed them with unease as potent symbols of the old religions.

ABOVE AND BELOW: *The two great stones unearthed by drain diggers in central Mexico City in 1792 were drawn by the Mexican historian Antonio de León y Gama a few years later. The upper stone is a circular calendar, the lower, a 'devilish image,' as the Dominican fathers called the goddess, the veritable Aztec Gorgon, Coatlicue.*

Consider the extraordinary history of this Zócolo, the splendid square at the centre of modern Mexico under which these two great blocks had lain for centuries. Once it was the heart of the city of Tenochtitlán, which had been founded by the Aztecs in 1325 after a long migration from the legendary ancestral Aztec homelands. At its height a century later, the huge stone city radiating from this central plaza, controlled an empire covering more than half of modern Mexico. On 13 August 1521, however, after eighteen months of siege and murder, Cortés and his regiments destroyed the Aztec empire and he built his own palace on the Zócolo, above the palace of the Aztec emperors. This is where the Palacio Nacional now stands, with its revolutionary murals by Diego Rivera. At right angles to it stands the Spanish-styled Metropolitan Cathedral and its sacristy, part-built of stone taken from the Aztec pyramids and temples that once stood on the site. Now, as the cathedral's architecture splits and cracks with uneven subsidence, you are again reminded of the bases of the ancient pyramids beneath, on whose remains the high colonial buildings partly stand.

When Cortés' small army had first arrived in Tenochtitlán they were greeted by a friendly emperor, but saw appalling spectacles of mass sacrifice reeking with the stench of rancid human blood. Later, however, after Cortés' commanders had murdered most of the Aztec court, they built their houses directly above the sanctuary and the skull racks of the Eagle Warriors, an élite core of the Aztec armies. Some of the Spanish officers who lived in these dwellings were later themselves executed in the Zócolo for high treason, hung and quartered in the traditional European manner.

In later centuries, the central square served as a marketplace next to the cathedral, a lively meeting place framed in grandiose European architecture. It was as if the Aztec temples

ABOVE: *Cortés' map of Tenochtitlán. 'The city,' wrote the admiring Spaniard, 'is big and remarkable. . .and much larger than Granada and much stronger, with good buildings and many more people than Granada. . .'*

underneath, with their bloody steps and sacrifices, and the murders and burnings of the Spanish invaders were so horrible a memory that everyone decided to forget the past.

And that is why perhaps, in 1792 those two great stones which just two centuries before had witnessed the arrival of Cortés and his regiments, had been greeted with such dismay. Not knowing what to do with them, the civic authority ordered them to be reburied at the university, lest they re-ignite paganism in the population. Ten years later, when the Prussian scholar Alexander von Humboldt arrived in Mexico City on his voyage of discovery, the two great stones had to be re-excavated so that he could see and study them. 'I would not have been able to examine them at all,' Humboldt said, 'had not the Bishop of Monterey listened to my plea and asked the rector of the university to have them dug up again.'

Humboldt's Europe, enlightenment Europe, in which modern archaeology was born, would not let the past stay buried. By the 1840s, Stevens, Catherwood and archaeology had arrived in the New World, along with Darwinism and a host of natural scientists, following in Humboldt's footsteps.

What though was this brave new world of Western scholarship to make of such a vivid and entirely alien past? Most of the first European visitors to the New World found the cultures there terrifying and only part-explained in terms of traditional European stereotypes of noble savages, witches, virgins, cannibals and kings. This was the frightening past, indeed, that Cortés had brought to a spectacular end. The single most curious thing, however, was that to early archaeologists this past, though comparatively recent, had taken place in a Stone Age; a Stone Age that had built rich architecture and maintained noble courts with kings and calendars and written histories. This then, was a past that all at once was savage and sophisticated, complex, contradictory and completely alien. 'When Cortés walked in Mexico,' one archaeologist wrote, 'he walked in an age comparable with ancient Egypt or Mesopotamia. It was as if Tutankhamun, his queens and courtiers and servants, rose up and offered the Conquistadors a cup of tea.'

How could such astonishing cultures, the Aztecs, the Maya and the rest, ever be fitted into Europe's comfortable and nicely ordered history of ancient Egypt, Greece and Rome?

ABOVE: *One of the so-called tzompantli altars that stand beside the precinct of the Eagle Warriors in the ruins of Tenochtitlán, discovered by Eduardo Matos Moctezuma in the late 1970s as part of his extensive excavation at the heart of modern Mexico City.*

ABOVE: *Sculptures left by the Aztecs at the great pyramid temple of Huitzilopochtli, now at the centre of Mexico City.*

LEFT: *The courtyard of the Eagle Warriors, an Aztec fighting clan. Some of Cortés' commanders later set up their own headquarters here.*

Explaining Civilisation. Tylor and Christy in Mexico: 1856

I N 1856, TWO ENGLISH QUAKERS, Mr Tylor and Mr Christy, travelled to Mexico to study some of the ancient cultures they had first seen in the books of Catherwood and Stevens. In their different ways, they were both great travellers – one of them engaged upon a lifelong search for the moral roots of humankind, the other in gathering information on all the peoples of the world, to form into universal theories.

They had first met in Cuba on a Havana tram. Henry Christy, the elder of the two, was a wealthy banker who had travelled around the world, writing books about India and China on the way, and bringing back to London the towels he had used in steam baths in Istanbul, the well-known 'Christy towels'. Seven years after his Mexican trip he would become world famous for his prehistoric excavations in the Vézère Valley which he financed and undertook with the great French prehistorian Lartet (*see pages 42–45*).

Edward Burnett Tylor was twenty-four when he arrived in Mexico, fleeing, on his doctor's advice, from incipient tuberculosis. Christy's companionship would help inspire his life-long enquiries into the foundations of human society. In the course of the next half-century, Tylor would become one of the world's greatest anthropologists, a man so vital to that science's academic progress, that in his lifetime it was sometimes known as 'Mr Tylor's (later Sir Edward Tylor's) science'.

Tylor's anthropology was a lucid synthesis of the ideas of many different scholars of the day. It proposed a kind of social Darwinism, a series of stages through which all humankind had passed on its way to civilisation. In the process of its explanation, Tylor virtually invented the definition of a 'savage' as an individual who was not necessarily violent or cruel as earlier meanings of the word implied, but simply an amoral person at an 'early' stage of human development on the path towards the civilisation of nineteenth-century Europe.

Tylor saw three basic stages in this progress; his savages were transformed into barbarians who in their turn, were civilised by city life and moral progress. In its archaeological dimension, it was proposed that this same pattern could be seen in the technological progressions from the Stone Age to the Bronze Age and on to the modern Age of Iron. A similar philosophical progression, Tylor later, and rather cynically, proposed, was the transformation of magic to religion and religion finally into its apotheosis – science!

Tylor's influential anthropology also taught that living examples of every stage of this long evolution were available for study right across the world. From familial relationships to court etiquette, all human institutions could be traced back to suitably 'primitive' beginnings. On Tylor's scale of human achievement, the Aztecs and their ancestors might first appear to be quite 'primitive'. Indigenous Mexico after all, had never 'progressed' beyond the Stone Age. At the same time, such beautiful and complex ancient monuments as those that Stevens and Catherwood had studied, suggested to many archaeologists that these vanished societies had been far more 'advanced' than any of their European counterparts.

It was all very puzzling and the observations of previous archaeologists were of little help. Captain Guillaume Dupaix, for example, a late eighteenth-century explorer in Mexico, a Bourbon soldier who had excavated both at Palenque and Pompeii, was so entirely bewildered by the former, so baffled by what he had seen in the rainforests, that even a description of Palenque's architecture had been beyond his powers. Even John Lloyd Stevens' sensible observation that the deserted cities had been made by the ancestors of the present inhabitants of Yucatan carried little weight; contemporary scientific opinion suggested that due to a lack of wheat for bread-making and large animals to roast, indigenous Americans would have been physically unable to build such monuments of stone. Neither did Stevens' observations begin to explain why, after building these astonishing memorials, the same people then abandoned and forgot them, and chose to live in simple huts in clearings in the jungle.

Tylor had an answer to the problem; an answer that was ultimately based on his deep personal belief in the unity of the human race, which had evolved, he thought, like a tree with many branches from a single trunk. A single trunk, one single beginning, for all of civilisation. Phenomena such as the Mexican pyramids, Tylor proposed, came about from short circuits across the branches of his evolutionary tree; short circuits in which more 'advanced' peoples from one branch visited the less 'advanced' on another, carrying plans for pyramids perhaps, and calendars, bows and arrows, even perhaps, notions of gods and fire. Tylor's theories were quickly taken up and amplified by a large number of lesser scholars. Somewhere, so their scenario went, somewhere in the distant past, ancient American 'primitives' had been presented with some disparate elements of a more 'advanced' civilisation by a group of people who may well have stayed to rule them for a while, but then had disappeared, leaving the forest to take over once again. This crossing of natural resources and foreign influence, this 'diffusion' of cultures, for that is what the process came to be called, accounted for ancient American pyramids and the courtly cultures that accompanied them.

In an age of exploration and empire-building, such an analysis of foreign cultures that appeared to Europeans to be both savage and sophisticated at one and the same time, seemed to make them easy to understand and certainly less frightening. It was also a most useful model for colonial administrators, for their work could now be explained as the last of a series of evolutionary short circuits by which 'primitive' people were brought into the light.

Diffusionism also inspired one of the burning questions of late nineteenth- and early twentieth-century archaeology: where precisely had world civilisation begun? Where had fire and architecture, pyramids and kingship been born? In the first age of patenting and industrial process, it seemed inconceivable that metal smelting, the bow and arrow or even the baking of bread could have had more than one inventor. The concept of diffusionism therefore, led many archaeologists to search for the source; to search for the one beginning. Just at this same time, some Middle Eastern archaeologists were beginning to suspect that somewhere in the ancient east there had once been a civilisation older even, than that of Pharaoh's Egypt.

Petrie at Nagada: 1894. Egypt and the Dawn of History

I N 1893 FLINDERS PETRIE WAS EXCAVATING on the east bank of the Nile in Upper Egypt, in the enormous temple enclosure of the ancient city of Coptos, behind the town of Quft. Coptos had guarded a long desert valley leading from the Nile to the Red Sea and Petrie was searching for evidence of a race of invaders who had entered most ancient Egypt from the east and established the pharaonic state. A theory, one of many of the time, composed, almost unconsciously perhaps, in the common vocabulary of 'Mr Tylor's science'.

As usual, Petrie was lucky in his digging, excavating three enormous un-Egyptian statues from the ruined sanctuary of a very ancient temple, strange figures with Red Sea seashells drawn along their bases, hinting precisely at the connections he had anticipated. In the evening after work, local people would often bring Petrie small antiquities hoping that he would buy them. At Quft he noticed these included ceramics of several types he had never seen before; shiny, hard and well-made pots, although never fashioned on a wheel, sometimes decorated in strange patterns and sometimes shining with a distinctive, hard, black finish. They came, the villagers told him, from the other side of the river and there were many more buried in the desert beyond the fields.

As the season progressed, Petrie often visited the other bank of the Nile, the western shore where the ancient Egyptians traditionally buried their dead, walking the desert, searching for the cemeteries of ancient Coptos. He knew that the ancient city cemeteries often lay at the end of ancient causeways that ran from the riverside straight into the desert. Sometimes too, they were marked by prominent natural features in the line of cliffs that fringed the river valley; a gap in the skyline perhaps, or a mountain standing by itself. Both these features were present on the western bank.

Petrie found many things on this desert survey: the accumulated residue of thousands of years of human life beside the Nile; some ancient tombs; a small temple whose hieroglyph-covered blocks were still buried in the sand; even a rough pyramid made of loose flints. What engaged him most though, were the large amounts of potsherds similar to those the villagers had brought to him in Quft. And as the low evening light grazed the surface of the desert, his excavator's eye perceived the subtle outlines of two vast cemeteries, still buried and untouched. Most puzzling was that even at the centre of these cemeteries, there were none of the usual ancient ruins of burial chapels and little altars, just the shallowest of indentations marking the grave pits, and everywhere, 'strewn potsherds on the surface'.

The following year he returned to the west bank with Hilda, his wife, and a full expedition staff – archaeologists to supervise the excavations and young draftsmen to number, clean and draw the antiquities they excavated. First Petrie divided the expedition into two halves, each with its own encampment and work force, equipped to excavate one cemetery apiece. Then, engaging the best of the workmen from his previous dig at Coptos, he built an expedition house, a simple row of cells, one for each member of his staff and two large halls to hold the men from Quft.

They started work in late December 1894 and were soon deluged by the sheer amount of antiquity they found; in five months, they would excavate nearly 3000 graves, as well as the little temple and two small ancient settlements. The centres of attention though, were the enigmatic and enormous ancient burial grounds. Petrie named the cemetery he would excavate after a nearby town famed for its fiery distillations of date wine and fine weaving, and so it is called today – the cemetery of Nagada. After its excavation, its irregular grave-pits, from two to six feet deep, give the impression of an antique no-man's-land beneath the blue hills of the valley's edge.

Day after day, the work was constant and precise. First, local villagers would clear the loose sand from the desert surface, stopping when they came across the edge of one of the grave pits that were cut into the hard mass of sand and pebbles of the desert floor. Then Petrie's Quftis – his workmen from Quft – would take over, clearing the pit of sand and pebbles and finally, with small knives and brushes, lay bare the ancient skeletons and their grave goods. Petrie or his assistant Ali el-Suefi, an Egyptian villager who had worked with him from his first years in Egypt, usually oversaw the careful Quftis, a process aided by Petrie's elaborate system of rewards and punishments for those who protected small precious objects from unwanted attentions and theft or damaged objects from the burials. So complete a course of archaeology was this, so practical and so intensive, that these same men were soon renowned throughout the Middle East as the finest of all archaeological excavators. To this day, some of their descendants are the backbones of many a Middle Eastern excavation, gently teaching callow foreigners the subtle art of excavation in the East.

After the graves had been cleaned, Petrie would go down into them and make a record of

BELOW: *Petrie's first working diagram of the 'Sequence Dating System' made from a careful statistical analysis of the pottery from the graves at Nagada. Following closely upon Pitt River's observations on similar processes of 'evolution' and 'degradation' in material he had found on Cranbourne Chase, Petrie's method of ordering the vast quantity of Nagada pottery has since been claimed as archaeology's sole original contribution to statistical analysis – and Petrie himself as one of the outstanding applied mathematicians of the nineteenth century.*

ABOVE: *Broken pottery from Petrie's excavations still lying on the stony desert wash of Nagada's great cemetery.*

their contents. Then he would clear all the objects from the tomb, work that took, he later recorded, between thirty minutes for smaller tombs to three hours or so for elaborate and multiple burials. The little drawings that he made, diagrams and pencilled notes in a series of small black notebooks have been described as minor masterpieces and are fundamental records of Egyptian archaeology.

This is the more remarkable when the sheer pressure of daily work is taken into account. All in all, Petrie's little team excavated more than 30,000 pots, some of them very large and still filled with their ancient contents of plaster, beeswax, sometimes animal and plant remains, and often weighing thirty pounds or more. Simply lifting them six feet to the desert surface, Petrie noted, in the salty sand, soon produced horny hands that split and bled.

Every evening the expedition members numbered and recorded the day's finds, which they then stacked around their little expedition house. Not only were there veritable fields of pots, but human bones as well, and stacked so high around the doorways of the house that their rooms became difficult to access. Inside each bedroom too, there were other objects under the beds, in heaps across the floor, piled on rough shelves; flat black palettes made of slate and shaped, sometimes into vigorous animal designs, fine flint knives, simple jewellery, ivory pins and combs. As Petrie had long since realised, the cemetery was best emptied of its ancient occupants and artefacts, for antiquities dealers followed hard upon the excavators' heels in those days, plundering everything that the archaeologists left untouched.

At the ending of the work at Nagada, Petrie's little team packed 300 crates of pottery to take away to Cairo, then after a few fine pieces had been selected for the National

Museum, the bulk was sent on to London, Chicago and Berlin, Philadelphia and Cambridge, along with seventy crates of bones and skulls as well. A great believer in the general theory of diffusion, Petrie also shared a belief common to his time that racial, and therefore cultural change could be studied by a comparison of skull measurements and even, in the general observation of human 'types' in sculpture and in painting.

Back home in Hampstead for the summer, Petrie wrote a brilliantly concise account of the excavation of the enigmatic cemeteries, setting a standard of archaeological recording in the Middle East that stood for decades and yet remains a vital volume to this day. At this same time he wrote one and a half volumes of a projected multi-volumed history of Egypt, collected an Honorary Doctorate of Literature from Edinburgh University and organised a petition, which was ultimately unsuccessful, against the building of the first Aswan Dam. Six months later he was back in Egypt, excavating again.

At Nagada, Petrie had posed the scholarly world a rare puzzle. He had found a culture never seen before. How old was it? Who had the people been who were buried in these cemeteries and what was their relationship to the pharaonic Egyptians? The graves had contained nothing recognisably ancient Egyptian in them. No writing either. Unlettered and with their bodies set in strange positions, curled up like babies in the womb, these mysterious people seemed to Petrie to be intruders, invaders in the Nile Valley. That the nearby small pharaonic temple which Petrie found and excavated had proved to be a temple of the god Seth, a god of foreigners and confusion, served to underline the theory; the god's identity reflecting in some 'primitive' way, as a Tylorian might have said, a half-memory of a genuine historical event. A few modest, intrusive ancient Egyptian burials in the cemetery were dated to around 1400 BC, which showed at least, that these unknown 'invaders' must have arrived at an earlier time than that.

Noting variations in skull size from typical burials in pharaonic cemeteries, Petrie proposed that the people buried in the Nagada cemeteries had been a 'New Race' in Egypt, a race that had sown havoc in Egypt at the end of the Pyramid Age. His theory however, was quickly disproved by a French archaeologist, Jacques de Morgan, who excavated a huge brick tomb close to the Nagada cemetery; a monument that Petrie's survey had missed. Like Petrie's cemetery, the tomb was of a previously unknown type. This time, however, it had writing in it; the crude hieroglyphs of a king whose name was close to that of the legendary Menes, the pharaoh who, so ancient Greek historians recorded, had been the first king of the first Dynasty of Egypt. This astonishing monument also contained large amounts of the same strange pottery that had filled Petrie's cemeteries, a fact that neatly and conclusively linked his 'New Race' to the first dynasties of ancient Egypt. At the same time, de Morgan's discovery also served to provide the occupants of Nagada cemetery with a name; they were now called, and quite correctly, simply 'pre-dynastic'.

ABOVE: *The open graves of Petrie's 'New Race' cemetery, near Nagada in Upper Egypt. Recent archaeology has shown that this cemetery was part of an elaborate series of mortuary complexes that served a huge town of the fourth millennium BC: a predecessor of pharaonic Egypt.*

Not used to being contradicted and usually well ahead of the academic game which he had impatiently described as 'log-rolling,' Petrie took some time to be convinced of the discoveries in the royal tomb. It was especially irritating to him that it had been a Frenchman who had come across the huge brick monument, especially one who headed the *Service des Antiquités d'Egypte*, which he mistrusted in all things. Then he was told that Professor Jacques de Morgan was the son of one Jack Morgan, a Welsh mining engineer, and this it seems, softened the blow.

Petrie still believed, however, that Nagada cemetery was populated with invaders whatever their date may have been, an idea he shared with most other archaeologists of the day. Earliest ancient Egypt, they now proposed, had been colonised by a new race with different-shaped skulls; people who, so Menes' great brick tomb suggested, had introduced writing and the skills of architecture into Egypt. In the common language of Mr Tylor's science, the 'primitive' dwellers by the Nile had been conquered by more advanced people from across the seas, who then formed the court and kingdom of pharaonic Egypt, the first nation state in all the world.

A single tell-tale cylindrical seal found by Petrie in a grave pit, a seal made to be rolled across the surface of wet mud to print an endless pattern in a line, hinted at the invaders' origins. The seal had been made in Mesopotamia. Had these ancient travellers come across the sea from the plain between the Tigris and the Euphrates? Had ancient Egypt then, the first Kingdom of the Bible, come from somewhere else? Had Mesopotamia been the birthplace of civilisation, the one beginning?

Sumer and the
Dawn of History

Ancient Sumer, the Mesopotamian culture so often described as the oldest in the world, was discovered in a German library in 1869. Studying a strange language inscribed on clay tablets from ancient Nineveh in north Iraq, the Assyriologist Jules Oppert realised that he was reading the records of a previously unknown civilisation, one that the ancient Assyrians had regarded as their most distant ancestor. Using part of an archaic phrase that the Assyrians themselves used as part of the royal title – 'King of Sumer and Akkad' – he named this lost culture 'Sumerian' and the archaeological notion of Sumeria was born.

A flat land of silt plains set between two great rivers, ancient Mesopotamia never had the resources to build large monuments of stone as had Egypt. What stone there was had been especially brought down into the great flat plain where it was carefully used to decorate large mud-brick palaces and civic architecture. Along with these vivid and exotic works of lapidary art, generations of European explorers had carried off thousands of ancient clay tablets. Their translation became the work of generations of scholars like Jules Oppert.

Following the naming of the Sumerians, various excavations working over the course of decades brought the ancient people slowly into focus. Thousands of their tablets were excavated from the deep dust of their ruined cities – Kish, Jemdet Nasr, Ur, Erech, Tutub and the rest. These Sumerians, it seemed, had been contemporaries of the early dynasties of pharaonic Egypt; they also seemed to have used writing before the ancient Egyptians had. Was this then, the world's first civilisation, from which all other cultures had diffused?

Ten years after Oppert named the Sumerians, an English scholar, the Reverend Arthur Sayce announced the discovery of another ancient civilisation, which he named the empire of the 'Hittites'. Sayce too, had conjured his ancient people from a mass of tablets brought back from the East. Just like the Sumerians, it was many years before the central cities of the Hittites were identified in Anatolia, their excavation undertaken, their own distinctive texts deciphered. These Hittites, it seemed, had been contemporary with the Theban Kings of Egypt, a millennium after the Sumerians had disappeared.

Slowly, throughout the final decades of the nineteenth century, a new picture of the ancient East was emerging. Unlike ancient Egypt, this new past was a complex place; a past of innumerable cities inhabited by many clever peoples, a past with rich literatures and a Babel of tongues, a past far older than the stories of the Book of Genesis which were partly set in this most ancient world and which, it was fast becoming clear, was partly based on some of the most profound and fundamental legends of the Sumerians. Was this then, where world civilisation had begun?

RIGHT: *Twelve Hittite gods, most beautifully sculpted on the natural rocks of the sanctuary of Yazilikaya, close to the Hittite capital of Hattusas, by modern Bogazkoy in central Anatolia. The sanctuary, and possible burial ground of the Hittite kings, Yazilikaya was at its height around the thirteenth century BC, when Hittite rulers fought and corresponded with the Egyptian kings. German archaeologists began work at Bogazkoy in 1906, and the Hittite language was deciphered a few years later.*

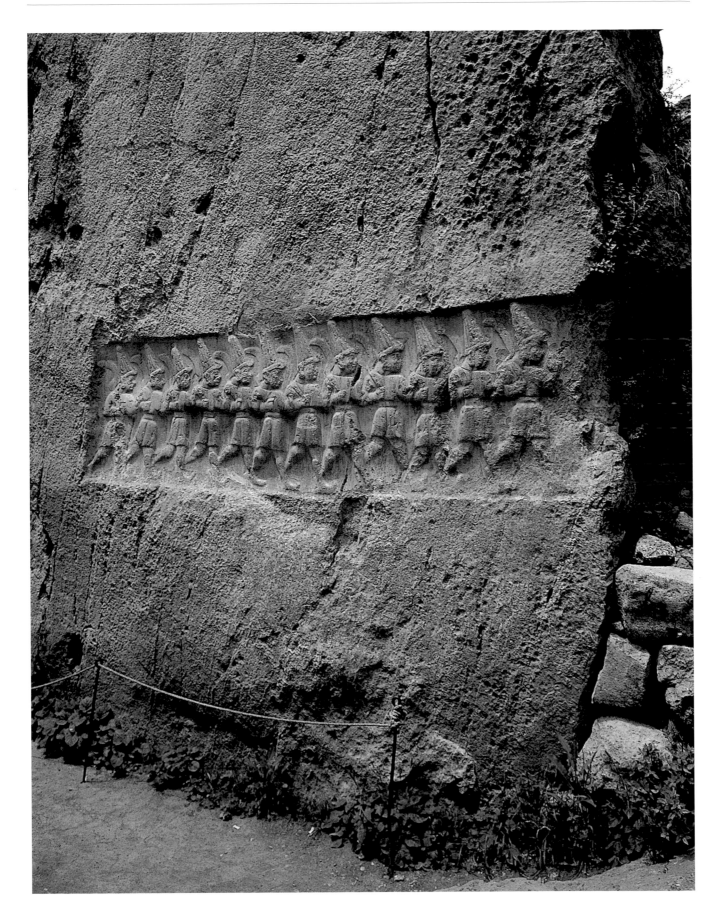

Breasted and the Rockefellers Chicago and the Ancient Orient

WHILE EXCAVATING THE CEMETERY at Nagada, Flinders Petrie was visited by Dr James Henry Breasted of the University of Chicago. A personable young Midwesterner on his first tour of the Middle East after his studies at Yale and Berlin, Breasted was destined to become one of the greatest of egyptologists and one of the finest advocates for archaeology the world has ever known. Though today his books are largely out of date, their mellifluous prose and intellectual span served to give them extraordinary resonance and influence. His five-volume translation of the historical texts of ancient Egypt, his splendid history of the pharaohs, his reflections on the 'dawn of conscience' and a clutch of lively text books, brought Breasted's personal vision of the ancient East to an entire generation of North Americans.

This though, was all in the future for the young man who observed Petrie working in the ancient cemetery. Petrie, he wrote in his diary, was genial, kindly and frugal, a forty-year-old as agile as a small boy who 'served a table so excruciatingly bad that only persons of iron constitutions could survive it'. A bohemian too, he recorded, and quite scandalously so, as far as Breasted's prim Midwestern companions were concerned.

Yet Breasted also saw a dedicated archaeologist working to his full capacities and achieving the very finest of results, he noted, for just $1500 US a season; a rare lesson on the value of careful archaeology which, at Nagada as in so many other sites, provided the world with exceptional historic information. Such archaeological precision in the field, followed by swift publication of material and a brilliant accompanying analysis, became a central theme of Breasted's public work which was to establish in the New World an institute dedicated to the study of the beginnings of civilisation in the Old World.

By 1919, Breasted was in a gloomy middle-age after twenty-five unrewarding years of teaching and penurious travelling for the purposes of personal study. He was also increasingly frustrated that he was utterly unable to embark upon a programme of archaeological exploration at the time when the Middle East was opening up to the West and its ancient

ABOVE: *James Henry Breasted, 1865–1935, the great Illinois egyptologist and fundraiser whose personal vision created the Oriental Institute of the University of Chicago, one of the leading centres of Middle Eastern archaeology.*

BELOW: *A doorjamb in the Imperial palace of Achaemenid Persia at Persepolis, burnt by Alexander the Great in 331 BC. Though outside his personal field of expertise, Breasted's great plan encompassed an archaeological programme of excavation and recording throughout the Middle East.*

monuments were suffering as never before. With little to lose, he broke a university rule and wrote to one of Rockefeller's senior advisors urging him to press the Rockefeller foundations for funding for American excavations and archaeological study in the Middle East. 'It is very distasteful to me to appear at all in such a crusade for funds. But do you not think I ought to do it, rather than to rust out during the last fifteen years of my life, thousands of miles away from the human records I ought to be saving and using?'

Breasted also wrote a long letter directly to his friend John D. Rockefeller Jr. In phrases Henry Christy would have been pleased to utter, and with a vocabulary that owed much to Tylor, the evangelising egyptologist observed that:

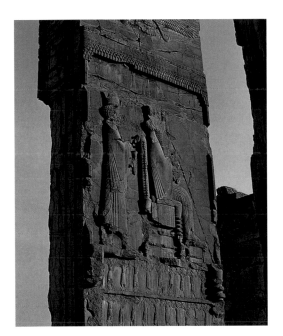

'…the noblest task in the study of man is to recover the story of the human career, which culminated in the emergence of a religion of divine fatherhood and human brotherhood…The materials out of which we can recover [the] lost chapters of the career of early man, lie scattered among the buried cities of the Near East. This whole region has just been delivered from Turkish misrule, and for the first time in history the birth-lands of religion and civilisation lie open to unobstructed study and research. In the entire history of knowledge, this is the greatest opportunity that has ever come for the study of man and his career.'

'The university teacher is as unable single-handed to cope with a situation like this, as would be the astronomer to study the skies without his observatory or his staff…A laboratory containing all the available early human records in systematically arranged archives is as necessary to a study of man's career as is an astronomical observatory with its files of observations and computations in the study of the career of the universe… The methods and the equipment of natural science should be applied to the study of man…'

'You are today one of the great forces in…social, economic and industrial history. The very principles of justice and fair treatment which you are so admirably applying…first grew up in the minds and hearts of men in that ancient world of the Near Orient around the eastern end of the Mediterranean…'

LEFT: *The remote Roman garrison city of Dura Europus in the Syrian desert on the banks of the Euphrates where, thanks to a telegram sent from Chicago, via Bombay and Basra, Breasted learned of the Rockefellers' decision to fund his schemes for excavating and recording the beginnings of world civilisation. That same day, 4 May 1920, Breasted also uncovered and photographed a series of ancient paintings in the ruins of Dura Europus that still stand as key monuments of the beginnings of Western art.*

After several months of waiting, Breasted was informed that John D. Rockefeller Jr. was indeed prepared to sponsor his dream and that same year, Breasted set out on an epic tour through the 'Fertile Crescent' – his own term for that vast arc of land that Abraham traversed on his journey from Iraq to Egypt. Breasted motored some 20,000 miles through wild and often dangerous country, meeting everyone from bandits to colonial administrators and always, surveying future possibilities for American archaeology. A devout Baptist like so many of his sponsors, Breasted always insisted that the core of the task was not to trace the early 'rise of man from the merely physical' but to chart man's early moral and technological progress: to excavate therefore, the sites and cities of the Bible. So he visited Megiddo in Palestine, the site of the biblical Armageddon, he drove to Babylon, wondered at the ruins, walked in its palm groves and sat in the shade of Koldewey's deserted excavation house. He also visited all the then-known cities of ancient Sumeria and was amused to find at Ur, the city of Abraham, a desert railway and a station called 'Ur Junction'. From this gruelling trip came plans for thirteen successful large-scale excavations in Egypt, Iraq, Turkey, Syria, Palestine and Persia. Years later, born of the equally gruelling tours of inspection of these same excavations, came plans to finance the building of national museums in Cairo and ultimately, in Jerusalem. Then of course, there were always the projects that were perhaps closest to Breasted's heart; lavish expeditions recording the crumbling monuments of Egypt, the country of Breasted's own scientific expertise. In Chicago too, the headquarters of this enormous enterprise, there were many major research projects in hand, involving numbers of the world's finest scholars and the study of a mass of ancient Middle Eastern languages and religious texts. The number of high-quality academic publications emerging from Breasted's institute in those years was extraordinary.

Beginning with an initial project that was little more than a personal tour of the Middle East, Breasted's relationship with the Rockefeller foundations grew until they were financing the largest archaeological programme of its time. Neither did Rockefeller ever visit Breasted's expeditions; contact with the man and his books, sometimes even through Breasted's works that Rockefeller's children were studying at school, was enough to make the funding flow.

ABOVE: *Breasted's archaeologists launch a meteorological balloon to obtain high-angle photographs of their excavations at Megiddo in northern Palestine. In the early 1930s, Breasted's Institute also used aeroplanes to survey archaeological sites, though in the days before helicopters, static and relatively inexpensive balloons provided more accurate images.*

In 1931, when Breasted was 66 and his expeditions were hard at work throughout the Middle East, the dream was laid out in Art Deco glory on a lintel above the main door of his research institute, the Oriental Institute of the University of Chicago. 'It is intended,' he wrote, 'to suggest the transition of civilisation from the Ancient Orient to the West. The East, on the left, is symbolised by the tall figure of an Egyptian scribe confronting the vigorous and aggressive figure of the West. . .Behind the West on the right are the Parthenon, a European cathedral, and a modern skyscraper tower. . .'

In one vital aspect, Breasted's archaeological programme differed entirely from Petrie's: maximum results for minimum cost was never the American way. 'Why,' the young Breasted had wondered at Nagada all those years before, 'should service to archaeology necessarily entail. . .almost total absence of the most rudimentary creature comforts.' A quarter-century later, bearing evangelist religion and the fruits of the free market, the New World had come to investigate the Old.

These expeditions of Breasted's Institute saw the birth of the style of Indiana Jones; these were leather-jacketed expeditions of young men and women with Chinese chefs and Chevrolets, with secretaries, photographers, business managers and laboratory staff. It was a world of grand parties too; one of the expedition chauffeurs recalled that his first task after being hired by Breasted from a luxury suite in a grand hotel in downtown Cairo, was to extract a limousine filled with crates of good champagne from the mud of an Egyptian canal. That would not have pleased Professor Breasted or his sponsors, who had decreed that all the Institute's excavations should be dry.

These self-same millionaires of course, were the high priests of industrial efficiency. They responded well to Breasted's plans because he wrote in ways they could easily appreciate. Each of his project's separate goals was outlined as if it was the prospectus for building a hotel or a steel mill, and if the scheme seemed to provide a satisfactory return, the archaeologists were given ample resources to fulfil them.

Some of the grandest expedition houses ever made were built for the Institute's archaeologists, permanent affairs quite unlike Petrie's monkish cells; houses designed by modernist architects from Los Angeles in the 'Arab style' and furnished from Liberty's of London and the chic ateliers of Erté's Paris. As well as Chicago House at Thebes in Egypt, where the finest of all the Rockefeller expedition houses was built with laboratories, drafting studios, photographic laboratories, a splendid library, tennis courts and a gramophone collection of recordings of the Great Composers, several lavish expedition houses were built in quite isolated locations in Iraq and northern Palestine.

The Chicago archaeologists also experimented with new techniques. Meteorological balloons were used for aerial archaeological photography, and a bi-plane was employed for an invaluable survey of ancient Persia. Air compressors were imported so that every ancient brick of Sumer's excavated temples could be cleaned, and this provided a level of architectural detail never before achieved in Middle Eastern sites. Industrial vacuum cleaners were used as well, that most American invention imported to prepare the ancient floors and walls for the attentions of professional photographers. And lavish methods for the accurate recording of ancient Egyptian reliefs were developed which remain the standard that all other expeditions aim to emulate.

Above all, however, Breasted's idealistic programme — the recovery of mankind's moral development — led to the selection of excavation sites that archaeologists had traditionally considered unpromising, but which, in Breasted's terms, promised important historical information. For the first time, the selection of sites for excavation in the ancient East was determined by an assessment of the potential information they might yield rather than the amount of antiquities they seemed to promise. Even Petrie at Nagada had been obliged to maintain the enthusiasm of his international sponsors by

providing them with the antiquities he found. For such ambitious projects, Breasted required the best archaeologists and as graduates in Middle Eastern archaeology were not common in America, Rockefeller money was set to lure some of the world's finest from other expeditions to lead the way. 'The job was done,' his son later remembered, 'with the ablest people available, regardless of nationality or temperament.'

These expeditions in the desert, multinational, well-equipped affairs, specialists and scholars working all together for many months, were unique. At worst, claustrophobic and chaotic, at best they were brilliant brains trusts that served, in time, to stimulate a new look at the cultures of the most ancient East and provide new answers to the old problems of beginnings and diffusions.

Aged seventy, exhausted by a final tour of inspection in the Middle East and suffering a severe infection, Breasted was taken off a transatlantic liner to a Rockefeller Medical Institute in New York, where he died in December 1935. Shortly after came the crash: Rockefeller had always maintained that he supported the man and not the Institution and in 1937 the money stopped. Telegrams were sent out from the Oriental Institute to its expedition houses informing the archaeologists and all the other staff that they were fired and with immediate effect. 'A man like me ought to have nine lives,' Breasted had written in those last years. 'I often wonder where I shall land with all these argosies I am loading with such reckless disregard of the fact that there is only one captain for the whole fleet. . .'

This then, was the downside of high capitalist archaeology, the reliance not on the frugal continuities of intellectual tradition with a penchant for the antique, but on the vagaries of personal contact and individual whim. Later on, more modest expeditions came to work in some of the Rockefeller houses once again, and to continue Breasted's high standards of research, but the great grand dream had gone.

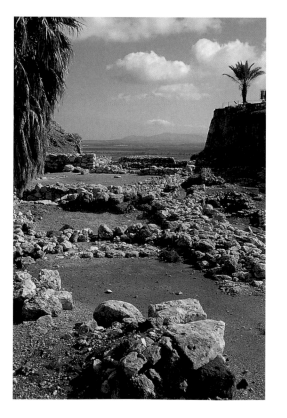

ABOVE: *The Oriental Institute's first expedition quarters in Egyptian Thebes, which, since the erection in the early 1930s of a more lavish establishment on the eastern bank of the Nile, now serves as the celebrated Hotel Marsan.*

LEFT: *The great Trench at Megiddo in northern Israel, part of the world's first million-dollar excavation, cut by Breasted's archaeologists. So large was this ancient Palestinian mound that even Rockefeller's resources were not sufficient to complete its archaeological investigation. The low round shape in the middle of the picture is the famous so-called Holocaust altar of a Canaanite temple; many more cities, and many more temples still lie beneath this venerable structure which dates from around 2000 BC. Between them, they hold much of the roots of Old Testament ritual and faith.*

Henri Frankfort, Bonded Brick and Senator McCarthy

ONE OF BREASTED'S MOST BRILLIANT international recruits had been Henri Frankfort, an Anglo-Dutch archaeologist trained by Petrie, who had a distinguished record of excavation throughout Egypt and the Middle East. Following the collapse of the Oriental Institute's archaeological programmes, Frankfort was gathered into the fold of the Oriental Institute. In Chicago, he was at the centre of a brilliant group of scholars, egyptologists, sumerologists and prehistorians, all of whom were taking a new look at the ancient world.

As part of this broad programme, Frankfurt undertook a re-examination of earlier theories of the beginnings of civilisation, especially the nineteenth century's quest for the origin of civilisation, carefully rehearsing the diffusionist arguments from the days of Christy and Tylor. In the 1940s, there was still very little archaeological evidence of ancient towns or villages older than those of Egypt and Mesopotamia, so the basic question had remained the same as it had been at the turn of the century: had civilisation really moved westward from Sumer into Egypt, as Petrie and others had believed? If it had, it would also have implied that civilisation really had begun in ancient Sumer.

Certainly, as Frankfort pointed out, the two ancient cultures shared a genuine commonality of brick architecture. Ancient Egypt's first-known buildings, such as the royal tomb that de Morgan found at Nagada, had been built under the direct influence of older Mesopotamian temples, such as those that Frankfort had excavated for Breasted in Iraq. Even the distinctive pattern and design of these grand Egyptian tombs, patterns that became the graphic symbol used in the hieroglyph denoting pharaoh's name and palace,

RIGHT: *Jacques de Morgan's reconstruction of the huge mud-brick tomb he found and excavated at Nagada, perhaps a tomb of Egypt's first pharaoh, the near-legendary Menes, and the monument that helped Petrie solve the riddle of the occupants of his 'New Race' cemetery (see pages 152–5). The patterns of the brick bonding on this monument, the so-called 'palace façade' design, was copied from earlier Mesopotamian monuments.*

had first been made of bricks and mortar in the ancient land of Sumer.

In ancient Mesopotamia, the meticulous work of the Chicago expeditions had revealed that in reality these patterns were ingenious designs of bonded bricks, employed to strengthen flimsy temple walls. In ancient Egypt, however, although the patterned walls looked similar to their Sumerian predecessors they were imitation; the Egyptian bricks simply stacked one upon the other, in simple patterns to imitate the appearance of the complex bondings of the originals. Here at last, Frankfort was able to show the diffusion of a genuine influence, crossing continents within the ancient world. A movement that, as more recent research and analysis has shown, was largely due to the far-flung trading networks of those early Sumerian city states, that reached to the very edges of the Nile Valley.

Frankfort also considered the genesis of writing in ancient Sumer, a process part-inspired, he suggested, by the linear patterns made by the rolling out of the patterns on cylinder seals on to wet mud. The use both of pictograms and of writing in lines was common to Egypt and Mesopotamia, Frankfort observed, and this seemed to suggest some kind of ancient linkage in which, once again, Sumer had priority and influence over Egypt. At the end of this old-style discussion of ancient to-ing and fro-ing, however, there comes a break with older ways of thinking – despite these influences, he concluded, there is no evidence that the state of ancient Egypt was not invented in the lands beside the Nile, that the religions and government of the two ancient cultures were entirely different; that two distinctive environments had produced two entirely different civilisations.

Frankfort's innovative analyses of ancient societies used modern methods of philosophical and anthropological enquiry, art historical analysis and the techniques of theological debate. Searching for the one beginning, earlier generations of archaeologists had concentrated upon analyses of trade, politics and conquest and had usually considered the ancient world to have been a simpler and poorer version of contemporary Western society and at lower stages of development than the present day. Frankfort broke right

ABOVE: *The Oriental Institute's expedition to Tell Asmar in 1934, led by the celebrated Anglo-Dutch archaeologist Henri Frankfort, who is seen smoking his habitual cigarette, leaning over the bench in the right hand side of the photograph. Amongst the international gathering of staff which was typical of many of Breasted's expeditions, were several scholars who would later write influential books of Middle Eastern scholarship including Seton Lloyd, far left; Rachael Levy, in the centre wearing a hat; and Thorkild Jacobson, later the doyen of Sumerian literary studies, who is seated on Frankfort's left.*

through such confining patterns of thought. Breasted's impromptu desert brains trusts were beginning to pay off and suddenly it seemed as if a new vision of the ancient world was about to come into existence.

Then the small group of people at the centre of this new enquiry into the past was suddenly fragmented. The investigations of Senator Joseph McCarthy and other related anti-communist crusades in the late 1940s and early 1950s in the US not only affected the military, the movies, the unions and the professions, but academic life as well. And archaeological theory bent under the strain. Inside Breasted's Institute, one young scholar was encouraged to change his cultural history of ancient Egypt to make pyramid building appear a little less 'communal'. Frankfort too, was under pressure. As a student in Amsterdam he had participated in left-wing politics. As the state investigators worked across American society and jealous colleagues gathered to attack him, he left for Europe and died prematurely just a few years later in 1954. In those last years, however, he poured out a series of brilliant books and articles that broke quite free from the savage nineteenth-century vision of the past, replacing it with a past of perfectly intelligent people with minds not one jot inferior to ours, but very, very different: the past then, became another place, a different country. After Henri Frankfort, a truly different picture of ancient humankind started to emerge.

BELOW: *The vast mortuary enclosure at Abydos in Upper Egypt, of King Khasekhemwy, a Second Dynasty pharaoh who ruled in the distant age before the pyramids, around 2800 BC. Here, the 'palace façade' denotes the eternal residence of the king. Until the very ending of ancient Egypt, almost three millennia later, the distinctive design of such panelling served as both a symbol of the royal name and to designate a link, a false doorway, between the living and the dead.*

Mars Attacks?
Pacal and Tutankhamun

I N 1949, A MARVELLOUS DISCOVERY at Palenque, deep in the rainforests of Yucatan in Mexico, revived many of the traditional theories of the diffusion of cultures from the Old World to the New. Excavating a stairway deep inside a jungle pyramid, Mexican archaeologist Alberto Ruz found a burial chamber as grand as many in the pharaohs' tombs in Egypt, and untouched since the days of burial. Nowadays, this celebrated tomb is believed to have been made for Pacal, an eighth-century AD monarch much given to erecting stone monuments, including parts of the so-called palace that housed Stevens and Catherwood during their visit to Palenque in 1839.

Pacal's stone sarcophagus was a marvel, grander yet than Tutankhamun's; his burial too, was decorated with jade jewellery and a mask as splendid as that of the celebrated young pharaoh. The opening of this completely novel tomb and the exhibition of its treasures became a media event, inviting obvious comparisons with Howard Carter's excavation of the tomb of Tutankhamun just twenty years before.

Had there then, after all, been an ancient connection and even perhaps an accompanying colonisation from Egypt into Mexico, as some nineteenth-century theories had proposed? Not surprisingly, after the Second World War, orthodox archaeological opinion had shied away from notions of a master race, the colonisation of 'savages' and skull measurement as an indication of intelligence and race. None the less, some of Tylor's outdated anthropological terms had also entered the popular vocabulary, just as some of Freud's jargon has done. The idea of ancient people and inventions travelling around the ancient world was a popular and well-trodden explanation of the past.

Just two years before the excavation of Pacal's tomb moreover, the Norwegian Thor Heyerdahl had undertaken a Viking-like voyage across the Pacific in an attempt to prove his theory that ancient South American culture was anciently diffused through Polynesia. The best-selling book that followed had made diffusionism part of common parlance, and a slew of books subsequently appeared, extending the same theory. Though Heyerdahl himself later proposed an ancient Egyptian crossing of the Atlantic, bringing pyramids and writing to the Americas, by that time, his rather antiquated proposal had been long outstripped by rather more exotic notions, with plot lines from

BELOW: *The jade death mask, reconstructed from the loose fragments that archaeologist Alberto Ruz found scattered over the skull of the man in the sarcophagus under the pyramid of Pacal at Palenque, and in all probability, the burial of that very ruler. The colour of fresh corn plants, jade appears to be transient and filled with natural life.*

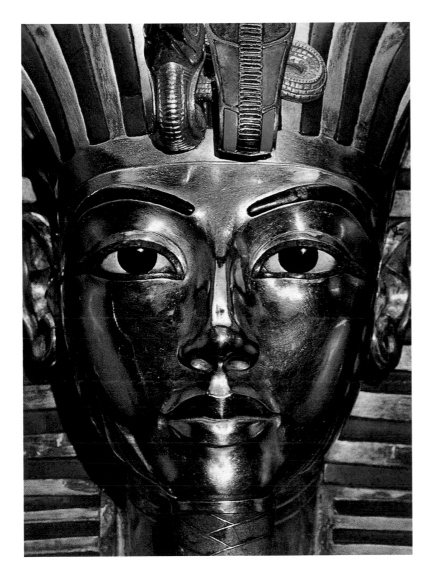

ABOVE: *Archaeology's most famous image, the golden death mask of the Pharaoh Tutankhamun from the Valley of the Kings, and a great work of sculpture in its own right. Gold, which the Egyptians called 'the skin of the gods,' was considered to be as bright and as eternal as the sun itself.*

Bulwer-Lytton and Madame Blavatsky. Eric von Däniken, for example, proposed that the image of Pacal on his sarcophagus lid was a picture of an astronaut on his way to civilise the savage earth – a proposal, now that modern astronauts no longer sit in the Pacal-like positions of Gagarin and John Glenn, has lost something of its immediate attraction. A slew of other esoteric colonisers followed, born of ancient legend and of science fiction: wise beings from Atlantis; white men from lost cultures who understood the wisdom of the spheres and brought it to a savage world; and all of them ultimately, harking back to the beginnings of 'Mr Tylor's science' (*see pages 149–50*).

Is there not in all of this, however, the slightest possibility of genuine connection between ancient Egypt and Mexico? Is it really beyond all doubt that these ancient monarchs, their priests and holy men had no connection whatsoever? Just as Frankfort's revolutionary methods of comparison between ancient Mesopotamia and Egypt revolutionised the language of Middle Eastern diffusionism, so they can also help to shed some light on the extent of ancient Egypt's influence on Mexico. Consider the two great tombs of Pacal and Tutankhamun.

On his sarcophagus lid, Pacal, our *cie-devant* astronaut is shown falling into the earth in disarray, falling down like an executed prisoner, falling headlong into the Milky Way, that endless scattering of stars like a cast of corn seeds in the night sky. Just as the space cut for Pacal's body in the stone of his sarcophagus is shaped like a womb, so this afterlife is as hazardous as the physical act of birth itself. Pacal's is an uncertain universe.

Tutankhamun's coffin, on the other hand, is a model of the entire Egyptian world; rectangular, entirely balanced and carefully delineated, with the pharaoh's place completely defined, his destiny as certain as the passage of the sun and stars. Here, nothing is out of balance, nothing left to chance. Even a great part of the glittering treasures in Tutankhamun's tomb are the residual paraphernalia of rituals performed in state temples and at the royal funeral; rituals designed to keep the state in tune with the universal order of the gods. Tutankhamun's destiny is an integrated part of state ceremonial and cosmic order. Provided pharaoh's mummy is correctly joined in rites and rituals to the eternal processes that regulated the Egyptian universe, there is no uncertainty in death at all. Consequently, Tutankhamun's shining mask is made of the metal that the Egyptians called the skin of their gods. All of Tutankhamun's golden portraits indeed, transform his earthly image into that of an eternal god.

Pacal's death mask, on the other hand, of light green jade, is the colour of a young maize plant which they termed 'the dancing prince', so his eternal destiny is personal, physical and organic. The tree of life drawn as growing from his chest on his portrait on the coffin lid, the first plant in the world, underlines this same organic concept of the Mayan universe. This was a hostile, fertile and ever-changing place. Pacal's destiny is one with the plants and animals of the rainforest. Life and death, growing and dying, both in nature and in humankind is one; human sweat and tears, milk and semen, the Mayans describe as the dew and nectar, as the very sap of plants and trees. The earth, they say, is 'warmed by bones' and in acts of self-mutilation and human sacrifice they offer human blood to it. And indeed, this ever-growing, ever-changing forest is a harsh environment; without due attention, you will bleed from pricks and scratches and the attentions of animals, reptiles and insects.

At Palenque, the Mayans called their green amorphous forest the 'Great Sea' and made their state, their civilisation by acting directly upon this dangerous and chaotic environment. Cut straight into the formless forest, their tomb-temples and their cities, a series of interlocking rectangles, were the very image of civilisation itself. It is hardly surprising that inside these carefully delineated symmetries they built observatories to watch the movements of the sun and stars. As Stevens said, these buildings seem like ships in a gale from which the ancient astronomers, cosmic navigators, looked anxiously for patterns in the sky on which they could fix uncertain human destiny.

Ancient Egypt, on the other hand, was an entirely symmetrical natural environment. The state lay symmetrically beside the flowing river that gave it life. And every day, the sun crossed the state at right angles; from east to west, from life to death. All that was required were rituals that allowed that state to join those natural symmetries.

The two different landscapes produced two very different ideas of time and history. Mayans believed their destiny to be woven inside a series of cyclic stellar patterns, both long and short, but all of them with endings and beginnings. For such histories, they required and thus invented the notion of absolute zero. Egypt, on the other hand, already fixed precisely on the compass points, and with its great pyramids locked in the grip of the sun and stars, had time with no beginnings, no endings and no zeros whatsoever; linear time, like the flowing of the Nile. In ancient Egypt, time was counted simply in the passing years of reigning pharaohs.

Two entirely different landscapes then, Nile and jungle, and two entirely different notions of eternity, of state, of life and death. Both original, both completely individual. Only crass insensitivity born of out-dated notions about ancient 'primitives' and 'master races' could fail to notice the essential differences between the two of them. What Pacal's tomb genuinely shares with Tutankhamun's and many other ancient monuments all around the world, are simply the preoccupations common to all ancient peoples; a concern with food and shelter, with the rhythms of the sun and the stars, a love of the vertical, the experience of sex and childbirth, the awareness of the omnipotence of death.

American Firsts
The Valley of Oaxaca: 1966–81

T HOUGH FEW PEOPLE EVEN NOTICED, the great grand theories of nineteenth-century diffusionism were effectively killed off within a few years of the discovery of Pacal's tomb, put to rest by the development of Carbon 14 and related dating techniques that for the first time provided fixed dates for all the ancient past, right around the world.

Just as Carbon 14 proved that the beginnings of Stonehenge were older than the pyramids of Egypt, and that it had not therefore, been planned by 'advanced' travellers from the East, so the same tests also showed that if the ancient Egyptians had taken the art of pyramid-building to the Americas, that their transatlantic crossing would have lasted for 1300 years: the time between the building of the last royal pyramid of Egypt and the first pyramid of Mexico. And that perhaps, is why modern diffusionists have come to propose that their various 'master races' came from outer space or Atlantis; anywhere, indeed, that avoids the icy gaze of modern scientific dating.

Modern archaeology, however, offers more than just a brake on the imagination. Though its practitioners seldom advertise the fact, they are slowly beginning to understand something of the true poetry of the past; something of the complexity and subtlety of what the ancients made on every continent on earth. And they are also starting to uncover evidence of civilisation's true beginnings; at different times, on different continents, with different peoples. Recent excavations near Mexico City, for example, have located traces of America's beginnings – flints dating from around 20,000 BC that are the direct descendants of prototypes brought to the Americas across the Bering Straits from Asia, out of Africa; part of that mysterious worldwide Stone Age culture, that a hundred thousand years ago, was manufacturing similarly shaped flints on every continent on earth.

In south central Mexico, excavations in caves above the Valley of Oaxaca under the direction of Minnesota professor Kent Flannery, have excavated the temporary shelters of hunter-gatherers, five or six individuals at a time, whose life spans have been dated by Carbon 14 measurement, to between 8765 and 6670 BC. These people ate deer and rabbit and a wide variety of seeds and plants, mainly acorns and agave, which they stored in pits within their cave. Careful excavation revealed that they differentiated various spaces in the caves for different tasks – food processing and cooking hearths in one area, butchery and weapon-making in another.

Other Carbon 14 dates taken from excavations in and around the village of San José Magote in the plains below, date the first known village settlements in this same area to around 1600 BC. The fields here are some of the most fertile in Oaxaca, well-watered and rich-soiled, an essential ingredient in the development of these early farming communities.

Just as rice was the dietary staple of the first Asian farmers and wheat the staple of the first farming communities of the Middle East and Europe, so maize was the staple indigenous diet of all ancient Americans. Further Carbon 14 dates from Flannery's excavations in the Valley show that maize had been cultivated in Oaxaca as early as 4000 BC, along with squash and chilli peppers, beans and avocado.

Inside the houses of these early villages, archaeologists have found work spaces that preserved the same divisions that had divided the caves of the hunter-gatherer communities 5000 years before; to the right of the door, stones for grinding maize and bone tools for shucking the corn cobs, as well as needles and spindle whorls. To the left, areas for butchery and making flint tools.

In the remains of its three centuries of life, before the ancient village of San José Magote was abandoned, archaeologists distinguished changes in house style and design. Egalitarian at first, the village slowly became a stratified community with relatively rich and poor households. At the same time, the villagers developed a public architecture, small buildings placed on stone steps and shaped like miniature versions of Mexico's celebrated stone temples, that contained pottery for religious rituals and many splendid works of art. Here then, are the first-known pyramids of the Americas in embryo.

Flannery's teams also excavated at the archaeological showplace of the Oaxaca Valley, Monte Alban, whose ending came with the Spanish conquest of Mexico. In its heyday it had been a great, grand ceremonial city with rows of pyramids, palaces, tombs and villas all set upon a mountain top at the very centre of the Valley. Similar works of art excavated at both San José Magote and Monte Alban have neatly connected the two sites, and Carbon 14 dating has shown that Monte Alban had been established at the same time as temple building ceased in San José Magote. This has led archaeologists to propose that some of the

ABOVE: *The fertile Oaxaca Valley, one of the oldest-known farmed landscapes of the New World. The blue hills behind hold the cave-settlements of the earliest-known hunter-gatherers of Central America, who seemed to have harvested maize in the millennia before farming communities settled in the Valley below.*

village communities in the plain may have migrated to the mountain top and there federated and established the grand new city at Monte Alban that still dominates the fertile plains below.

Flannery's teams have estimated that the population of Monte Alban grew to some 30,000 people in the twelve centuries of its existence. Writing was developed in the city at a very early stage; this script, the first in all of Mexico, has still not been properly deciphered. At just this same time, the people of Monte Alban also seem to have conquered other cities, to make what is now known as 'the Empire of the Zapotecs'.

Here then, is something of the real beginnings of American civilisation. It did not come in spaceships, nor with ancient Egyptians in their leaky boats, nor even with Columbus. Even the division of space employed in the caves of the first hunter-gatherers, and inside the first houses of the valley, is maintained in some village houses to this day. This most ancient culture was born of continuities that have lasted for thousands upon thousands of years. Born too, of an environment that first shaped these first Americans and then, in turn was shaped by them into their own distinctive landscapes. Never did this process require outside contact for its advancement. Until the coming of the Spanish, the ancient people of the Americas shaped their cultures by themselves, in their own way, from the elements of the lands in which they lived. One of the many independent and unique civilisations that ancient people created all around the world.

ABOVE: *One of the hundreds of Monte Alban's small pyramids awaits the attentions of the restorers.*

LEFT: *A basket of maize, the unique staple crop of the Americas. Maize requires a specific and individual technology for its cultivation and preparation, just as do rice and wheat, which were developed independently and at quite different times in Asia, Europe and the Middle East. To this day, maize stands at the centre of an unique indigenous culture that, until the Spanish invasions of the sixteenth century, had an entirely self-contained economy.*

PART V

At the Service
of the State

Königsplatz, Munich: 1935
Acropolis Germaniae

N 1915, GENERAL VON HINDENBURG, the Chief of the German High Command, took time off from the First World War to give a short speech over a freshly excavated Iron Age cemetery on a windy plain of northern Germany: 'As we gaze at these heroic graves of the high ancient German warrior culture, we realise that we are only Germans as long as we keep our swords sharp. . .' Used like this, archaeology can quickly generate and sustain popular sentiment, and become a truly terrifying force. The Chief of the German High Command was using the deep power of the buried past to sustain the slaughter of the First World War.

The Iron Age cemetery that inspired the General's peroration had been excavated by Professor Gustav Kossinna who devised the common archaeological concept of the 'culture group', that is, the theory that groups of ancient objects sharing the same designs, patterns and material can provide evidence of the history and movements of a single human culture. Using his theory of culture as his guide, Kossinna traced a prehistory for his beloved 'German race,' from 'Aryan' beginnings in Asia, to Europe where, so his followers would later claim, this race's 'natural genius' triggered the two great civilisations of ancient Greece and Rome.

Such 'archaeology' with its pseudo-scientific jargon – 'racial movement', 'high and low cultures', 'folk memories' and all the rest of it, greatly influenced Hitler, whose speeches were filled with such phrases. Many of the crack regiments and fraternities of the Third Reich designed their symbols and rituals to reflect such archaeological pseudo-truths. Secret fraternities of SS knights mixed their nasty ideology with the excavated signs and symbols of the past. Archaeology appeared to give all this a spurious depth and resonance, a true, a secret history – archaeology, that is, mixed with Wagner's operas, Nietzsche's aphorisms, the tales of the Teutonic Knights and Madame Blavatsky's version of Tibetan Buddhism.

Like most canny politicians, Adolf Hitler liked to place his party in the context of the past; part of a living, growing natural order. In the elegant Königsplatz at the heart of Munich, his voice echoing round the ancient marbles, Hitler gave his most memorable speeches. Around the Königsplatz, the State Music Academy of Bavaria is housed in what was once the official Munich residence of Adolf Hitler. A hundred yards away, in an identical building was the Munich headquarters of the Nazi Party, Hitler's spiritual homeland from where he graduated to Berlin.

In front of these two identical façades were two Greek-styled temples. On 9 November 1935, in a vast mock Roman ceremony, sixteen martyrs, Hitler's companions shot down in the streets of Munich in the unsuccessful putsch of 1923, were laid to rest in sixteen bronze sarcophagi. Before the move to Berlin, Hitler too, had wanted to be buried here.

The Königsplatz had been laid out a century before in the 1830s by the court architects of the kings of Bavaria. Facing the Nazi buildings was a grand classical gateway, giving entrance to the city's most splendid nineteenth-century suburb. Down the long sides of the square, two fine classical façades face each other: the Pinakothek, which housed the Bavarian picture gallery, and the Glyptothek, a choice collection of classical sculpture. The old museums, their ancient sculptures and the fine paintings stood at the very centre of the Nazi state. Paved in granite in place of its original grass, the once gentle space became the Nazi's Tiananmen Square; in Nazi parlance, the 'Acropolis Germaniae'. On 10 May 1933, books were burnt here in an official Nazi ceremonial.

Following in the footsteps of Kossinna and other German nationalist archaeologists, the

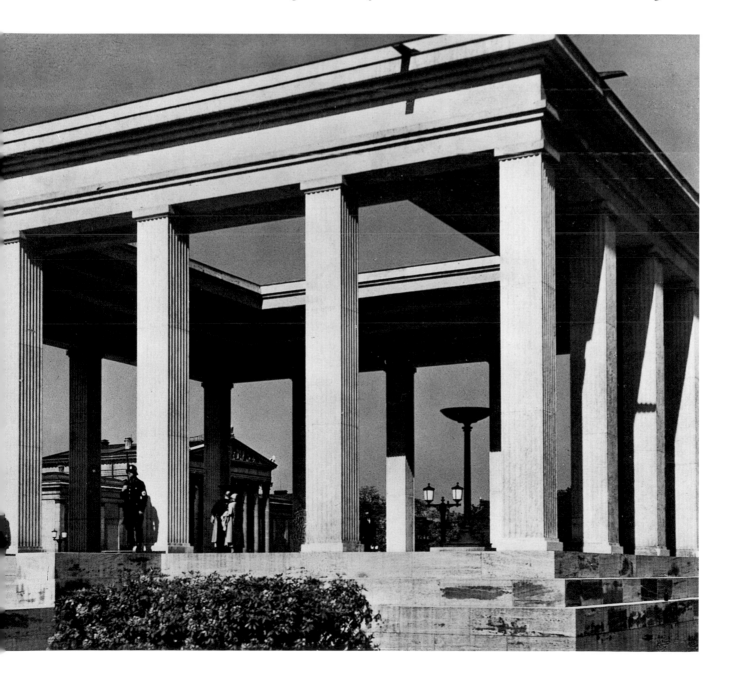

Nazi state taught that ancient Greece and Rome had been built by people of Germanic stock, and the Fall of Rome was due to pollution of the Aryan blood stock by Semitic blood, following the Roman conquest of the Middle East.

The very language of Nazi expansion, its racial theories, its *raison d'être*, came from popularist versions of a handful of nineteenth-century nationalist historians and archaeologists. In perhaps the world's most terrifying use of archaeology, Hitler and his Reich insisted on their own specific vision of the past. This misdirection of a basically benign science emphasises the amazing power and influence of archaeology; the power of the buried past and the power of its interpreters. This is a science that can seem to tell us where we have come from and show us how we got to be the way we are.

Not surprisingly, some of the first SS units into Poland hunted down not Jews, but archaeologists. In Czechoslovakia, when the SS historians could not find Professor Józef Kostrzewski of Poznan University, who had been a particularly tenacious opponent of Kossinna's racial theories, they killed his family in his stead. As had happened for the previous decade in Germany, university archaeologists were careful vetted, and many were dismissed or killed. Archaeological sites used in the support of alternative theories of history were 're-excavated' to recover the 'real truth'. A sage once said that those who do not know history are condemned to repeat it. The greater problem is, under these circumstances, whose history are you supposed to believe: Hitler's? Marx's? Roosevelt's? Churchill's?

As archaeologists deal in concrete truths, scientific, provable bits of history, they surely are the ones, perhaps indeed, the only ones who can provide hard evidence of what the past was really like. Or can they? Seen in this light, archaeology is not merely interesting, but inherently political and has many different uses. The danger of distortion lies in two basic choices that all archaeologists must make: firstly, how the evidence of the past is interpreted; secondly, what you choose to dig up in the first place.

A Nazi, for example, would regard the excavation of a working-class district of an ancient Egyptian palace not only as a dangerously Marxist preference, but one that would provide no meaningful data for his particular version of history. On the other hand, the excavation of an ancient Greek running track or an early German fortress could potentially provide fresh evidence of ancient Aryan invention, bravery and athleticism; areas worthy of excavation.

Sometimes though, even the best laid histories can go awry. On 25 May 1936, at the Berlin Olympics, which Hitler had personally proclaimed as a showcase for Aryan supremacy, the black American athlete Jesse Owens achieved the finest ever one-day showing in track history, equalling the 100-metre sprint world record, breaking the world 200-metre sprint record, setting a new long-jump record that stood for twenty-five years and earning a total of four gold medals. Jesse Owens had never read a Nazi history that would have told him that, at best, his place within the world was that of a 'black auxiliary' to the white races: he was running in a very different version of the past.

PHOTOGRAPH ON PAGES 172–3: *The very air of ancient Greece; some of the seven hundred or so names of schoolboys scratched on the stone walls of an ancient schoolroom in the model city of Priene in western Turkey.*

Olympic Games. Adler and Curtius at Olympia: 1874–1944

T HE STADIUM OF ANCIENT OLYMPIA, the locus of the first Olympic games, was excavated in the 1940s by Nazi archaeologists during the dreadful German occupation of Greece. The haul was enormous and unexpected; the ancient Greeks had hung armour captured in battle along the embankment above the running track for several centuries, and there it lay beneath the ground, the finest collection of Greek armour ever discovered, one of the greatest treasures of the Olympia Museum. As well as these trophies, the ancient stadium was revealed, the space in which the first Olympics had been held.

Ancient texts tell that athletic festivals were held at Olympia for a thousand years until in AD 393, Theodosius, that most Christian Emperor, put an end to all such pagan obscenities. Unlike the modern Olympics, these games celebrated the identity of a single culture, that of Greece, by using religious offerings and feats of strength. This is not to say that this was a celebration of statehood, however, since the ancient Greeks were never a simple, single state. The games of Olympia took place every four years and lasted four days. Chariot racing, the famous five-mile race, took place on the first day, along with bareback horse racing. The second day was the day of the pentathlon, javelin and long jump, with the final two events, sprinting and wrestling, left until the last day. The third day always took place on a full moon, and this dictated the day the games began. The third morning was reserved for ceremonial; in the sacred precinct set beside the Stadium, a hundred oxen were slaughtered and eaten, and their bones were burnt upon an altar. Pausanius, that invaluable ancient guide to Greece, tells us that in his day, the centuries-old ash heap was some twenty feet in height, a great grey mound standing amidst a splendid gathering of temples and a host of statues.

Long-distance races took place on the morning of the fourth day, with the finale of the pentathlon and wrestling and boxing following in the afternoon. The referee patrolled the wrestling ring with whip in hand; no eye-gouging was allowed. The games' finale was a 400-metre foot race. All successful athletes were fêted with laurel wreaths and some with statues. A few came to be worshipped in the cities that they represented as deities in their own right. The Greeks believed that the games had started in the eighth century BC, and that Hercules himself had slept under Olympia's olive trees before performing prodigious feats of strength. True or not, for many centuries, Olympia and its festival was a hub of Greek identity.

Although hundreds, if not thousands of ancient texts celebrated and described the ancient games, the location of Olympia was utterly unknown until an eighteenth-century traveller, Dr Richard Chandler, from the Society of Dilettanti, noticed some old columns in a vineyard planted in the mud of a meandering river floor. Many historians, including the indefatigable J.J. Winckelmann, had made imaginative reconstructions of the place; by 1829 a French expedition had actually excavated and measured part of the buried temple and sent some of its statues back to the Louvre.

By the 1890s the site was already on the tourist path. 'Two trenches marked the excavations of the French,' the young Flaubert recorded in 1849 on his journey through the East. 'Traces of enormous walls, some huge upturned stones and a fluted column base of enormous girth were all that remained of ancient Olympia.' Serious excavation began in 1874, just as Schliemann was starting work at Troy, the work being undertaken by two Berlin professors of the Prussian Academy. First financed by the Kaiser and the government exchequer, they would continue for over a century. This, the first excavation in the world to be undertaken under the terms of a diplomatic agreement between two modern governments was the outcome of a lengthy dialogue between the two states, Greece and firstly, Prussia and later, united Germany. Basically, the Greek government granted permissions and received all the finds from the work; the Germans being granted copyright of first publication and paying all the costs of excavation.

The most celebrated monument of Olympia, which the French had part-dug out in the 1820s, was the legendary Temple of Olympian Zeus that, for almost a thousand years had sheltered the gold and ivory image of that god – the legendary statue by the artist Pheidias, one of the Seven Wonders of the ancient world.

In the late 1870s the Germans excavated the entire temple, waiting for the vintage to be completed, so that their labour force was not distracted. Digging stratigraphically, they recovered its entire history. Beneath the nineteenth-century vineyard, with its few standing columns still holding up the vines, they found Byzantine levels, relics of town buildings, churches, houses and the rest that had grown up around the pagan ruins and which, in their turn, had been robbed to make a wall to keep out Slavic invaders in the fifth century. The walls were unsuccessful, the tribes not only destroyed the town on the ancient site, but by depleting the local population, ruined the upkeep of the agricultural terracing of the area so that after a thousand years of productivity, the fertile earth flooded over the ruins, burying them in yellow mud and slowing the river so that annual floods became inevitable. That is how Olympia was lost.

Underneath this band of yellow mud lay the ancient levels, and these were remarkably preserved. The Germans found the great statuary of the temple façades, still lying where an earthquake had shaken them down, some of the greatest masterpieces of Greek art. Under and around these precious marbles were the great columns of the temple, lying like slices of salami down the temple steps. Friable and fragile, the archaeologists left most of them where they had fallen fifteen centuries before.

All this history had come from a simple, yet very careful stripping of four strata of ancient filling. The German publication became a yardstick for all archaeological investigations of such sites. These excavations were truly ground-breaking – the first time that northern prehistoric archaeological methods were employed on a major classical site and the work of the Prussian Academy would influence everybody from Schliemann at Troy to Flinders Petrie in Egypt. Even the way the site itself was treated too, would have a vast effect. After excavation, the Germans carefully landscaped the site. Here too, with private Greek funding, they designed and built the world's first site museum to hold the astonishing collection of statuary and other antiquities that, year by year, to the amazement of the archaeologists and the Kaiser, they were taking from the earth.

By the 1890s, Olympia had become a favourite tourist site of Greece, the Germans having

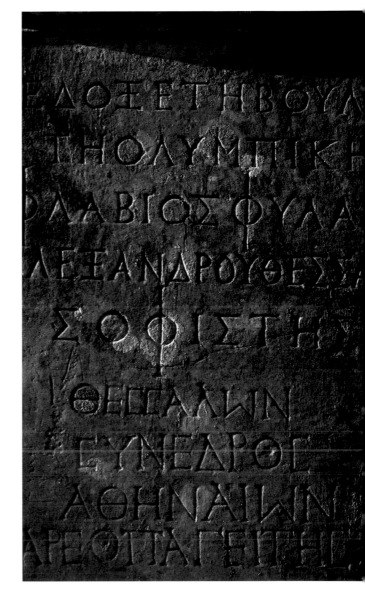

ABOVE: *One of Olympia's five thousand surviving statue bases, it honours an Athenian athlete.*

RIGHT: *The powerful doric order of the Zeus temple at Olympia. Careful excavation by the Berlin archaeologists Curtius and Adler between 1875–81, recovered the entire history of this temple, and of its destruction. These groundbreaking excavations were the first in the Mediterranean world to be conducted with the care and method developed by northern archaeologists, and demonstrated the value of these methods when excavating celebrated classical monuments. They were also the first excavations to be conducted by the now-standard contract, in which the host nation retained all antiquities discovered, whilst the visiting archaeologists held first rights of publication.*

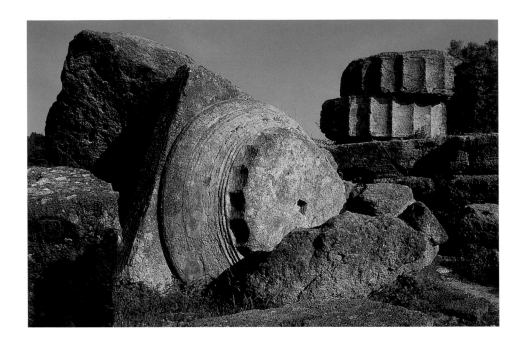

excavated the greater part of the sacred enclosure, anciently called the Altis, and cleared the tunnel that, so Pausanius informed them, led to the buried Olympic stadium. At this same time, a Frenchman, Baron de Coubertin visited the excavations not for the purposes of archaeology, but as part of his plan to revive the ancient games. Olympia, the Baron de Coubertin conceived, could be the panacea of modern male youth, helping to strengthen them and provide them with ideals they had lost. In Greek times, as every educated person knew, the sons of the élite had formed a military and athletic bond that served them and their country through thick and thin. In his own time, France had been invaded and heavily defeated by Prussian force of arms – a defeat he thought had occurred because French schools were excessively intellectual. A misfortune that did not afflict the British, de Coubertin observed, as they, like the ancient Greeks, played a great range of sports, even inventing many of their own like rugby and cricket and football. The English word 'sport' was used in almost every country in the world to describe the religious festivities that took place in the stadium at Olympia. The word came from the old English *disport*, which in turn, came from the French and means 'to divert or amuse'. As part of the social revolution that accompanied the Industrial Revolution, the British had applied sets of rules and regulations to what had been village pastimes, they had given them rules, referees, and leagues and clubs. The 'noble and chivalrous' religion of 'sport', de Coubertin believed, could well transform the 'softness' of so much modern youth, simply by physical fitness and hard competition.

So de Coubertin reinvented the Olympics Games and in 1900, in a charmingly amateur and innocent celebration, the ancient stadium of Athens was rebuilt and the Olympic Games were held again. Down the years, the idea grew. Although de Coubertin and the Vatican opposed it, women were admitted to the games. Then in Berlin in 1936, the long drawn-out ceremonial of torch-lighting and parading was introduced – a misrepresentation of similar-looking scenes on ancient vases and other ceremonies.

The ancient Olympian space was excavated and filled with modern dreams. Where had these visions come from?

Dreams of Greece
Regensburg: 1842

THE ASTONISHING TEMPLE OF VALHALLA at Regensburg in Bavaria, a misty Parthenon standing high above the Danube, a shrine to the greatness of the German Genius, was built by order of King Ludwig of Bavaria and opened by him in October 1842. The building's true beginnings, however, date from 1807, when Napoleon and the French armies were cutting through Germany and central Europe, and kings and princes like Ludwig's father, Maximilian, were forced into an accommodation with the realities of a new order in Europe.

ABOVE: *The Valhalla of Regensburg, built upon a vineyard on the slopes above the Danube valley. Based on the Parthenon of Athens and built of alpine granite and conceived in the first years of the nineteenth century, Valhalla was designed by the Munich architect and archaeologist, Leo Klenze.*

Today, the idea of building a northern, *faux* Parthenon might seem absurd, at the least. At the time of its conception, however, it had simply been the patriotic reaction of a twenty-year old Crown Prince to what he saw as a national humiliation. He would build a monument named Valhalla, after the hall in which dead German heroes were feasted by the Valkyries, the maidens who had taken up their bodies from the heat of battle. And his Valhalla would be filled with the names and portrait busts of the greatest Germans. The prince was no architect, all he knew was that this Valhalla should be 'great, not merely colossal...but with a greatness that is in the architecture, a dignified simplicity combined with pomp...'

The prince first commissioned an architectural competition for Valhalla's design, but none of the entries were sufficiently impressive. A few years later though, when the young archaeological enthusiast, Baron Haller von Hallerstein, returned from Greece where he had sat and drawn at the Acropolis of Athens alongside the English architects Stuart and Revett, he showed Prince Ludwig his drawings of the Parthenon, high on its hill and the die was cast. The form of a Greek temple expressed perfectly the prince's idea that his Valhalla should have a 'dignified simplicity'. By 1825, when Ludwig became king, Leo Klenze, his friend and state architect was already working on the plans.

In the days when the Valhalla was under construction, it was considered entirely sensible for mythic German heroes to leave paradise each day to hunt and fight, to return each evening, not to a northern long house, but to a reproduction of the Parthenon of Athens. The Greek style had come to stand for Paradise itself. Drawings of the ionic capitals on the Acropolis of Athens had decorated the pages of the first printed editions of the French Revolution's *Rights of Man*. The same forms also decorated the tombs and houses of both liberals and conservatives right through the Western world. As Winckelmann had written

LEFT: *Klenze's splendidly rich design for the interior of Valhalla of Regensburg, a marble hall in which visitors walk through the reconstructed past of the nineteenth-century history painters to pay homage to the German Genius.*

LEFT: Pheidias and the Parthenon *by Lawrence Alma-Tadema, 1868. An imaginative reconstruction of ancient Athenian elders 'viewing' the celebrated frieze that Lord Elgin was to take from the temple and ship to London. Carefully based upon the findings of contemporary archaeology, such paintings served to breathe life into the distant past — a past though, replete with the values of nineteenth-century society. Alma-Tadema's Pheidias, for example, the supposed sculptor of this celebrated frieze, is pictured as if he was a Victorian artist at the annual vernissage of the Royal Academy in London.*

RIGHT: *Valhalla's southern pediment shows not the gods of Olympus but, in similarly classical pose and costume, the creation of the German Federation, the gods of the River Rhine and Moselle, and the seated divinities of Württemberg, Saxony and Hesse.*

in the previous century, these timeless forms had been the creation of an ideal society whose arts expressed a 'noble simplicity and serene grandeur'. Certainly they were far from the mendacities and miseries of the nineteenth century, and the growing industrial revolution. That is why a Greek temple was given the name Valhalla.

Inside Valhalla, in the holiest of holies, clad in multi-coloured marbles of black, gold and red, beside the sculptured busts of two field marshals, a poet and a mystic preacher, stands the bust of J. J. Winckelmann; the 'first to regard archaeology as a science, and founder of the modern history of art,' as Valhalla's handbook informs us. A real German hero. With a giant leap of the imagination, Winckelmann had been the one begetter of this disembodied vision of an imagined ancient Greece; he was the man who projected that dream with such romantic power and force that it is still with us today. Although having seen Greek sculpture only through Roman copies, he imagined masterpieces and confected visions from descriptions of lost statues written by ancient connoisseurs. He also made a personal Greek paradise in which these same lost statues seemed to come alive.

Here then is the root of Europe's dreams of Greece, the Greece of the Olympic Games and of Hollywood, of gravestones, banks and great dictators. Certainly not the Greece of those vibrant fragments of the ancient culture that the Prussians excavated at Olympia, dark, lively and strange; but the Greece of the imaginings of northern Europeans longing for the everlastingly sunny south.

Königsplatz, Munich: 1816
Greece in Bavaria

I N 1816, WHEN LEO KLENZE, THE ARCHITECT OF VALHALLA, was asked by King Ludwig to design a gallery for his collections of Greek and Roman statues, he settled upon a scheme to make the building perfectly square, reflecting Winckelmann's literary divisions of classic art into four separate periods. Earlier galleries of classical sculpture were usually designed around the subject matter of the statues; there might be a Room of Muses, Apollo, the Seasons and the like, one following on the other, sometimes with a special salon for Roman portraits, such an obviously individual category of their own. Klenze's museum, however, was above all else a museum of ideas, one showing an 'improved' past carefully organised according to the order of a history book.

Klenze's Glyptotek was the first large-scale purpose-built public art gallery in the world. There is hardly a major city in the world today that has not organised its museum along similar lines. And not only has this four-sided scheme influenced the design of most later public galleries of classical art, but through them, the way that we still see classical sculpture. Winckelmann's four eras of classical art now seem as if they are natural divisions in themselves. As excavators catch their first sight of sculptures half buried in the earth, most will first assess what they see in terms of the same quadripartite scheme that Leo Klenze so elegantly memorialised in brick and stone in Munich.

Klenze designed his gallery on the Königsplatz of Munich around the same time as the Valhalla at Regensburg. Turn left at the entrance and you enter Winckelmann's 'archaic' period with its straight and simple statuary. Moving through, visitors come into two galleries of later sculpture; Winckelmann's 'grand' period which is derived from the 'archaic', though less abstract; then the more flamboyant and sensual works, the more realistic 'beautiful' period. Completing the square is the gallery of later statuary, including Roman sculptures, with marvellously vivid portraits of people 'warts and all' – the period Winckelmann characterises as being of 'imitation and decay' that ended with the fall of Rome.

King Ludwig's pride and joy, and the especial jewel of his collection was set up in the 'archaic' galleries – a large group of sculptures which he had bought in Rome when he was Crown Prince. These sculptures were among the fruits of Haller von Hallerstein's trip to Greece, where he had travelled in the spring of 1811 as part of a group of young Englishmen, Danes and Germans come to draw and excavate the ancient temples and dance in the evening moonlight. Before they had left their base at Rome, the young noblemen had formed themselves into an association called the Xeneion, the first and quite possibly the liveliest international association of archaeologists in the world, dedicated they proclaimed 'to Greece, ancient literature and the fine arts', although others were later to observe that,

RIGHT: *The entrance to the galleries of Munich's Glyptothek. One of Leo Klenze's elegant doorways frames the celebrated Barberini Faun, perhaps the finest piece of classical sculpture north of the Alps. A beautiful mix of archaeology and design, the doorway bears Klenze's name upon its lintel.*

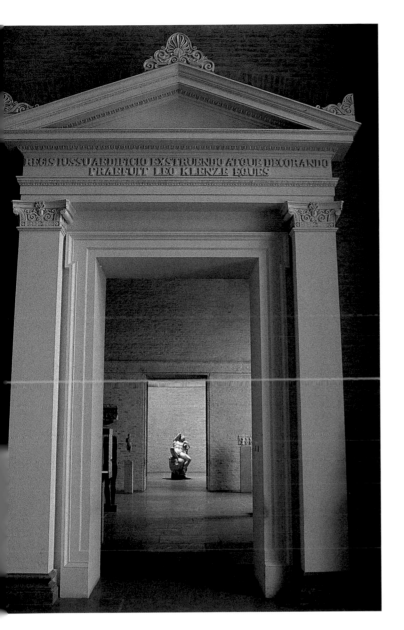

in reality, they were an association of robbers. It is true that they took many fine sculptures and antiquities, which they sold on their return to Rome, a common occurrence of the period.

Not only did Haller von Hallerstein suggest the design of Valhalla to the Crown Prince, but also that he should buy, at considerable cost, the superb sculptures that Xeneion had found when they had excavated the lovely Temple of Aphaea on the Isle of Aegina. Ludwig asked his Roman agent, his friend, the painter Martin Wagner, who had already bought him many fine sculptures, to examine and then purchase Haller's finds, then finally to have them restored and 'improved' as was the fashion of the day, by a man they called 'the god of artists', the Danish sculptor Bertel Thorvaldsen, another follower of Winckelmann.

The problem with the Aegina sculptures was that they had fallen from the temple's pediments in an earthquake, and were damaged. At Rome there were several sculpture studios restoring, some said even making, antique sculptures for the northern collectors. However, it was unusual to ask such a man as Thorvaldsen to undertake the work; at that time the Dane was considered to be one of the greatest sculptors alive.

Some of the Aegina sculptures lacked heads and limbs and even more importantly, despite the careful drawings that Haller and his friends had made during their nine-day excavation, no one knew exactly how they had all been set up in the triangular angles of the temple's pediments; there was much that was still uncertain. With the king advising every step of the way, Thorvaldsen made the sculptures new heads and helmets, hands, limbs and armaments and set the sculptures upon individual plinths. That years later, when the Dane had finally finished, no one could really tell the difference simply confirmed his reputation as 'greatest-ever sculptor'.

The fact that we today can so easily distinguish between ancient Greece and nineteenth-century Denmark, simply shows how tastes have changed and grown. Ancient sculptures were not made, in the manner of nineteenth-century sculptures, as simulacra of real life – in the sense that an airbrushed *Playboy* picture is a simulacrum – but as another sort of life, one independent from the real world. Thorvaldsen's heads appear softer than the ancient Greek originals. They seem as gentle as a Raphael; their smiles give fresh personalities to the ancient bodies. The real Greek heads though, look straight through you, like a cat does. This past is quite another universe. And that, of course, is the trouble with fakes. Greece recast in the Munich of Ludwig's day, makes ancient Greece a little more familiar to us than it was. Fortunately, in an act of archaeology inside a museum, the Glyptothek's post-war curators had the courage to strip off the much-loved nineteenth-century restorations. The truth is, there is hardly a major museum today that does not knowingly exhibit fakes or restorations – sometimes they are not removed for fear of upsetting the public, or even, to avoid looking foolish. Yet it is important to separate them out from the genuine articles, for fakes detract from the real past and bring confusion to it.

When the marbles were stripped of Thorvaldsen's reworkings they were also reset using evidence from later excavations on Aegina that finally established how the groups had really stood upon the ancient temple. However, this rearrangement still caused a great deal of alarm and public criticism, just as the restoration of major monuments so often does today.

It is simply a question of choice: do we want to see the things as they once were, or how we first remember them? Do we wish the ancient object to be presented as an approximation of ancient reality, or as a slice of our own past? Do we wish to see classic art arranged by Klenze and his mentor Winckelmann, or by modern archaeologists ? But here, one has to stop, for the distant past can only ever be presented in the context of more recent times, whether in museums or by archaeologists in excavations, or in books.

ABOVE: *The Danish sculptor Thorvaldsen in competition with the classical Greeks. The second, fourth and fifth heads in this line are genuine archaic Greek work, and were excavated on the Isle of Aegina in 1811. The other two were made on commission at Rome around 1820, part of Thorvaldsen's reconstruction of the sculptures of the Aegina Temple, for their joint exhibition, half ancient, half neoclassic, in King Ludwig's Glyptothek.*

LEFT: *The Temple of Aphaea, on the Island of Aegina, most perfect example of late Greek archaic temple architecture, built in the early years of the fifth century BC. The temple was first excavated and stripped of most of its sculptures by Xeneion, the world's first International Association of Archaeologists – in reality, a group of like-minded young Europeans, romantic neoclassicists who undertook several excavations in Greece in the first decades of the nineteenth century.*

Improving Athens: 1834
Bavaria Restores the Acropolis

L EO KLENZE, THE COURT ARCHITECT OF BAVARIA, first walked up the steps of the Acropolis in 1834, thirty years after Lord Elgin's men had last come down them, carrying off the marbles of the Parthenon. Klenze had been sent off to Athens as part of a team of ministers and advisors to King Ludwig's son, Prince Otto, who had been created King of Greece.

Since Elgin's day, the War of Greek Liberation, that bitter fight with Ottoman Turkey, had further ruined the Acropolis which now had garrisons and gun emplacements, siege towers and castles built all over it. Piles of rubble and marble chip littered the sides of the stony hill. Klenze though, was in ecstasy. 'God has blessed me,' he wrote in his diary 'there is not a word within me to express the feelings in my soul.' He had finally come to the land and the very buildings which, through the drawings of archaeologists and architects, had inspired some thirty years of his work.

In Klenze's day, Athens was little more than a village overshadowed by the vast hill of the

RIGHT: *Since medieval times, the great rock of the Acropolis of Athens had served as a fortress. Its present manifestation, starkly stripped of everything but its fifth-century BC monuments framed by a low surrounding wall, was planned by Leo Klenze and his archaeological successors.*

Acropolis and its towering ruined monuments threaded about with mosques and bastions. King Otto and his ministers had decreed that this little town with its hill of temples, with its shepherds and their flocks of sheep, should become the capital of Greece. Klenze, the court architect of King Ludwig of Bavaria, Otto's father, was to control the plan of its rebuilding. He started at the top, upon the Acropolis, bringing regiments of troops to free the two great standing temples, the Parthenon and the Erechtheum, from the ruins of the buildings of the Turkish administration and the fortresses built by medieval counts around the ancient gateways, the Propylaea.

Amidst the rubble of the ancient gateways, the king's soldiers found an entire small temple dismantled and serving as a gun emplacement. Using the old drawings of 'Athenian' Stuart as his guide, Klenze rebuilt the little jewel, setting it up again upon its ancient plinth. Archaeologists though, are seldom satisfied with their predecessors' restorations; since Klenze's time the Temple of Athena Nike has been dismantled and resurrected three times over, as archaeologists make changes to its precise position and proportion.

Inside the Propylaea, the plateau of the hill was covered with the abandoned, ruined buildings of the Turkish administration. Klenze's drawings show a mosque still standing in the middle of the Parthenon, the little mosque that had replaced the old Byzantine cathedral which had been destroyed when the great temple was blown to pieces in the siege of 1687. The Turkish town that Elgin had known, and which had long supported and covered this destruction in picturesque streets and alleys had been shattered, partly exposing the great white blocks of the broken Parthenon and the graceful Erechtheum. Klenze's men demolished all the surviving walls and houses of the Turks and, after carefully gathering all the fragments of the ancient marble from the temples, tipped the remainder off the top of the Acropolis walls, which, in their turn were also stripped of their medieval battlements.

What to do then, with the extraordinary ruins now brought to light again, set half-way

LEFT AND RIGHT: *Freed from their re-use in the masonry of later buildings erected on the Acropolis, demolished and sorted by Klenze's gangs in the 1830s, these marble blocks quarried in the Peloponnesus by ancient Greeks, await restoration as part of the present archaeological programme of conservation and rebuilding.*

BELOW AND RIGHT: *Time and incident shape every one of the surviving stones on the Acropolis of Athens. One of the Parthenon's marble columns (below) displays the devastating effects of the huge explosion that occurred when an ignited gunpowder store inside the temple blew the entire structure apart in 1687. Long before that time, however, the Byzantines had already converted the great temple into the Cathedral of Athens, as this Byzantine Greek inscription on a loose fifth-century BC block of marble (right) so eloquently testifies.*

between heaven and earth? King Otto's brother-in-law, the Prussian Crown Prince had the idea of living up on the Acropolis inside a great new palace, and the renowned court architect of Prussia, Karl Friedrich Schinkel, was asked to design one. It was, you might say, a prestige development; a neoclassic Las Vegas with genuine standing ruins. The king would entertain his guests in a series of Roman-style courts and salons, whose inner construction Schinkel had copied from the brick and steel of Manchester's industrial buildings. A formal French garden was planned to fill the gap between the ancient temples, along with a race track for horses and a small forest, especially planned to hide half of the Erechtheum, placing it as though it were the subject of a romantic painting. This pretty conceit was to be carefully reflected in a rectangle of water, a pool beside whose golden waters one might read Goethe on a summer's evening, as one would do in Munich or Berlin. Topping off the whole, was a vast Germanic rendition of the Statue of Athena, a gloomy reminder of an ancient colossus that once stood high above the temples on the rock. Klenze said that it was marvellous, a *Midsummer Night's Dream*; its architect, the 'divine' Schinkel was indeed a genius. And then, in what was probably his greatest single gift to Greece, Klenze put the plan away. However, this did not solve the problem of what to do with these great shattered lumps of archaeology.

One day, writes Klenze in his diaries, he had been working away on the Acropolis when 'the blue flag of hope appeared on the horizon. Lo! The king was coming with his ministers. As if by a miracle,' he says, 'the gigantic stones began to obey the masons and harmonise again, with the hymns that saluted the coming of the King.' The Greeks of course, already knew it: the Acropolis was a national shrine, a shrine to that view of ancient Greece as the unassailable height of human civilisation, just as Winckelmann had written a century before. During the War of Independence, when Turkish troops had started to tear down the venerable stones to take the ancient lead fillings of the binding cramps to cast as musket balls, the Greek troops besieged high up on the Acropolis had sent their enemies fresh bullets ready-made, with a message to leave the sacred stones alone. This then, as Klenze saw, was archaeology on the very grandest scale, and certainly no candidate for redevelopment.

Klenze's task, and that of his successors, was laid out from the beginning. The Acropolis was to be stripped of everything but its greatest classical monuments, stripped right down to the living rock. Although one of Otto's ministers complained that 'the archaeologists would destroy all the picturesque additions of the middle ages in their zeal to lay bare and restore the ancient monuments,' all the later history was thrown away. The Italian castles, the little mosque, the Byzantine cathedral that now exists only in a book of splendid sermons by Michael Cloniates, the twelfth-century Bishop of Athens. Yet, it was said as late as the 1900s, you could still find tesserae, golden squares of glass from the mosaics of the cathedral that Cloniates knew, flashing in the small cracks in the rock of the Acropolis beneath your feet.

Along with many later archaeologists though — many of them brave Greek nationalists — it was Klenze, who in clearing the great white rock, first set the stage on the Acropolis of Athens for the succeeding generations who came to see this reconstructed ancient world, standing high above the modern city.

As the century progressed and European tourism grew enormously, travel writers like John Addington Symonds, erudite and breathless all at once, fixed its mood precisely for the century to come: '. . .Athens wears for her garland the air-empurpled hills Hymettus, Lycabettus, Pentelicus. . .The Acropolis is the centre of this landscape, splendid as a work of art with its own crown of temples. . .Athens, like the Greeks of history, is isolated in a sort of self-completion: she is a thing of the past, which still exisits, because the spirit never dies, because beauty is a joy forever. What is truly remarkable about the city is just this, that while the modern town is an insignificant mushroom of the present century, the monuments of Greek art in the best period, the masterpieces of Ictinus and Mnesicles [the Parthenon's ancient architects]. . .are so unencumbered with subsequent edifices that the actual Athens of Pericles absorbs our attention.'

Klenze's work, however, did not stop at the Athenian Acropolis. After laying out the Glyptothek of Munich according to Winckelmann's theory of art history, he now oversaw the design of an entire city as if it was a history book. Nineteenth-century Athens was planned to exhibit and display a contemporary and largely German view of the 'classical world'. All the city's ancient standing monuments were fitted into a system of long straight roads which led from the city's symbolic heart on the Acropolis, out into the hills behind. Inside this scheme, the little alleyways of Byzantine and Turkish Athens were left alone in the shadow of the Acropolis, a village at the city's heart soon decorated with the villas of King Otto's modest court.

Klenze planned the great new city as if it were a walk around the Glyptothek; a square set sideways, with the rock of the Acropolis on its southern corner. The plan revealed itself as visitors drove in their carriages up the long, green avenue from the harbour of Piraeus, the road set at just the correct angle for a fine view of the Acropolis on their approach. Then suddenly, with the Acropolis on the left hand, up loomed the enormous Roman temple of Zeus, the largest classical building in Greece lying in romantic ruin. To ensure that the view was unobstructed, as it still is today, Klenze carefully restored the temple's platform.

Years later, as the city grew, Athens' ancient stadium lying in the fields beyond the Zeus Temple would be restored, and the pastures beside it with the famous Kallirrhoë Spring, were covered by a complex of gymnasia, tennis courts and swimming pools, all in the ancient manner, to house the first revived Olympic Games. The modern high road from Piraeus still follows Klenze's basic plan, running alongside the city parks beside the Temple of

Zeus. And on your left, beside a group of little houses, there still stands a small Protestant church built by one of Haller von Hallerstein's English friends, in an appropriately English gothic style.

The centre of the town was planned to hold the grandest of the capital's new buildings, comfortable nineteenth-century archaeological visions of the classic past. On the same spot, where it is said Aristotle taught in the Lyceum, Klenze's colleagues built the Greek parliament building and the central offices of the administration. Beyond them, Klenze himself designed the city's Catholic cathedral in the Roman manner; and a Greek cathedral too, in Roman-Byzantine style. Later architects added Otto's modest palace and a great gathering of universities and public libraries; the ancient worlds of Greece and Rome as revealed by contemporary archaeological excavations and brought to life again with paint and sparkling marble.

Today, the enormous city completely covers the great green plain with noise, dust and moving traffic. The Parthenon still stands above it all, stripped, serene and slowly shedding its fine marble skin in the polluted air. Here Winckelmann's Museum of the Mind has made it into the street and archaeology has become a national celebration and a pageant. And high on the pediment of the great Archaeological Museum, the building that now holds Schliemann's treasures from Mycenae and a host of other wonders, there is a copy of a group of statues in the Vatican; the statues that Winckelmann considered to be amongst the finest in the world.

BELOW: *The beauty of the Parthenon, shattered, restored and now dissolving slowly in the polluted air of Athens, stands as the supreme modern symbol of the human past, as UNESCO'S logo and as a moving testament to the fragility of human achievement.*

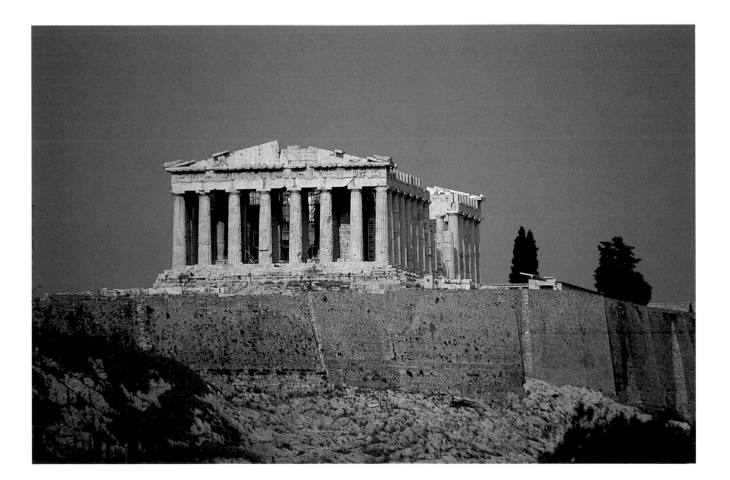

Improving Athens: 1931 America Restores the Agora

O N KLENZE'S ADVICE, KING OTTO'S MINISTERS set aside several areas of ruins for future excavation; one of them, the urban heart of the ancient city, was the site of the Agora at the foot of the Acropolis. Over the years, sporadic excavation revealed many individual buildings; in 1931, however, the American School of Classical Studies took over twenty-four acres of the site for excavation and the full extraordinary extent of what remained there was revealed. At that time, there were 600 houses on the land, the homes of some 7000 people. These were compulsorily purchased by the Greek government, then bought, planned and photographed and demolished by the American excavators.

In the 1950s, after two decades of extraordinary discoveries, one of the ruined marble porticoes that had stood beside the Agora was rebuilt according to the original specifications, the twenty-one shops in its long arcade being restored and adapted to hold the product of the American excavations. Called the Stoa of Attalus after the king who had presented it to Athens in the second century BC, the ancient building had offered shade and shelter along the edge of the open square and also separated this grand public area of the city from the dense alleyways and streets behind.

Suitably enough, the Stoa's rebuilding was also funded with US dollars; no other modern nation has used so many signs and symbols of the ancient Greeks on their public buildings or trumpeted the virtues of their ancient political system – democracy – that in truth, was born on archaeological sites like the Agora of Athens. In just such public squares, coinage and the market economy had been born alongside ideas of democracy and freedom – this last being the reverse of that other novel Greek condition, slavery. Here then, was born the basis of the modern notion of what it means to be human.

Miraculously, the American excavators found the apparatus of the modern democratic state in embryo still lying in the ruined buildings along the edges of the Agora. Here was an altar from which all distance was measured, perfect

BELOW: *The rock of the Acropolis viewed from the reconstructed buildings of the Agora of Athens.*

examples of standard weights and measures, the municipal water clock. Here too, were the foundations of the state mint, the Athenian council chamber for elected representatives, public notice boards, law courts with the elaborate machinery to permit secret jury voting, a ministry of war with dockets exchangeable for state armour and armaments; even what appeared to be the state prison where Socrates was executed – a small bust of the philosopher was found in one of the cells along with what might have been a pharmacist's jar for hemlock!

In all of this, the smallest details were the most amazing; a complicated machine for the automatic and public selection of juries with small dockets bearing individual names, a sculptor's tool bearing his name, sets of pottery for state occasions marked as public property, tax assessments, law codes, sculptors' kilns. Season by season, the extraordinary detail transformed older literary views of ancient Athenian life and times and turned it into something you could touch. Nor was there anything to suggest that this fascinating view of ancient life stopped at the edge of the twenty-four acres of the American site. Fanning out from the Agora, the public streets and squares of ancient Athens ran northwards across a railway line and eastwards under the oldest surviving part of central Athens called the Plaka, the last remnants of the little town of Elgin's days.

ABOVE: *A detail of a marble column top bearing the pattern of an acanthus leaf, excavated in the Agora, the ancient marketplace of Athens.*

So just as they had done before, the American archaeologists started to buy areas of land beside their excavations, and pull down the dilapidated nineteenth-century houses standing on them to excavate the ancient city underneath. One fascinating marble-covered highway ran from the Agora, beside the Stoa of Attalus, away to a Roman marketplace and an ancient public library, donated by the Emperor Hadrian, where a notice had been excavated telling the hours of opening and listing fines for overdue books. Along this marble street, sheltered by elegant colonnades, they found rows of ancient shops and houses: cobblers, wine-sellers, bronze workers, even the philosophers' schools. Slowly, slowly, house by house, the fascinating work progressed.

During the 1960s though, an alarm sounded. Although the Plaka was a largely run-down and part-abandoned quarter of the city inhabited by hippies and small eccentric shops, modern Athenians now saw that the precious remnants of the nineteenth-century city were disappearing. These were the oldest houses of the modern city, the little houses that Klenze had admired, he had even designed some of them. King Otto had ridden down these streets. They were part of the history of modern Athens. So the modern Athenians now had to decide which version of the past they wanted – their past, the nineteenth-century past, or the very ancient past. In the event, excavation was stopped. Today, concrete bulks hold up the houses and the streets on the edges of the excavations; land prices have since boomed, smart restaurants spill into the streets, the old houses are beautifully restored, their gardens filled with palm trees and the scent of jasmine. And the ancient past is balanced by the city of the present day.

Just Like Old Times
Via Imperiale, Rome: 1924

I N 1922, MUSSOLINI AND HIS FASCISTS marched on Rome and took over the government of Italy. Their ambition was to turn the country into a modern state at the centre of an international empire, just like the ancient Romans had done two millennia before. Just like the ancient Romans then, Mussolini's Fascists needed parading grounds; marching space for departing armies, marching space for victory celebrations. What better parade ground than through the very heart of ancient Rome, the scene of the triumphs of the Caesars and the centre of their ancient empire.

The trouble was, that in the 1920s, the heart of ancient Rome was covered by a dense historic maze of streets and buildings. Underneath, however, beneath this deep rich city lay the vast open squares and markets of the ancient Romans, the physical foundations of urban life in western Europe, and some of the most influential edifices of the modern world. Undaunted by this obscuring mass of later histories, Mussolini decided to cut slices through the ancient city. First though, he declared a third epoch in Roman history, after that of the caesars and the popes; a Fascist Rome that required new roads, new schools, new baths and gardens, and above all, new greatness and new majesty! The programme would of course, he declared, need much love and sacrifice, and calling upon the city mayor, he exhorted: '*Governatore! al lavoro!*'

Mussolini's promise to carve great slices through the 'squalor and poverty' of old Rome gave archaeologists a unique opportunity. As Professor Corrado Ricci, eminent restorer of so many celebrated Italian monuments would later put it, he relied on Fascism to realise the dream of his lifetime – the excavation of the marketplaces, the Fora, of Imperial Rome. Lending their reputations and their professional skills to Mussolini's grand idea, Ricci and his colleagues swiftly seized the day.

In the event, for this single theatrical effect, living neighbourhoods were rendered into dust to make a great grand highway to the Coliseum, the Via del Impero, Mussolini's marching ground. At the beginning of the work, Mussolini himself appeared on the rooftops of the demolition site, on that most beautiful Roman skyline, pickaxe in hand and

RIGHT: *Having wielded a ceremonial pickaxe at the beginning of the project, Il Duce visits his Roman excavations on the newly emerging Via Imperiale, and is hailed by the happy workers. The artist also shows us the now-familiar view of the Coliseum that Mussolini's project first revealed.*

ABOVE: *Mussolini's Via Imperiale in the process of being cut through the centre of old Rome in August 1932. A view from the top of the vast nineteenth-century monument, the so-called Vittoriano, the national symbol of the unification of Italy.*

ABOVE: 'The columns of the temple of Venus Genetrix beside the Via Imperiale, are restored to their architectural splendour. The Duce is turning Italy into a teeming factory,' proclaimed the caption of this plate from a newspaper colour supplement in 1932.

smashed through an elderly skylight to initiate the work. As demolition continued, the archaeologists extracted and restored many of the surviving fragments of the ancient architecture and Mussolini's ministries built their great parading ground and left the part-restored and propped-up ruins of the archaeologists for its backdrop.

Still standing by the side of Mussolini's great wide roadway is a mock-Roman column inadvertently celebrating the destruction of this section of the city. 'In the reign of King Victor Emanuele III, Benito Mussolini, Capo di Governo & Francesco Boncompagni-Ludovisi, Governor of Rome opened this Via dell Impero, in the 10th year of the era of Fascism, 28 October, 1932.' On that sunny day, Mussolini rode on horseback around the bright new road way that has transformed the ancient Coliseum into a traffic island and, scissors in hand, cut the ribbon to release a roaring flow of traffic that has hardly ceased to this day; a vast artery joining the Coliseum to the centre of the modern city.

Some said that Mussolini's great Street of Empire, with its marble maps of ancient Rome's expansion, its grand saluting podium and its municipal rose gardens was a manifestation of the triumphant rebirth of modern Italy. Not, one imagines, the inhabitants of the ancient *quartiere* that the dictator's pickaxes had smashed into the ground. It has been called the Rape of Rome. Though the results of these excavations have indeed proved vital for our modern understanding of the layout of ancient Rome, as Ricci knew they would, they destroyed much of modern Rome, as well as several ancient Roman monuments that happened to get in the way of the parading Fascist armies, these monuments being declared 'illogical and unaesthetic'!

When faced with the fragments of ancient architectural masterpieces that Ricci and his colleagues brought into the light – picturesque sections of celebrated long-lost marketplaces of the Caesars, raw, exposed, dragged blinking into the sunlight and crudely bisected with Mussolini's tarmacadam marching ground – you don't know whether to laugh or cry. Built one after the other by a succession of emperors, these great grand marble marketplaces were, for a thousand years and more, the most celebrated complex of buildings in the Western world. Visiting emperors were invariably impressed; there is a tale of a Byzantine ruler who, when inspired to erect an equestrian statue of himself inside one of the ancient marketplaces, was told that he should first make a stable of his own to hold it! Trajan's market had been the last to fall; a visiting French bishop records that in his day, in the seventh century, Romans out for their evening stroll still came to listen to public readings of Virgil on its marble steps. This though, was the market's last appearance for several centuries. The area is low and tends to damp. As Rome's population shrank, it was amongst the first to be abandoned and fell victim to earthquakes and the stone robbers whose kilns rendered the ancient marbles to building lime. In the fifteenth century though, when the popes finally returned from Avignon to Rome, and the city quickly grew in size again, extensions to the city were planned that incorporated the ruins of the ancient marketplaces. These were the ancestors of Rome's *quartieri*. Corrado Ricci's archaeologists and wreckers destroyed the quarter known as the Alessandrino, after the renaissance cardinal who had designed it, a fact surprisingly commemorated in a nearby street that still bears Ricci's name in celebration of his labours. Many of the buildings of the Alessandrino had been miniature histories in themselves, with

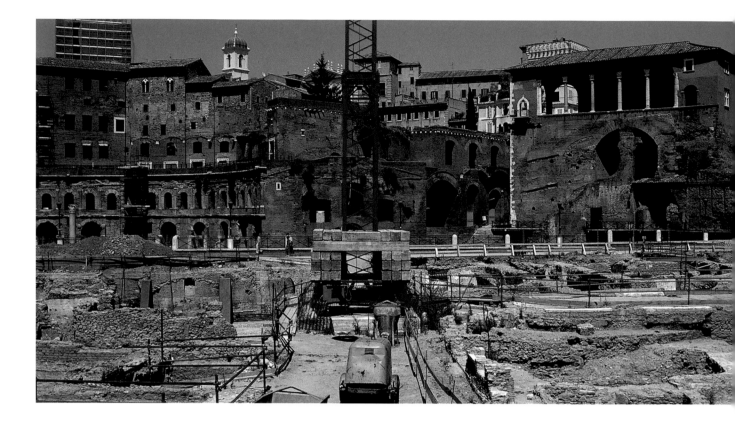

great, ancient Roman basements, baroque façades, eighteenth-century apartments and Art Deco roof gardens. Small shops and apartments, entire neighbourhoods living inside buildings set amongst the massive ancient Roman ruins. In the eighteenth and nineteenth centuries, foreign artists had come to live alongside Roman families, often in studios and apartments built directly into the ancient rooms of the venerable Roman markets. The whole quarter was dense with accumulated history, myth and local lore. In the nearby ruins of the marketplace of the Emperor Nerva, for example, there had been a rare survival from magic medieval Rome, an arch that centuries of pilgrims had venerated, where a half-visible inscription that proclaimed the *Arca Nerva* had been wrongly identified as the original Ark of Noah!

There have long been plans to clear away Mussolini's outrageous film set; to turn the centre of ancient Roman into a single vast archaeological zone and rid the standing ruins of the continuous vibration and pollution generated by the traffic on the Via del Impero. Then, at least, when the grand parading ground is cut away, for the first time in some fifteen hundred years, something of the real pomp and splendour of most ancient Rome, that grand imperial advertisement, will once again come into view. Sometimes though, as a fresh generation of archaeologists clean and clear the relics of the ancient marketplaces and dig up Mussolini's rose gardens, the sad relics of the basements of the Alessandrino come into the light again; fragments of peoples' lives that were arrested in the 1920s; small tiled kitchens, bathrooms and apartments; this then is the real archaeology of Fascism.

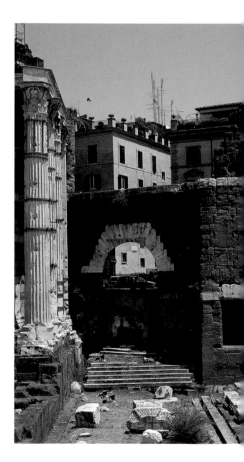

LEFT: *Fresh excavations beneath the Fascist parade grounds of the Via Imperiale in the late 1990s uncovered the foundations of the homes destroyed to make the great wide road. A new generation of Roman archaeologists now hopes to complete the archaeological explorations of the 1920s, and finally, to transform the heart of modern Rome into an archaeological park.*

BELOW LEFT: *In the vast ruins of the Imperial Roman marketplaces, parts of which served as a backdrop for the Via Imperiale, Mussolini's archaeologists dug out some thirty feet of fill to part-reveal the astonishing ancient architecture. The great arch at the centre of this photograph once crossed a small shadowed alleyway, the Via Bonella, in the now-vanished quarter called the Alessandrino.*

RIGHT: *The priests of the Emperor Augustus lead members of his family to the dedication of the Ara Pacis, the Altar of Peace, on 4 July 13 BC. A small part of the reliefs recovered by Mussolini's archaeologists and set into the reconstructed altar once again, in commemoration of Augustus' 2000th birthday, on 23 September 1938.*

The Altar of Peace, Rome: 1938. The Shadow of Augustus

The year 1938, the sixteenth year of Mussolini's rule, was the 2000th anniversary of the birth of the first Roman emperor, Augustus. A man after Mussolini's heart, Augustus had founded both the Roman Empire and the dynasty of emperors who first ruled it. Augustus, like Mussolini, was a tremendous propagandist. In his day, however, propaganda was building in the grand style. The Imperial tomb, Augustus' family tomb, was at the heart of the rebuilding schemes that changed Republican Rome forever.

Since ancient Roman times, the great brick cylindrical core of Augustus' tomb, with rows of niches in its interior walls designed to hold the imperial ashes, has served the Romans somewhat inventively, as a bull ring, a circus and finally, as an opera house whose acoustics were claimed to be the finest in the world. The last concert was held on 13 May 1936. The next day, the archaeologists moved in; Mussolini again making an appearance, on this occasion with a spade and a wheelbarrow shovelling away under the direction of his archaeologists. The plan was to restore the imperial tomb in time for the emperor's 2000th birthday.

Once again, Mussolini's archaeologists stripped the building down to its ancient bricks and cleared the area all around of many historic buildings. Here, however, they found virtually nothing. The sad old ruin, so mysterious that no one really knows its original appearance, was ill-set into the centre of a monstrous Fascist square, the Piazza dell Augusto Imperatore, whose sole redeeming feature is Alfredo's Restaurant, an elegant 1950s interior set underneath Il Duce's heavy porticoes.

Careful excavations over the past twenty years have proved that Augustus' tomb once formed part of a careful scattering of separate monuments linked together in Augustus' time by magic patterns of sun and shadow that held especial significance for the emperor and his dynasty. An enormous ancient Egyptian obelisk erected at the centre of one of the largest squares in ancient Rome, bound this astonishing light show together, casting its shadow over a white stone pavement some 525 feet long, all carefully marked with bronze insets, in an elaborate network of lines and letters and words of Greek, the traditional language of Roman astrology.

Thus marked, the obelisk's shadow counted out the hours, the days and the months, the zodiac and the emperor's horoscope and biography. Extended to the outer boundaries of Rome, one of the obelisk's geometries touched the dead centre of Augustus' mausoleum on a particularly auspicious day, whilst another marked the corner of the nearby field where the bodies of the imperial family were ceremonially cremated before their emplacement in the niches of the family tomb. The day that controlled these sight lines was 23 September, the day of Augustus' victory over the Egyptian armies of Anthony and Cleopatra which consolidated his rule over the Roman Empire. On that day, as if in homage, the shadows of his Egyptian obelisk ran right up to the bottom of a flight of steps that rose up to a vast marble altar dedicated to Peace. In Mussolini's day, however, no one knew of these magical alignments; only that the celebrated Altar of Peace – the *Ara Pacis* – still lay deep within the earth, and this too, would be resurrected along with the Imperial tomb as part of the imperial birthday celebrations. The story of its excavation is one of the wonders of twentieth-century archaeology.

For most of its long history, the *Ara Pacis* lay close by the main street of Rome, packed in the damp earth some forty feet beneath the pavements of the Via In Lucina. To bring it to the light again, Mussolini's archaeologists had to use some magic of their own, all the resources of a modern 1930s state. And this perhaps, has been the only time in history when archaeology was provided with funding and expertise usually reserved for the military or the media.

Archaeologists had known that Augustus' famous altar lay under the corner of an elegant *palazzo* in the Via In Lucina ever since the foundations of the palace had been laid directly on top of it in 1568. Ever since that time indeed, odd blocks of the altar covered in the most elegant reliefs had been extracted by the excavation of a series of tunnels extending ever further underneath the street and the

foundations of the palace. There was, however, an obvious limit to this process. By the 1900s it was already clear that the Palazzo Fiano, a beautiful renaissance building, which was already badly cracked, would collapse if any more subterranean excavations were undertaken. A year before Augustus' 2000th birthday, however, the order was given to extract the *Ara Pacis* from its renaissance prison and the archaeologist-engineer Giuseppe Moretti was given the unenviable task.

Moretti began his work by setting new foundations for the old *palazzo*, supporting the corner of the palace above the altar with steel girders and hydraulic jacks, repairing the damage in the palace walls and, finally, casting a great bridge of reinforced concrete beneath

ABOVE: *A detail of the exquisite vegetation that covers the lower portions of the Ara Pacis. The Greek sculptors who carved the altar imported the century-old traditions of Greek art to Rome. The designs have had vast impact on the European arts, from early Christian mosaic and medieval Bible illumination to the present.*

LEFT: *The Palazzo Fiano in the Via In Lucina at Rome, whose foundations once rested on the marble blocks of the Emperor Augustus' Ara Pacis*

BELOW: *The tomb of the Emperor Augustus and his family. Used as a fortress and a Roman bull ring, then converted to an opera house in the nineteenth century whose acoustics were said to be the best in Europe, Mussolini's archaeologists stripped the ancient building down to its imperial foundations. At the end of the work, even the Duce's architects admitted that the venerable old tomb, home of a thousand legends, looked like an old and rather rotten tooth.*

it all to act as a support. Then, he planned, the altar stones could simply be removed from underneath by further excavation. Yet as they dug, their trenches filled at once with water.

At this point, the normal procedure of archaeologists would be to bring in pumps and drain the entire site. Here though, under part of central Rome, this would remove the water and sand that held up all the surrounding buildings and destabilise the neighbourhood. Moretti's solution to the problem was unique. He froze the area solid. First, his engineers dug a rectangular trench some five feet wide and twenty-four feet long right around the corner of the palace. This was filled with a network of three-inch pipes which, on filling with refrigerant and controlled by compressors, produced a wall, a coffer dam, of ice. Then the pumps were brought in again, the small central area that held the altar was drained and digging out the altar was resumed. Even after this extraordinary effort, Moretti was forced to leave the massive foundations of the altar where they lay – they were just too deep, and too large to move. But one by one, the precious marbles were extracted from the ice-cold earth and the *Ara Pacis* was re-erected in a glass pavilion set beside the mausoleum. Opening in 1938, on the fateful 23 September, it was the sensation of the emperor's 2000th birthday party.

Augustus famously claimed to have found Rome a city of brick and left it a city of marble. The *Ara Pacis* – the finest single monument of ancient Rome, made by Greek craftsmen from Italian marble – is the epitome of his boast. Even today, in its airless box, a traffic island adjacent to the ruined tomb which even its Fascist architects despondently described as

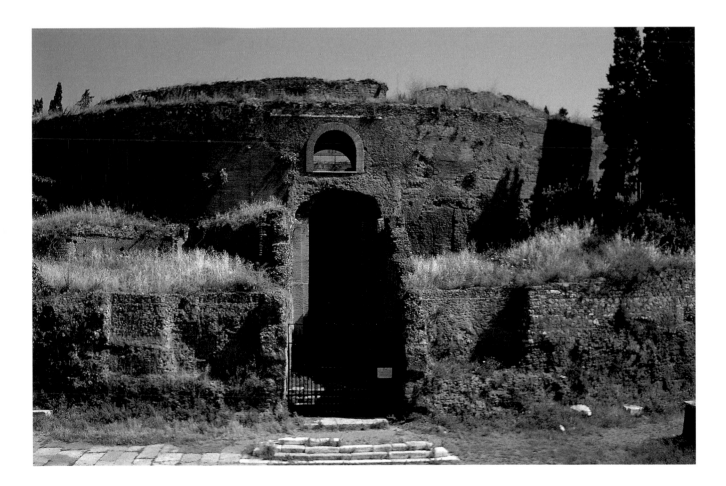

looking like a rotten tooth, the great altar still seems strange, mysterious, a marble screen with a single dark doorway at its centre. In fact, the high marble bench of the altar itself where the Roman priests offered slaughtered animals to the gods is hidden at the centre of a rectangular enclosure. A high wall of finely decorated marble that memorialises a temporary shelter of wood and garlands erected in AD 13 when, in great procession, the *Ara Pacis* was dedicated by the emperor. Although elegant enough, the altar is but a functional form; the marble screen, however, is an ancient masterwork that commands attention.

High up on one side of the altar screen is a relief portrait of Augustus himself, his face a little cracked now, after the Palazzo Fiano had rested on his head for centuries. He is shown walking in procession with his priests, the state fortune tellers and his numerous family, each one of them, man, woman and child, is well-known from gossipy contemporary records. Though carved by Greeks, this procession has none of the cool vigour of the Parthenon's processions. Here the atmosphere is incredibly Italian, a clear-sighted portrayal of a powerful family group walking in public procession; informal, dignified and human.

Carved over the greater part of this great marble enclosure, the palmettes twisting and turning, and the garlands seemingly swinging in a breeze have been imitated so many times, from Florence to New York, in banks and churches and so many paintings, that at first glance they are easily overlooked. Although it is difficult to see them anew, look again at their freshness, at the natural life that fills every inch of the carvings, and you will enjoy some of the finest sculptures ever made in Rome. 'The earth's overwhelming gifts' Augustus' court poet Virgil called the natural abundance that the artists here portrayed. Other scenes on this altar screen show some of the central images of Rome's ancient mythic history, recast with the faces of Augustus' family. Nature's abundance coupled with the divinity of the emperor and his family, promises prosperity to all who live in peace inside Augustus' empire.

This, Mussolini, this is propaganda on a cosmic scale!

The Boats of Nemi: 1927–1944. The Ashes of the Past

Of all of Mussolini's archaeological enterprises, the most extraordinary took place at Lake Nemi, south of Rome, the heartland of the ancient Latin tribe that founded Rome. It's a strangely sinister place. An extinct volcano, a round lake sitting in an inverted cone of wooded hills, a lake the ancient Romans called the Mirror of Diana. In Virgil's day, there was a vast terraced Temple of Diana by the lakeside, enlivened with lurid tales of ritual

ABOVE: *The ingenious plan of the archaeological engineer Giuseppe Moretti, which enabled him to freeze the ground under the buildings of the Via In Lucina in Rome, and enable the extraction of the Ara Pacis, and its replacement in the renaissance foundations with ferro-concrete. Moretti's rough rectangular trench held banks of refrigeration tubes, fed from the compressors and cylinders of carbon dioxide that stood in the street above.*

murder, buried treasures, sinister rites and sacred golden trees. Escaped slaves who fought and killed the high priest here became high priest in his place. But first, the slave had to snap off part of a sacred tree that grew here in this wood.

Today, it still seems sunk deep in half-forgotten myth. Sir James Frazer's famous *Golden Bough* was part-inspired by the awesome tangle of legends lapping around this strange lake. Virgil, too, was clearly moved by such unfathomable antiquity. Although the Romans did not know the origins of these savage stories they still believed their power; one of them noting sagely that such stories 'might not be true, but they had certainly existed'. A suitably dark place then, for a great dictator to come to excavate the past, especially when there were stories of great treasures lying on the bottom of the lake.

Down through the ages, many people had caught glimpses of two near-legendary boats, two enormous barges in the mud of the lake, and some had tried to raise them. In the process, a collection of the boats' bronze fittings, some of the finest, heaviest and most fantastic ever made, some odd statues and ritual equipment had been snatched from their decks by divers and brought up to the surface.

According to small inscriptions engraved on some water pipes, another great dictator, Augustus' nephew, the Emperor Caligula, had built the two great boats and put them on this lake where, surely, they formed part of the temple complex. Proportioned like supertankers, the two boats were some 230 feet long, very broad and very heavy. Their decks were decorated with precious marbles and bronze life-sized palm trees. Marble columns had

BELOW: *The Archaeological Museum at Lake Nemi, built in 1932 by Mussolini's military architects to hold the ancient Roman boats that the state archaeologists had retrieved from the waters of the lake.*

supported great pavilions, like arcades in a grandiose garden. A splendid reconstruction of one of them had served as a floating restaurant in the 1911 International Exhibition at Rome.

Mussolini wished to raise them both intact, and called in Corrado Ricci, Giuseppe Moretti and some of Italy's finest engineers to take charge of the work. After a competition was held to discover the most efficient way of bringing the two boats into the light, it was decided to drain the lake away. An ancient Roman water system, designed to keep the water by Diana's temple at a constant height, was cleaned, restored and put to work again. Then with a battery of four vast electric water pumps working over several years, the lake was drained and the giant boats appeared again. And as the lowering waters lapped along their sides once more, which, miraculously preserved, appeared to be as good as new, it seemed as if Caesar's boats were floating once again on the tide. In 1932, they were a wonder of the international press, and kings came to visit them. No one had ever seen anything quite like this before.

In 1933, a most elegant simple double hanger was set beside the lake to house these two fantastic tokens of the might and ingenuity of ancient Italy. Protected by temporary shelters, with the flag of Italy flying from their roofs, cradled in gigantic slings and set on a enormous system of rails, the two huge boats were slowly slid into the exhibition. For a few years, millions came to see them beside the dark lake. Then, when war came to Italy, the boats inside their hangers gave shelter to hundreds of refugees. Finally, in 1944, after Allied aeroplanes had bombed them, some retreating German soldiers set fire to the two splendid boats. They were completely consumed by the flames. Only the splendid empty space inside their hanger still remains, along with two small models, a desultory display of faded photographs and a vast incongruous anchor, a token of the boats' vast size.

ABOVE: *One of the vast barges, probably built during the reign of the Emperor Caligula, standing exposed on the mud of Lake Nemi in September 1929, after Mussolini's archaeologists had drained Lake Nemi of its water.*

But of course, there is also the archaeologists' publications of the work at Nemi. Mussolini's plans for the past always included archaeologists. They, after all, gave the seal of respectability to the dictator's schemes. Like Speer, the Nazi architect, many professional archaeologists were delighted to work with state resources that colleagues in other countries could only ever dream about. And many of them too, it must be said believed the grand words of the Fascists' special version of the past. Today of course, all that has been discredited. At Nemi, only the archaeologists' books remain; annual reports of the work in progress, two volumes by Corrado Ricci, and a final summing up, after their destruction, published now by the offices of the Italian State.

Here, and only here, is our record of the lost boats; a scientific description in words and charts and photographs of what was found. The books tell you, as any good archaeological publication will, about the work of excavation. They describe precisely, scientifically, the details of what was found and where. Experts provide analyses of various specific details of the bronze fitments and the iron nails, of the lead pipes and anchors, the wood of the boats, the coins found inside the hulks. Moretti discourses on the splendid bronzes that were found; naval architects write about the details of the rigging, steering and the rest.

Nemi's magic boats now live in books, in Mussolini's empty hanger and a story more improbable than any told by Diana's ancient priests. Is it in the books then that the ancient reality lies; this paper picture of the past? That perhaps, is archaeology's single greatest paradox – the gap between the real past and the science that records it.

ABOVE: *The scant remains of one of the terraces of Diana's temple that stood beside Lake Nemi. Intermittently examined by travellers and archaeologists since the eighteenth century, immortalised by Turner's great paintings and the anthropological speculation of Sir James Frazer, the ruins still hold a sinister sun-speckled beauty.*

LEFT: *The elegant empty interior of Lake Nemi's archaeological museum, burnt out in 1944.*

Minoan Postscript:
A Microcosm in Archaeology

THE WORLD-FAMOUS PALACE OF KNOSSOS on the island of Crete was excavated and restored over a period of some twenty-five years from the turn of the nineteenth century by Arthur (later Sir Arthur) Evans. Son of the wealthy and distinguished antiquarian Sir John Evans, an eminent scholar and museum curator in his own right specialising in gems and coins, Arthur Evans was interested in the very roots of ancient Greece. Struck by the fact that Schliemann had found no archaic texts at Mycenae or at Troy, Evans felt that even at a slightly later period, such pre-Greek writing must have existed. Evans had first been drawn to Crete by some exquisite engraved gemstones which he had seen in museums and in antiquary shops, gems of types that were common on the island where they were collectively known as 'milk stones' and were worn on necklaces as an aid to lactation. Not only did these stones seem extremely old but also Evans was convinced their engravings included signs that were part of a pictographic writing system. So, like the legendary youth of ancient Athens who had sailed to Crete and killed the Minotaur, in 1894 Evans focused his entire attentions on that neglected island, still under Turkish domination: 'A clue was in my hands, and like Theseus, I resolved to follow it, if possible to the inmost recesses of the Labyrinth.'

Evans took with him to Crete the orthodox view of the ancient Mediterranean world, one formed from the writings of the Greeks and Romans, amplified by the research of Tylorian anthropologists and above all by recent archaeology: 'In Dr Schliemann the science of classical antiquity found its Columbus. Armed with a spade, he brought to light from beneath the mounds of ages a real Troy: at Tiryns and Mycenae he laid bare the palaces and the tombs and treasures of Homeric Kings... Professor Petrie's researches in Egypt have conclusively shown that as early at least as the close of the Middle Kingdom, or approximately, the beginning of the second millennium BC, imported Greek vases were finding their way into the Nile Valley. By the great days of the Eighteenth Dynasty, in the sixteenth and succeeding centuries BC this intercourse was of such a kind that Mycenaen art, now in its full maturity of bloom, was reacting on that of the contemporary Pharaohs.'

Evans' ambition was to fill the gap in history between

RIGHT: *Part of the Grand Northern Gateway to the complex of buildings at Knossos, restored by Evans and his team of international architects and local craftsmen, employing the most advanced building technology of the day.*

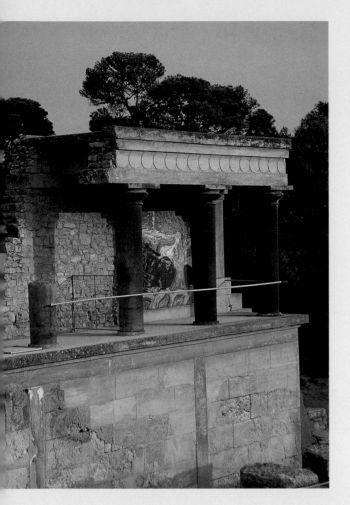

LEFT: *Sir Arthur Evans, 1851–1941, the excavator of the Palace of Knossos on the Isle of Crete with some of the treasures that he found. Evans had the time and money to work according to his own archaeological desires. D. G. Hogarth, at that time director of the British School of Archaeology in Greece, wrote to Evans that 'these expensive methods are yours in digging, as in collecting. . .You are a rich man's son. . .At the other pole to you stands Petrie – I see advantages in the methods of both.' At Knossos, Evans' personal vision and connoisseurship led him to undertake a reconstruction of the so-called Palace of the Bronze Age Kings of Knossos.*

Schliemann's Mycenaeans and the coming of the tribes that had brought iron and classical Greek culture down into the Mediterranean and mainland Greece.

He walked over the beautiful isle of Crete for several seasons before settling on a large artificial hill called Kephala, set in a valley behind the port now called Heraklion, the island capital. The hill had large ancient stones sticking out of the ground with marks on them that seemed to Evans to be similar to those on the milk stones that he had studied and collected for many years. Expending a great deal of time, effort and expense, during which time Crete underwent the trauma of being freed from Turkish rule, Evans bought the hill of Kephala, engaged an experienced team of professional archaeologists, hired 150 local farmers and mine workers and began to excavate.

From the very first day, 23 March 1900, breaking the soil on the very tip of the hill, extravagant and beauteous ancient treasures flowed from the ground. Evans and his archaeologists soon saw that they were excavating the centre of an enormous complex of buildings: 'A prehistoric palace,' wrote Evans, 'but a palace on a far larger scale than those of Tiryns and Mycenae.' The first room they had found, just a few inches beneath the top soil, was filled with the scattered fragments of fine wall paintings of a completely unknown type, extravagant and exquisite pottery and a throne-like chair of stone; Evans enthusiastically called it Europe's first throne room. Wonder followed wonder. To his especial delight, by the end of the first season, after the excavation of several acres of buildings, the archaeologists had recovered more than a thousand written texts of three different types of archaic writing , some of them found in little libraries of clay tablets, all cemented together into large blocks that required the most careful handling. It would, however, be another fifty years or so before anyone succeeded in translating just one of these types of writing. By the end of the first season, they had uncovered two acres of buildings and Evans had realised that he had found the remains of a previously unknown civilisation, a civilisation with fine arts, splendid architectures and sophisticated writing systems. A lost world brought into the light.

What was most riveting was the liveliness, the beauty, the sheer immediacy of the images on the antiquities they found. These were not solemn images from ancient Egypt or dark Troy, but animated, even risqué fragments of a sparkling, chattering and sometimes, it seemed, curiously modern population. 'To the north of the Palace,' wrote Evans, 'in some rooms that seem to have belonged to the women's quarter, frescoes were found in an entirely novel miniature style. Here were ladies with white complexions – due, we may fancy, to the seclusion of harem life; *décolletées*, but with fashionable puffed sleeves and flounced gowns, and their hair as elaborately curled and *frisé* as if they were fresh from a coiffeur's hands. "*Mais*," exclaimed a French savant who honoured me with a visit, "*ce sont des Parisiennes!*"'

As he excavated the individual rooms of the buildings on the hill of Kephala, he gave them all picturesque labels. The entire complex was always called the Palace. He had long since adopted the habit of calling the ancient ruins of Crete 'Knossian,' after the legendary palace of Knossos, where Greek legend told, King Minos had once lived. Now Evans called his palace the Palace of Knossos and its ancient inhabitants Minoans, after that legendary keeper of the Labyrinth. The largest decorated rooms inside the Palace of Knossos were called the Chambers of the King, medium-sized rooms the Chambers of the Queens and yet smaller ones dubbed Guard Houses and the like. The most numerous rooms of all, however, and by far the longest, with rows of storage pots for oil and grain, were known as magazines. As befits a palace, there were also gate houses and rooms for staff and ceremony. There was even an empire too, for King Minos' Palace to rule. By the 1900s, however, all the lands of the ancient eastern Mediterranean were already occupied by well-documented empires, so Evans gave his Minoans an empire of the sea, in academic parlance, a thalassocracy. It was plain common sense: as Evans remarked, 'Why is Paris strongly fortified, while London is practically an open town? The city of Minos, it must be remembered, was the centre of a great sea power, and it was in "wooden walls" that its rulers must have put their trust.'

Most famously of all of course, Evens rebuilt the ancient ruins on the hill of Kephala as his Palace of Knossos, a worthy capital for an empire of the ancient sea. One of the showpieces of world archaeology, visited by millions every year, the creation of a great archaeologist, scholar and philanthropist it is, none the less, a past built by an Edwardian gentleman.

It was also, it must be said, a most remarkable solution to an archaeological dilemma. As Evans soon discovered, the stone blocks sticking out from the gently rolling hill of Kephala, which had so intrigued him, were the topmost portions of high walls still buried in the earth; the walls of buildings several stories high. As they dug, they uncovered corridors and deep stairwells still attached to these same walls, with fragments of fine frescoes and rows of columns. Employing a technique of his own invention called 'architectural stratigraphy' that not only plotted the position of every object in the precise manner of his father's friend, Pitt Rivers, Evans had each floor level thoroughly cleared before his archaeologists cut down into the next one. This enabled him to recover the entire history of the buildings over a period of some five centuries, from 1800 BC; a history whose dates were certified by the numerous Egyptian objects they uncovered.

As they went further down into the buildings, however, the structures that they had isolated became increasingly unsafe. The root of the problem lay in the way the ancient people had constructed these buildings. Evans' Minoans had built the greater part of Knossos with enormous wooden beams, something like the timbers of a medieval house. These beams had edged, consolidated and, sometimes even supported, heavy stone walls. These ancient timbers, however, had long since been burnt away and rotted out, leaving walls that were held only by the earthen fill that Evans' workmen were removing. Unless he had restored the buildings' structure as he excavated, and restored it in a substantial way, Evans would never have been able to excavate without demolishing the buildings of each stratum as he went. A museum curator at heart, involved in both conservation and in presenting the past to a popular audience, Evans now went his own way, employing his substantial family fortune in the process. As he wrote to his father in the very first season, 'The Palace of Knossos was my idea and my work…I must have sole control of what I am personally undertaking.'

Evans' way was to employ the most modern architectural methods of his day, and call in competent young architects to take charge of the restorations. They replaced the missing

BELOW: *Evans, his arm proprietarily poised on one of the hundreds of splendid storage jars he excavated at Knossos, sits beside Theodore Fyfe, one of his archaeological architects, and the suede-booted Duncan Mackenzie, the brilliant Scottish archaeologist who supervised and recorded Evans' excavation of Knossos, and whose methods made possible the elaborate restorations with such a great degree of accuracy.*

wooden beams with costly imported steel and concrete. They remade parts of the Palace, row upon row of the distinctive Minoan pillars, which had originally been made from wooden beams and faced with painted plaster. An effort that today is similar to the work of the proprietors of a computer encyclopaedia reconstructing explanatory sections of ancient buildings.

Almost as soon as such work is begun, however, the restorers find themselves facing choices for which the archaeological evidence cannot supply the answers. Here, it must be said, Evans took the bull by the horns. Rather than discreetly fitting steel into the surviving fragments of ancient walls, steel sufficient to allow excavation to continue safely underneath, Evans made the palace of his dreams. New walls were built upon traces of the old, new protective ceilings were installed and all was replastered and repainted. Where all archaeological evidence was lost, the architects took their cue from ancient models and paintings of Minoan buildings. By the end of this extraordinary enterprise, Evans had given the world a sun-filled place filled with the shades of ancient courtiers, of young men and women dancing through the light and shadows of stairs and courtyards, palaces and throne rooms.

This, of course, was when middle-class Europe was rediscovering sun and sea and sex, when Picasso was motoring down from Paris to moonlit Riviera parties, when Corbusier was preaching the merits of walking naked in the sunlight and Matisse, following Cézanne, was painting warming canvases filled with Mediterranean light. Knossos with its archaeology, its ancient pedigree was a vital part of this brave new world: Europe was turning to its beginnings. In Proust's carefully constructed memoirs, Knossos became one of old Europe's sunlit ancient memories; lesser writers transformed Sir Arthur's island civilisation into Atlantis risen again above the waves; most saw this ancient world as an idyllic, rather sexy, dream. And naturally enough, all Mediterranean cruise lines were delighted with the prospect of offering a brand-new stopover on the old familiar sea lanes. A small museum was hastily erected in Heraklion to accommodate Sir Arthur's treasures, an asphalt road was laid to his ancient palace, the cruise boat passengers now came to the little-visited island of Crete to see the Palace of King Minos for themselves, and Evans' successors made small desultory excavations at the edges of the tourist site.

In 1953, a marvellous thing happened to the ancient Palace of Knossos; it began to talk again. Michael Ventris, a young English architect, had finally managed to decipher one of the three languages on the mysterious inscribed tablets that Evans had excavated more than fifty years before. To the surprise of all, it seemed that the people of Knossos had used a form of Greek; even their cows had good Greek names! This would have amazed Sir Arthur Evans. Like all other serious scholars of his time and many still today, he believed that the people who had made classical Greek culture had come down into Greece following, and probably provoking, the ending of the ancient cultures that Schliemann and himself had excavated. Books, theses, entire careers, university departments and many, many excavations had been built and undertaken to investigate these ancient invaders who stood at the very roots of Western culture. The fact that the people who had made Knossos and the Parthenon of Athens were related by a common language thus raised the most fundamental questions. That a form of ancient Greek had been spoken in the eastern Mediterranean a thousand years before most scholars had thought possible – and more modern research suggests that their linguistic ancestry is yet far older even than that – spelled the ending of an era, the ending of nineteenth-century explanations that saw war, plague, disaster and invasion as the main movers of ancient history.

In 1979, even the cosy popular image of Knossos as an archaic Riviera paradise with added empire, took a nasty knock. The Greek archaeologists Yannis and Efi Sakkellarakis found the well-preserved remains of the body of a bloodless youth, an ancient Minoan with his throat cut, still lying on the altar of a sanctuary on a Cretan mountain pass. Close beside him, was what appeared to be the body of the officiating sacrificial priest, the victim of an earthquake that seems to have interrupted that violent ceremonial. The Minoans had practised human sacrifice! A year later, excavating in an ancient house right next door to Evans' palace, a British archaeologist, Peter Warren, uncovered the bones of two small children along with a fine collection of splendid associated Minoan objects. The tiny skeletons, which had been deliberately disarticulated, had knife marks on them: the two children had been butchered, just as a carcass would be for consumption. As a leading authority on ancient butchery later agreed, however, these knife marks were not those of an expert butcher. In all probability therefore, they were the work of an amateur, a priest perhaps, preparing the two children to be cooked and eaten as a ritual meal.

Sacrifice and cannibalism in the kingdom of good king Minos! Many Minoan archaeologists simply refused to accept the evidence. Yet, as their excavators well knew, it was completely true. At the Palace of Knossos, it was not just Sir Arthur Evans' restoration that was crumbling, pounded by the weather and millions of tourists, but his powerful vision of the ancient world and that of generations of historians. The ancient palace and its kings and princes that Evans had so carefully constructed, had become something of a grand illusion.

In the last three decades, modern archaeologists have begun to question the very language of their subject; those common nineteenth-century images and terms that have imprisoned historical thought and potential for so long, and presupposed the answer to every question that you might ever ask about the past. Had Knossos really been an ancient palace, an imperial palace, the home of mighty kings and queens? The truth is there was no evidence at all of Minoan kingship nor, even that royalty was itself a common institution in the ancient world. The so-called Empire of Knossos, seems to have been an assumption based upon Evans' terminology and vision of the world.

A palace, of course, is not merely a home for kings, but the centre of an administration, with ceremonial and administrative quarters, with soldiers, scribes and servants, with large dining rooms and living quarters and sometimes too, high surrounding walls, a sort of a fortress. There is very little resembling that in the architecture of Knossos. Just acre upon acre of store rooms, a few decorated chambers with seats and benches and a few more modest rooms that seem to be connected with a kind of ceremonial. There is, however, an enormous paved road leading to the complex, and wide and splendid stairways that suggest considerable traffic in and out of it.

To an anthropologist, all this would intimate that the buildings at Knossos were sacred store rooms; a temple set in a fertile valley. The great temples of ancient Thebes in Egypt provide a clear analogy. They too had huge storage areas whose contents were collected as tax under the aegis of the gods. At Knossos, the amount of grain and oil that could be stored in the huge magazines whose capacity it has been calculated, would hold half the produce of the island at that time, could have supported tens of thousands of people for several years, just as was done at ancient Thebes. Seen in this light, Knossos begins to assume a fresh dimension, although it remains a most extraordinary, enigmatic place, still difficult to understand. But now at least, there is a possibility of a fresh understanding of ancient reality.

Similarly, the image of Knossos as the capital of a so-called 'empire of the sea', bears further questioning. For this is an empire without a single visual record of its existence, without a mention in contemporary texts. This then, is presently a phantom empire built from ancient pictures of Minoan ships, the reputation of the legendary King Minos and the assumption that the widespread influence of Minoan arts denoted earthly power. Yet neither splendid boats nor artistic influence imply an empire, any more than echoes of the architecture of the Palace of Versailles in London, Vienna and New York imply that the Sun King ruled in England, Austria or America.

What then, were the realities of the well-established so-called 'empires' of the ancient world, those of Egypt, China and the Americas? Were they ever really national empires as marked out on modern maps with lines round their boundaries. Did such concepts exist in the distant past? What too, of the concept of nationality itself, three and four thousand years ago? From the available evidence, it presently appears that most ancient people counted what we today call culture as ethnicity, a notion very foreign to the modern world where ethnicity is commonly believed to be the same as race. What evidence is there of the existence of the modern notion of the individual? Like Evans' Palace, these are all ideas from a much more recent past. Is it then correct to assume their presence in distant history?

Traditionally, archaeologists made their history in much the same way as Sir Arthur Evans made the Palace of Knossos, from genuine fragments of this and that all held together with modern glue to form a single edifice. That of course, is a CNN sort of history, a patchwork of wars, coronations, politics and trade. Yet there are many other histories to be told about Knossos, just as there are about every other archaeological site on earth.

One of these modern histories, for example, deals in far longer spans of time than used to be the case. As Evans himself observed, the walls of King Minos' Palace stood on much older residues that were never excavated: 'A primitive settlement of still greater antiquity…this "Neolithic" deposit was over twenty-four feet thick, everywhere full of stone axes, knives of volcanic glass, dark polished and incised pottery…' People had lived on this hill long,

long before King Minos' day and in all probability, the memories and manners of those more ancient times were held in the buildings that Evans remade, just as most ancient memories are held still in the Mexican Valley of Oaxaca (*see pages 169–71*). Somewhere near the bottom of these most ancient levels, although archaeologists have yet to excavate them, there should be the first olives trees brought to the island and the bones of the first sheep too – those two staples that, coupled with wine, enabled the Minoans, their successors and contemporaries to live so well on the poor soil of the Mediterranean.

The prehistoric people of paleo-Knossos would have farmed quite close to the stream that runs below the palace. The wider landscape was not terraced then and would have supported very little. This would have altered, however, in the time of the so-called Palace. There is evidence of road and bridge building right through Crete at this time; in all probability, terracing for grain and olive trees and grapes began in this same period as well – although this still awaits archaeological confirmation. Classical Greek culture brought iron to Crete, the Romans set aqueducts into the ancient valley of Knossos and so provided immense amounts of water and agricultural prosperity. Arab and Turkish domination brought new crops – citrus, sugar, cotton; Sir Arthur too, brought a novel prosperity – asphalt roads and electricity to light the ancient ruins and the excavation house; in his day the richest dwelling on the island, a little palace. This new history deals in daily life and not in politics, kings and war. As Fernand Braudel, that great French historian had realised back in the 1940s, there are vast histories to be made for the great majority of humanity; all those people who previously, have never had a history.

Nowadays then, most serious archaeologists work at sites that seem to hold no gold, no treasure, but simply information about how people lived; they work in middens and in pigsties, in castles, in peasant hovels, in fields and graveyards, and at the bottom of the sea. They are gathering basic information about changing diets, changing populations, about trade and faith, myth and magic and the processes of making things. And this very different

ABOVE: *White-suited Evans standing amidst his workmen as they rebuild the Grand Staircase of Knossos. Iron joists, previously unknown on the Isle of Crete, were an expensive importation, as was concrete; materials that are presently causing the conservators of Evans' legacy fresh headaches of their own. At the ending of this work, the staircase would stand some twenty-five feet high, to serve three separate stories of Evans' palace.*

BELOW: *The lonely Roman city of Madaura, in the Algerian hinterland. In the fourth century, St Augustine came to Madaura, a sophisticated university town, to study the arts of literature and rhetoric. Recent archaeological surveys across northern Africa have shown how the Romans changed this lonely landscape from a semi-desert to a rich countryside of wheat, vines and olives, whose proceeds inspired a citizen of the region to celebrate this new world in Roman script on imported marble; 'The hunt, the baths; play and laughter; that's the life for me.' The desolate city is still set inside a network of ancient roads connecting dozens of ancient and unexcavated farms.*

data is beginning to provide surprising information. One thing that has already emerged is that most of the images of daily life delineated by ancient writers and artists bears about as much relationship to reality as do Hollywood movies.

Sometimes this new archaeology will require surveys through vast landscapes: deserts, valleys, sea beds and mountain tops; the investigation of huge spans of time and the tiniest traces of ancient life. These though, are the processes by which we will prove that the 'Fall of the Roman Empire,' Europe's slow progress from slavery to serfdom, from emperors to chiefs, was something more than an ancient soap opera set in an Imperial court. The same broad-based archaelogy might also show us something of what the pyramids and temples cost ordinary ancient Egyptians and Mesopotamians to build, placing their mighty constructions in a genuinely human context for the very first time. In Australia, archaeologists have already begun to excavate some 40,000 years of rich and varied social history to set beside contemporary memories of Dreamtime. In the Americas too, archaeologists are building entirely new histories of the ancient cultures of their continent, without a single master race to help them on their way.

It will take generations of excavators to extract the basic information required to build those new histories from the same old earth which has already yielded so many treasures and fine monuments. Clearly, the discoveries of this new archaeology will require very

different spaces for their exhibition from those of the old. This new science will not be held in grand galleries and glass cases. After two centuries of dedicated scholarship, however, almost everything in the cupboard of those great collections has been catalogued and numbered and history now has a base of chronologies and kings. Modern archaeology then, has firm foundations and a vast potential: the power to recover the pith of ancient life, to show us people who were once as intelligent and as contradictory as ourselves, and to share in some small way, the experience of their lives. That is the true treasure that future archaeology can find for us.

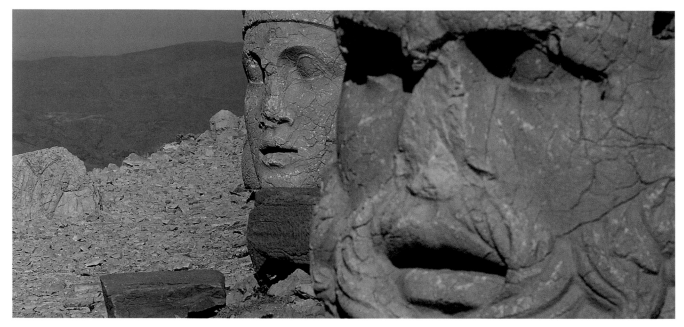

Index

PHOTO PAGE 212: *Two of the colossal heads that decorate the tumulus of Antiochus I of Cammagene at Nemrud Dagh in south-eastern Turkey.*

Bibliography

Many of the volumes listed here, especially the older ones, do not necessarily provide balanced, up-to-date or even correct, information about the ancient sites and cultures that they describe. They have been chosen for their significance for the history of archaeology and as indications of the sources of the narratives of this book. Most of the more recent volumes, however, contain reliable bibliographies dealing with various aspects of ancient history and the archaeological sites described in this book. Unless no translation is available, the English editions of the works are generally listed below. Works cited only by author and date have been given in full in a previous section of the bibliography.

General Works

Glyn Daniel, *150 Years of Archaeology*, London, 2nd ed., 1975

Encyclopaedia Britannica, 1768–

Illustrated London News, 1842–

Massimo Pallottino, *The Meaning of Archaeology*, London, 1968

Colin Renfrew & Paul Bahn, *Archaeology, theories, methods and practice*, London, 1991

Introduction

F. Debono, *Prehistory in the Nile Valley*, in, (ed.) J. Ki-Zerbo, *General History of Africa* I, London, 1981

Charles Rollin, *The Ancient History of the Egyptians, Carthaginians, Assyrians, Babylonians, Medes and Persians, Macedonians and Grecians*, 10 Vols., Paris, 1740 [last edition, London, 1925]

Alain Schnapp, *The Discovery of the Past, the origins of archaeology*, London, 1996

PART I: Into the Past

Dieter Arnold, *Gräber des Alten und Mittleren Reiches in El-Tarif*, Mainz, 1976

Paola Barocchi & Daniela, Gallo (eds,), *L'Accademia etrusca*, Milan, 1985

Fritz Eckart Barth, *The Prehistoric Cemetery of Hallstatt*, Vienna, 1994

Ofer Bar-Yosef, *On the Nature of Transitions: the Middle to Upper Palaeolithic and the Neolithic Revolution*, in, *Cambridge Archaeological Journal* Vol. 8, No. 2, October, 1998

Geoffrey Bibby, *The Testimony of the Spade*, New York, 1956

Lewis R. Binford, *In Pursuit of the Past*, London, 1983

Mark Bowden, *Pitt Rivers, the life and archaeological work of Lieutenant-General Augustus Henry Lane Fox Pitt Rivers, DCL, FRS, FSA*, Cambridge, 1991

Don Brothwell and Eric Higgs, (eds.), *Science in Archaeology*, London, 1969

C. W. Ceram, *A Picture History of Archaeology*, London, 1957

Georges Charbonnier, *Conversations with Claude Lévi-Strauss*, London, 1969

Gordon Childe, *What Happened in History*, Harmondsworth, 1964

Edith Clay (ed.) *Sir William Gell in Italy, letters to the Society of Dilettanti*, London, 1976

Austin Claverhill, *Rushmore – Then and Now*, privately printed, 1988

James Clifford, *The Predicament of Culture, twentieth-century ethnography, literature, and art*, Cambridge, Mass., 1988

Glyn Daniel, *The Origins and Growth of Archaeology*, London, 1967

Glyn Daniel, *Stone, Bronze and Iron*, in, (ed) J. V. S. Megaw, (ed.) *To Illustrate the Monuments, essays on archaeology presented to Stuart Piggott*, London, 1976

Glyn Daniel, *Writing for Antiquity, an anthology of editorials from Antiquity*, London, 1992

Joseph Jay Deiss, *Herculaneum, Italy's buried treasure*, London, 1985

Margaret Drower, *Flinders Petrie, a life in archaeology*, London, 1985

Clive Gamble, *The Palaeolithic Settlement of Europe*, Cambridge, 1986

D. A. E. Garrod and D. M. E. Bate, *The Stone Age of Mount Carmel, excavations at the Wady el-Mughara*, Vol. I, Oxford, 1937

Monique Goudet-Ducellier, *Terra Amata, un campement de chasseurs prehistoriques a Nice il y a 400,000 ans*, Nice, 1987

Michael Grant, *Bourbon patronage and foreign involvement at Pompeii and Herculaneum*, in Edward Cheney & Neil Richie (eds.) Oxford, *China and Italy, writings in honour of Sir Harold Acton*, London, 1984

Michael Grant, *The Visible Past, Greek and Roman history from archaeology 1960-1990*, London, 1990

Paolo Graziosi, *Palaeolithic Art*, London, 1960

Bo Gräslund, *The Birth of Prehistoric Chronology, dating methods and dating systems in nineteenth-century Scandinavian archaeology*, Cambridge, 1987

Harold St. George Gray, *General Pitt Rivers*, in L. H. Dudley Buxton, *The Pitt Rivers Museum*, Farnham, Dorset, 1929

Jacquetta Hawkes, *Adventurer in Archaeology, the biography of Sir Mortimer Wheeler*, New York, 1982

Peter James, et al. *Centuries of Darkness*, London, 1991

Jørgen Jensen, *Christian Jürgensen Thomsen; an appreciation in the Bicentennial of his Birth*, Acta Archaeologica, 1986

Jørgen Steen Jensen (ed.) *Christian Jürgensen Thomsen 1788–29. December – 1988*, Copenhagen, 1988

Ole Klindt-Jensen, *A History of Scandinavian Archaeology*, London, 1975

Carlo Knight, *Sir William Hamilton's Campi Phlegraei*, in Edward Cheney & Neil Richie (eds.) Oxford, *China and Italy, writings in honour of Sir Harold Acton*, London, 1984

Adam Kuper, *The Invention of Primitive Society, transformations of an illusion*, London, 1988

Édouard Lartet and Henry Christy, *Reliquiae Aquitanicae, being contributions to the archaeology and palaeontology of Périgord and the adjoining provinces of Southern France*, London, 1856-75

Richard Leakey, *Origins*, New York, 1977

Wolfgang Leppmann, *Pompeii in Fact and Fiction*, London, 1968

Claude Lévi-Strauss, *Totemism*, Harmondsworth, 1969

Hakon Lund, *Mindelunden ved Jægerspris*, Jægerspris, Denmark, 1976

Henry de Lumley, *A Palaeolithic Camp Site at Nice*, in, *Scientific American*, no. 220.

Alexander Marshack, *The Roots of Civilisation*, London, 1972

Ronald Millar, *The Piltdown Men*, London, 1972

Stephen Mithen, *The Prehistory of the Mind, a search for the origins of art, religion and science*, London, 1996

Erwin Panofsky, *Studies in Iconology, humanistic themes in the art of the renaissance*, New York, 1962

W. M. Flinders Petrie, *Diospolis Parva*, London, 1901

Stuart Piggott, *Ancient Europe, from the beginnings of agriculture to Classical Antiquity*, Edinburgh, 1965

A. H. L. Fox Pitt Rivers, *On the Discovery of Chert Implements in Stratified Gravel in the Nile Valley Near Thebes*, in *Journal of the Anthropological Institute*, No. II, 1881

A. H. L. Fox Pitt Rivers, *Excavations in Cranbourne Chase*, 4 vols. (privately printed), 1887–98

August Mau, *Pompeii, its life and art*, London, 1899

Amadeo Mauri, *Herculaneum*, Rome, 1977

Bodil Bungaard Rasmussen, Jørgen Steen Jensen & John Lund (eds.) *Christian VIII & Nationalmuseet*, Copenhagen, 1999

Colin Renfrew, *Before Civilisation, the radiocarbon revolution and prehistoric Europe*, London, 1973

Avraham Ronen, *Mt. Carmel Caves – the first excavations*, in, Avraham Ronen (ed), *The Transition from Lower to Middle Palaeolithic and the Origin of Modern Man*, Oxford, 1982

Schnapp, 1996

Karel Sklenár, *Archaeology in Central Europe: the first 500 years*, Leicester, 1983

Timothy Taylor, *The Prehistory of Sex, four million years of human sexual culture*, London 1996

M. W. Thompson, *General Pitt Rivers; evolution and archaeology in the nineteenth century*, Bradford-upon-Avon, 1977

Raleigh Trevelyan, *The Shadow of Vesuvius, Pompeii AD 79*, London, 1976

Bruce Trigger, *Gordon Childe, revolutions in archaeology*, London, 1980

Mortimer Wheeler, *Archaeology from the Earth*, London, 1954

Mortimer Wheeler, *Alms for Oblivion, an antiquaries scrapbook*, London, 1966

J. S. Weiner, *The Piltdown Forgery*, London, 1955

Mina Weinstein-Evron, *Early Natufian el-Wad Revisited*, Liège, 1998

PART II: The Treasure Seekers

S. A. [Sarah Atkins] *Fruits of Enterprize, exhibited in the travels of Belzoni in Egypt and Nubia interspersed with the observations of a mother to her children*, London, 1825

Al-Jabarti, *Chronicle of the French Occupation*, New York, 1993

Dieter Arnold, *Moses und Aida. Das Alte Ägypten in der Oper*, in, *Ägypten – Dauer und Wandel*, Mainz, 1985

Joseph Alsop, *The Rare Art Traditions, the history of art collecting and its linked phenomena wherever these have appeared*, New York, 1982

Salvatore Aurigemma, *Villa Adriana*, Rome, 1984

Baedeker Guides, Egypt and the Sudan, Leipzig, 1929

G. Belzoni, *Narrative of the Operations and Recent Discoveries within the Pyramids, Temples, Tombs and Excavations in Egypt etc. etc.*, London, 1820 & 1822

Deborah Bull & Donald Lorimer, *Up the Nile: a photographic excursion 1839–98*, New York, 1978

Ceram, 1957

Kenneth Clark, *The Art of Humanism*, London, 1983

Elisabeth David, *Mariette Pacha, 1821–81*. Paris, 1994

Dominique Vivant Denon, *Voyage dans la Basse et la Haute Égypte, pendant les Campagnes du Général Bonaparte*, Paris, 1802

M. Wilson Disher, *Pharaoh's Fool*, London, 1957

W. N. Edwards, *The Early History of Palaeontology*, London, 1967

Charles Gillespie & Michel Dewachter, *Monuments of Egypt, The Napoleonic Edition, the complete archaeological plates from La Description de l'Egypte*, Princeton, 1987

E. H. Gombrich, *Tributes, interpreters of our cultural tradition*, Oxford, 1984

Jeanette Greenfield, *The Return of Cultural Treasures*, Cambridge, 1989

Julia Van Haften (ed.) *Egypt and the Holy Land in Historic Photographs, 77 Views by Francis Frith*, New York, 1981

Francis Haskell & Nicholas Penney, *Taste and the Antique, the lure of classical sculpture 1500–1900*, New Haven, 1981

J. Christopher Herold, *Bonaparte in Egypt*, London, 1962

Erik Iverson, *The Myth of Egypt and its Hieroglyphs in European Tradition*, Copenhagen 1961

T. G. H. James, *The British Museum and Ancient Egypt*, London, 1981

John Kenworthy-Browne, *Private Skulpturengalerien in England 1730–1830*, in Klaus Vierneisel & Gottlieb Leinz (eds.), *Glyptothek München, 1830–1980*, Munich, 1980

Richard Lepsius, *Discoveries in Egypt, Ethiopia and the Peninsula of Sinai in the years 1842–45*, London, 1852

André Malraux, *The Voices of Silence*, Princeton, 1953

Auguste Mariette, *The Monuments of Upper Egypt*,

London, 1877

Gaston Maspero, *Guide to the Cairo Museum*, Cairo, 3rd ed. 1906

Gaston Maspero, *New Light on Ancient Egypt*, London, 1908

Stanley Mayes, *The Great Belzoni*, London, 1954

Isabel McBride (ed), *Who owns the Past?* papers from the annual symposium of the Australian Academy of the Humanities, Melbourne,1985

Timothy Mitchell, *Colonising Egypt*, Cambridge, 1988

Massimiliano Pavan, *l'Aventura del Partenone un monumento nella storia*, Florence, 1983

David Roberts, *The Holy Land, Syria, Idumæa, Arabia, Egypt & Nubia*, 6 vols., London, 1855

Samuel Rogers, (ed. Dyce) *Recollections of the Table-Talk of Samuel Rogers, to which is added Porsoniana*, London, 1856

John Romer, *Valley of the Kings*, London, 1981

Kenneth Setton, *Athens in the Middle Ages*, London, 1975

Sacheverell Sitwell, *Conversation Pieces, a survey of English domestic portraits and their painters*, London, 1936

Sacheverell Sitwell, *British Architects and Craftsmen, a survey of taste, design and style during three centuries 1600 to 1830*, London, 1945

E. Scheicher, *Die Kunst und Wunderkammern der Habsburger*, Vienna, 1979

James Stuart & Nicholas Revett, *The Antiquities of Athens, and other monuments of Greece as measured and delineated*, London, 1762–1816

John Summerson, *Architecture in Britain, 1530 to 1830*, Harmondsworth, 1970

John Summerson, *The Unromantic Castle, and other essays*, London, 1990

Fani-Maria Tsagakou, *The Rediscovery of Greece, travellers and painters of the romantic era*, London, 1981

Klaus Vierneisel & Gottlieb Leinz (eds.) *Glyptothek München, 1830–1980*, Munich, 1980

Eugène-Melchior de Vogüé, *Lettre de Mariette Pacha*, Paris, n.d., circa 1885

Theodore Vrettos, *The Elgin Affair, the abduction of antiquity's greatest treasures and the passions it aroused*, London, 1997

John A. Wilson, *Signs and Wonders upon Pharaoh, a history of American egyptology*, Chicago, 1964

J. J. Winckelmann, *Geschichte der Kunst des Altertums*, 1764 [English translation, *The History of Ancient Art amongst the Greeks*, Boston 1880].

Francis A. Yates, 'Oracle to the Cock of France' in *Collected Essays*, Vol. 2, London, 1983

PART III: Digging by the Book
William Foxwell Albright, *The Archaeology of Palestine*, Harmondsworth, 1960

Irina Antonova et al, *The Gold of Troy, searching for Homer's fabled city*, London, 1996

Nahman Avigad, *Discovering Jerusalem*, New York, 1980

Michael Avi-Yonah & Ephraim Stern (eds.), *Encyclopedia of Archaeological Excavations in the Holy Land*, 4 vols., Oxford, 1975-8

C. J. Ball, *Light from the East, or the Witness of the Monuments*, London, 1899

Ceram, 1952

Moshe Dothan, *Terminology for the archaeology of Biblical periods*, in, *Proceedings of the Symposium Biblical Arch*, (ed) Janet Amitai, Jerusalem, 1985

S. R. Driver, *Modern Research as illustrating the Bible* (Schweich Lectures 1908), London, 1909

Drower, 1985

Hervé Duchêne *The Golden Treasures of Troy, the dream of Heinrich Schliemann*, London, 1996

Joan Evans, *Time and Chance, the story of Arthur Evans and his forebears*, London, 1943

Joan Evans, *A History of the Society of Antiquaries*, London, 1956

Exhibition Catalogue, *Troy, Mycenae, Tiryns and Orchomenos; the hundredth anniversary of Schliemann's death,*

[in Greek] Athens, 1990

J. Lesley Fitton, *The Discovery of the Greek Bronze Age*, London, 1995

H. J. Franken & M. L. Stiener, *Excavations in Jerusalem, 1961–1967*

Vol II, *The Iron Age extramural quarter on the south-east Hill*, Oxford, 1990

William H. C. Frend, *The Archaeology of Early Christianity, a history*, London, 1996

Vronwy Hankey, *From Chronos to Chronology: Egyptian evidence for dating the Aegean Bronze Age*, in, *The Journal of the Ancient Chronology Forum* Vol. 5, 1991-2

David Hogarth (ed), *Authority and Archaeology, Sacred and Profane*, London, 1899

James, 1991

Kathleen M. Kenyon, *Archaeology in the Holy Land*, London, 1985

Kay Kohlmeyer et al, *Wiedererestehendes Babylon, Eine antike Weltstadt im Blick der Forschung*, Berlin, 1991

Georg Korres, *Das Mausoleum Heinrich Schliemanns, auf dem Zentralfriedhof von Athen*, in, *Boreas 4*, Münster, 1981

Caroline Moorehead, *The Lost Treasures of Troy* London 1994

George E. Mylonas, *Ancient Mycenae, the capital city of Agamemnon*, London, 1957

W. M. Flinders Petrie, *Tell el Hesi*, London, 1891

W. M. Flinders Petrie, *Ten Years Digging in Egypt*, London. 1893

W. M. Flinders Petrie, *Six Temples at Thebes*, London, 1896

W. M. Flinders Petrie, *Seventy Years in Archaeology*, London, [1933]

John Romer, *Testament, the Bible and history*, London, 1988

A. H. Sayce, *Reminiscences*, London, 1923

Heinrich Schliemann, *Troy and its Remains*, London, 1875

Heinrich Schliemann, *Mycenae*, London, 1878

Heinrich Schliemann, *Ilios: The city and country of the Trojans*, London, 1880

Heinrich Schliemann, *Troja, results of the latest researches and discoveries on the site of Homer's Troy*, London, 1884

Yigal Shiloh, *Excavations at the City of David I, 1978–82*

Qedem 19, Jerusalem, 1984

George Adam Smith, *The Historical Geography of the Holy Land*, London, 1895

Morton Smith, *Jesus the Magician*, London, 1978

David Trail & W. M. Calder III, *Myth, Scandal and History: the Heinrich Schliemann controversy*, Detroit, 1986

Alan J. B. Wace, *Mycenae, an archaeological history and guide*, Princeton, 1949

Alan J. B. Wace, et al, *Excavations at Mycenae 1939–1955*, London, 1979

Keith W. Whitelam, *The Invention of Ancient Israel, the silencing of Palestinian history*, London, 1996

Yigael Yadin (ed.) *Jerusalem Revealed, archaeology in the Holy City*, Jerusalem, 1976

PART IV: Looking for the One Beginning
William Foxwell Albright, *From the Stone Age to Christianity, monotheism and the historical process*, New York, 1957

Charles Breasted, *Pioneer to the Past*, New York, 1943

James Henry Breasted, *Development of Religion and Thought in Ancient Egypt*, London 1912

James Henry Breasted, *The Oriental Institute of the University of Chicago*, Chicago, 1931

James Henry Breasted, *The Dawn of Conscience*, New York, 1947

Bernadette Bucher, *Icon and Conquest, a structural analysis of the Illustrations of de Bry's Great Voyages*, Chicago, 1981

Jean Capart, *Primitive Art in Egypt*, London, 1905

Frederick Catherwood, *Views of Ancient Monuments in Central America, Chiapas and Yucatan*, London, 1844

Ceram, 1952

Erich von Däniken, *Chariots of the Gods?* London, 1969

Leo Deuel, *Flights into Yesterday, the story of aerial archaeology*, London, 1971

Brian Fagan, *Elusive Treasure, the story of early archaeologists in the Americas*, London, 1977

Kent Flannery & Joyce Marcus, *Zapotec Civilisation*, London, 1996

Henri Frankfort et al, *The Intellectual Adventure of Ancient Man*, Chicago, 1946

Henri Frankfort, *Kingship and the Gods*, Chicago, 1948

Henri Frankfort, *Ancient Egyptian Religion*, New York, 1948

Henri Frankfort, *The Birth of Civilisation in the Near East*, New York, 1951

O. R. Gurney, *The Hittites*, Harmondsworth, 1964

Victor Wolfgang von Hagen, *Frederick Catherwood archt.*, London 1950

Victor Wolfgang Von Hagen, *Search for the Maya, the Story of Stephens and Catherwood*, Farnborough, Hants, 1973

H. R. Hall, et al, *How to Observe in Archaeology*, London, 1929

Margaret T. Hodgen, *Early Anthropology in the Sixteenth and Seventeenth Centuries*, Philadelphia, 1964

Samuel Noah Kramer, *Sumerian Literature, a general survey*, in, *The Bible and the Ancient Near East: Essays in Honor of William Foxwell Albright*, (ed. G. Ernest Wright), Baltimore, 1961

Seton Lloyd, *Foundations in the Dust*, London, 1980

Max Mallowan, *Mallowan's Memoirs*, London, 1977

Joyce Marcus, *Zapotec Chiefdoms and the Nature of Formative religions*, in, *Regional Perspectives on the Olmec* (ed. David Grove & Robert Sharer), Cambridge, 1989

Eduardo Matos Moctezuma, *The Great Temple of the Aztecs treasures of Tenochtitlan*, London, 1988

Jacques de Morgan, *Recherches sur les Origines de l'Égypte*, Vol II, *Ethnographie Prehistorique et Tombeau Royal de Négadah*, Paris, 1897

Jacques de Morgan, *Prehistoric Man, a general outline of prehistory*, London, 1924

W. M. Flinders Petrie, *Naqada and Ballas*, London, 1896

W. M. Flinders Petrie, 1901

W. M. Flinders Petrie, [1933]

Sayce, 1923

Linda Schele & David Freidel, *A Forest of Kings, the untold story of the ancient Maya*, New York, 1990

Linda Schele & David Freidel, *Maya Cosmos, three thousand years on the shaman's path*, New York, 1993

Grafton Elliot Smith, *The Ancient Egyptians and the origin of civilisation*, London, 1923

John Lloyd Stevens, *Incidents of Travel in Central America, Chiapas and Yucatan*, New York, 1841

John Lloyd Stevens, *Incidents of Travel in Yucatan*, New York, 1843

J. Eric S. Thompson, *Maya Archaeologist*, Norman, Oklahoma, 1963

Richard Townsend (ed.), *The Ancient Americas, art from sacred landscapes*, Chicago, 1992

Bruce G. Trigger, *Early Civilisations, ancient Egypt in context*, Cairo, 1993

Charles Truman, *The Sèvres Egyptian Service 1810–12*, London, 1982

Gordon R. Willey & Jeremy Sabloff, *A History of American Archaeology*, New York, 1993

Wilson, 1964

C. Leonard Woolley, *Ur of the Chaldees*, London, 1929

C. Leonard Woolley, *Spadework, adventures in archaeology*, London, 1953

PART V: At the Service of the State
Peter Betthausen, *Karl Friedrich Schinkel*, Berlin, 1985

Sabine Brantl, *Haus der Kunst 1937–97*, Munich, 1996

John M. Camp, *The Athenian Agora, excavations in the heart of classical Athens*, London, 1992

Filippo Coarelli, *Roma Sepolta*, Rome, 1984

Roland and Françoise Etienne, *The Search for Ancient*

Greece, London, 1992
Joachim C. Fest, *Hitler*, Harmondsworth, 1977
Pierre Grimal, *In Search of Ancient Italy*, London, 1964
Haskell & Penney, 1981
Eric Hobsbawm & Terence Ranger (eds.), *The Invention of Tradition*, Cambridge, 1983
Adolph Hitler and Bartin Bormann, *Hitler's Table Talk, 1941–44*, London, 1953
Iris Lauterbach (ed.) *Bürokratie und Kult, Das Parteizentrum der DSDAP am Königsplatz in Münich, Geschichte und Rezeption*, Munich, 1995
Kenneth Setton, *Athens in the Middle Ages*, London, 1975
Paul Mackendrick, *The Mute Stones Speak, the story of archaeology in Italy*, New York, 1960
Paul Mackendrick, *The Greek Stones Speak, the story of archaeology in Greek lands*, London, 1962
Elena di Majo et al, *Bertel Thorvaldsen, 1779–1844 scultore danesi a Roma*, Rome, 1989
Fani Mallouchou-Tufano, *The Restoration of Ancient Monuments in Greece (1834–1939)* [in Greek], Athens, 1998
Daniele Manacorda & Renato Tamassia, *Il Piccone del Regime*, Rome, 1985
Cyril Mango, *Byzantinism and Romantic Hellenism*, in, *Journal of the Warburg and Courtauld Institutes* XXVIII, London, 1965
A. L. Mongait, *Archaeology in the USSR*, Harmondsworth, 1961
Donald M. Nicol, *Byzantium and Greece*, in, *Nicol, Studies in Late Byzantine History and Prosopography*, London 1986
Hans Peter L'Orange, *The Roman Empire, art forms and civic life*, New York, 1985
Thomas Raff & Annegret Hoberg (eds), *Ein griechischer Traum, Leo von Klenze der archäologe*, Munich, 1986
Ronald T. Ridley, *The Eagle and the Spade, archaeology in*

Rome during the Napoleonic era, Cambridge, 1992
Giuseppina Pisani Sartorio et al, *Dalla Mostra al Museo, dalla mostra archeologica del 1911 al Museo della della Civiltà Romana*, Venice, 1983
Sklenár, 1983
Michael Snodin (ed.), *Karl Friedrich Schinkel: a universal man*, New Haven, 1991
State Monuments Commission, *Regensburg, Valhalla, official guide*, Regensburg, 1998
Richard Tomlinson, *The Athens of Alma-Tadema*, Stroud, Glos., 1991
Tsagakou, 1981
Trigger, 1980
Yannis Tsiomis (ed.), *Athenes Ville Capitale*, Athens, 1985
Guido Ucelli, *Le Navi di Nemi*, Rome, 1950

Minoan postscript: a microcosm in archaeology
Graeme Barker et al, *The Biferno Valley Survey*, Leicester, 1995
Graeme Barker et al, *A Mediterranean Valley, landscape, archaeology and Annales history in the Biferno Valley*, Leicester, 1995
George F. Bass, et al, *A History of Seafaring*, London, 1972
John Bintliff, et al, *The Annales School and Archaeology*, London, 1991
Andrea Carandini, *Settefinestre, una villa schiavistica nell'etruria Romana*, (3 vols), Modena, 1985
R .A. Crossland & Ann Birchall (eds.), *Bronze Age Migrations in the Aegean, archaeological and linguistic problems in Greek prehistory*, New Jersey, 1974
Robert Drews, *The End of the Bronze Age, changes in warfare and the catastrophe ca. 1200 BC.*, Princeton, 1993
Arthur John Evans, *The Palace of Minos*, 4 Vols., London 1921–36.
Arthur John Evans, *The Palace of Knossos and its Dependences in the light of Recent Discoveries and*

Reconstructions, in, *Journal of the Royal Institute of British Architects*, Vol. 36 #3, Dec 1928
Joan Evans, *Time and Chance, the story of Arthur Evans and his forebears*, London, 1943
Grant, 1990
Rachel Hood, *Faces of Archaeology in Greece, caricatures by Piet de Jong*, Oxford, 1998
Sinclair Hood & David Smyth, *Archaeological Survey of the Knossos Area*, British School at Athens, Supp. Vol. 14, London, 1981
R. W. Hutchinson, *Prehistoric Crete*, Harmondsworth, 1962
Hugh Lloyd-Jones, *Blood for the Ghosts, classical influences in the nineteenth and twentieth centuries*, London, 1982
J. P. Mallory, *In Search of the Indo-Europeans, language, archaeology and myth*, London, 1989
Mark Patton, *Islands in Time, island sociogeography and Mediterranean prehistory*, London, 1996
J. D. S. Pendlebury, *A Handbook to the Palace of Minos at Knossos*, London, 1933
J. D. S. Pendlebury, *The Archaeology of Crete, an Introduction*, London, 1939
Dilys Powell, *The Villa Ariadne*, London, 1973
Colin Renfrew, *Archaeology & Language, the puzzle of Indo-European origins*, London, 1997
Colin Renfrew, *Word of Minos: the Minoan contribution to Mycenaean Greek and the linguistic geography of the Bronze Age Aegean*, in, *Cambridge Archaeological Journal* Vol. 8, No. 2, October, 1998
Yannis & Efi Sakellarakis, *Minoan Crete in a New Light*, Athens, 1997
Michael Shanks & Christopher Tilley, *Re-constructing Archaeology, theory and practice*, London, 1992
Peter Throckmorton, et al, *The Sea Remembers, shipwrecks and archaeology from Homer's Greece to the rediscovery of the Titanic*, New York, 1991

Acknowledgements

A great number of archaeologists, curators and historians were interviewed especially for this book; to all of them, Elizabeth and I offer our thanks for their time, patience and great good humour: Soeren Anderson, Graeme Barker, George Bass, Ofer Bar-Yosef, Manfred Beitak, Anna Belfer-Cohen, Mark Bowden, Austin Claverhill, Alfonso Morales Cleveland, Jean-Pierre Corteggiani, Jules Dassin, Andrew Deathe, Jose Galan, Hans Goedicke, Norman Golb; Zahi Hawass, Jorgen Jensen, Jorgen Steen Jensen; Daniel Kaufman, Flemming Kaul, Manfred Korfmann, Francois Larché, Eduardo Matos Moctezuma, Guadalupe Pech, Mark Roberts, Jeremy Sabloff, Yannis Sakellarakis, Bruce Watson, Mina Weinstein-Evron. To all those other archaeologists who, over the past thirty years or so, have alternatively educated and entertained us, many of whom are our friends and whose names are too numerous to mention, we would also like to offer our sincerest thanks.

It is fitting too, to record here the names of some of those whose skills and talents helped to make the TV series *Great Excavations*. At Channel 4 our thanks are due to Karen Brown, Tim Gardam, Andrew Brann, and especially our commissioning editor Alan Hayling whose fine judgement and good sense contributed enormously to the success of the series. Co-producers: Nicholas Barton, Cathy Haslam. Director: Sonali Fernando. Production: Iona Campbell, Alison Fletcher, Elizabeth Flowers. Editors: Sally Hilton, Steven Stevenson. Camera operators: Marcus Birsel,

Roger Chapman, Lawrence Gardner, Barbara Nicholls. Camera assistants: Noel Balburnie, Andy Banwell, T.C. Thomas, Michael Timney, Sound recordists: Andy Cottom, Trevor Hotz; Lucy Pickering, David Welch. Music: Dario Marianelli. Fixers: Banu Avar (Turkey), Liane Baur (Germany), Bruna Camarena (Italy), Christine Desdemène-Hugon & Pierre Salive (France), Mary & Romany Helmi (Cairo) Hamdi Mohamed Mousa (Luxor, Egypt), Mouns Overgaard (Denmark), Hara Palamidi (Greece), Chloe Sayer & Francisco Torregrosa (Mexico), Elia Sides (Israel).

We would also like to thank our friends at Cassell & Co and at A. P. Watt who helped make this book: Michael Dover, publisher; Marilyn Inglis, editor; Nigel Soper and Austin Taylor, designers; and Caradoc King, literary agent.

Credits

The publishers would like to thank the following photographers and organisations for permission to reproduce their material. Every care has been taken to trace copyright holders. However, if there are any omissions we will be happy to rectify them in future editions. All photographs are by Elizabeth Romer except the following on the pages listed:

Michael Maslan Historic Photographs/Corbis, 10; Museo Archeologico Nazionale, Naples/Bridgeman Art Library, 13; from *La Destruccion de Pompeya* by Micato de Zamarcois, Mexico, 1871, 15; Corbis,18, 19t, 121, 145, 158, 212; Bettmann/Corbis, 19b, 55, 161; National Museet, Copenhagen, 23, 25; from *Urgeschichte des Menschen* by M. Hoernes, Vienna, 1892, 31; Pitt Rivers Collection at the Salisbury and South Wiltshire Museum, 32, 33, 34, 36 37, 38; Geological Society/Bridgeman Art Library, 41; from *Reliquiae Aquitanicae* by Edouard Lartet and Henry Christy, London, 1856, 42, 43, 44; AKG, London, 47, 99t, 108t&b, 110t, 147, 175; Mary Evans Picture Library, 52, 76, 80b, 94, 102; Sinclair Stammers/Science Photo Library, 56; Hulton-Deutsch Collection/Corbis, 60, 61, 62, 112, 126, 204 ; Royal Castle, Warsaw/Bridgeman, 68; Towneley Hall Art Gallery/Bridgeman, 69; Stapleton Collection/Bridgeman, 71, 79; Versailles/Giraudon/Bridgeman, 77; Sonia Halliday Photographs, 78b, 80t, 91r, 113t; Royal Geographical Society/ Bridgeman, 84; Francis Frith Collection, 98b, 99l, 101t; Private Collection/Berko Fine Paintings, Belgium/Bridgeman, 106; Petrie Museum, University College, London, 122, 124, 151, 153b; Robert Harding Picture Library, 127t&b, 146t&b; from *First Photographs of Jerusalem* by Ely Schiller, Jerusalem, 1978, 137; Gianni Dagli Orti/Corbis, 143t&b; Oriental Institute of the University of Chicago, 160t&b, 162b, 164; Museum of Anthropology, Mexico/Werner Forman Archive, 166; Birmingham Museums and Art Gallery/ Bridgeman, 182t; from *Bertel Thorvaldsen*/de Luca Edizioni d'arte, Rome, 1989, 186; Charles E Rotkin/Corbis, 192; Giancarlo Costa, 194, 195t&b; from *Le Navi de Nemi* by Guido Ucelli, Instituto Poligrafico e Zecca dello Stato, Rome, 1940, 202; Ashmolean Museum, Oxford, 207, 210